THE TELLER IN THE TALE

The Teller in the Tale

A HALF-JEWISH CHILD
IN NAZI GERMANY

Elizabeth Heyn

Herstory WRITERS WORKSHOP

First American edition published by Herstory Writers Workshop, Inc. 2009

CENTEREACH, NY

Manufactured in the United States of America

ISBN 978-0-9821385-1-9

In memory of my mother, Charlotte Heyn

PART ONE

CHAPTER ONE

Fɪʀꜱᴛ ᴛʜᴇʀᴇ ᴀʀᴇ always the spaces. As in a painting of a country scene or that of a city, in which almost as an afterthought the painter has placed a person, a child stands, painted very small and vague somewhere in the tableau, shadowy, edges blurred. Everything else is prominent and purposeful. The child is often alone, although sometimes in some of these memory paintings other human figures appear in the landscape: Mother, grandmother, aunt, other adults. Only rarely are there any other children. As the child grows, she begins to appear clearer, more prominent, better defined. Gradually her world expands to include others, gradually that world will shape the adult she will become.

ɪ ᴡᴀꜱ ʙᴏʀɴ in Bremen, a medium-sized city in the north of Germany, and spent the first few weeks of my life there in the elegant old house of my mother's long-time friend Lili. I used to wonder why I wasn't born in Hamburg, the city where my mother lived together with my grandmother and her younger sister Bertha. I would have wanted to have spent the first days of my life at home instead of in a stranger's place. I don't know why I never asked for an explanation, only much later did I figure it out: the time-honored reason why a young woman used to give birth to her child away from home.

No one, except perhaps my family, thought that I was an adorable little girl. People found me neither pretty nor winsome, with my short straight mousy hair and a rather ordinary little face once I had lost the charm of babyhood. Strangers usually ignored me; now and then I would overhear someone say to my mother something to the effect that, even though I wasn't very pretty, at least I had a lively personality and seemed to be quite clever. Perhaps I didn't hear those words; perhaps there was only something in their behavior or in my mother's attitude that told me. In any case, that is how I came to think of myself. Much later she told me that I had been a comical little toddler, who had enjoyed making funny faces and remarks to make her laugh and that I had laughed a lot myself. That came as a surprise to me, for I could not imagine myself like that. I thought of myself as serious, thoughtful and a little sad.

IT IS A WARM SPRING AFTERNOON. I am sitting all alone on the stoop of our apartment house looking up and down the narrow deserted street. The children with whom I had played, have gone home for their afternoon snack and I am bored. Maybe I'll go in too. But no, only my Grandmother, my *Oma*, is home, and she is probably reading her book. I sit some more and think of what I could do next. The street is too quiet; even the Schmidt's yellow cat has gone to sleep in a puddle of warm sun on their balcony. I wish there were at least some sparrows as in the park. "Sparrows like trees," Mutti had said when I asked her once why there were no sparrows on our street. I look up and down the street once more. No, no trees. Maybe there are trees on some other streets?

4

I decide to take a walk by myself. Out of our street, along the next larger street, for many blocks. This is more interesting. There at the corner, some big trees. And yes, on the lower branches, birds. Sparrows? Or maybe they are those other birds from the little song I learned: "Blackbird, thrush, finch and starling . . ." I sing to myself as I keep walking and walking. Now and then I count my steps, one, two, three, four . . . to twenty, at which point my number knowledge becomes hazy, and then I start anew, one, two, three, four . . . When I get tired of that game I try not to step on the cracks between the paving stones. That's hard, because the stones are large and my legs are short and I have to hop. I don't know how many corners I turn, but I am not the slightest bit afraid and not at all worried about finding my way back. Some passersby look at me in a funny way, but I pay no attention. Here and there the lights in the shops are being turned on, and still I keep walking, without a thought of wanting to turn back. I look left and right before crossing a street, the way I've been taught. See, I don't need to hold hands like a baby!

When toward dusk my grandmother calls me to come in for the evening meal, I am nowhere to be seen. She panics, runs into the street to find me, but without success. When my mother comes home from work, she calls the police.

I don't remember who brought me home, nor how far I had traveled, but on my return I couldn't understand what all the fuss was about. My mother was angry with me for being so thoughtless, but naturally also relieved to have me back. "You must never, never do this again," I remember her saying as she held me close, and tears ran down her cheeks. She couldn't understand why I had wanted to go off like that by myself.

"Why did you do that? Didn't it occur to you that Oma and I would worry?"

"But Mutti, I had to get to know the world!" had been my

answer according to the family anecdote. Wasn't I four years old, already since winter? It seemed to me that wanting to take a walk alone had been such an ordinary thing to do. What was all the fuss about? Only later, as the story of my escapade was and retold did I understand how worried they must have been.

Was that the first time that I needed to do something on my own? Was this the first time that I felt an urge to rely only on myself in the great world outside? The first time that I felt everyone else would quite naturally understand and trust me? Perhaps already then the seeds of my long struggle for personal independence had begun to germinate.

☙

I AM FIVE. We are on our way to Lili's house. The streetcar to the station and then a long ride on the train and now a streetcar again. I can see that Mutti is very happy. She smiles a lot and promises me that we will really enjoy ourselves.

"Remember last year?" she asks. "We had fun together, didn't we?"

I don't remember much fun. Mutti was so busy talking with the others that she didn't have any time for me. Usually I like to listen to grown-ups, but I didn't know what they were talking about and no one wanted to explain. No, not much fun.

Now the grown-ups are sitting again around the table on the garden terrace. The table is set with an embroidered cloth and there is a vase with flowers on it. In the garden there are beds of all kinds of beautiful flowers and the sun is shining. They are drinking coffee and are talking a lot. I would like to sit down too, but there isn't a chair for me.

"Go and say hello to the cats. Go ahead," my mother suggests as I hover around her chair.

"And look at the fish in the big aquarium in the sunroom

too. We have some new pretty ones. I think you'll like them," Lili adds.

Why do they want me to play with the cats and watch the fish? Why are they sending me away? I can feel that they don't want me with them. My lower lip protrudes in a pout; I am mad at them, I am jealous. I don't mind sharing my Mutti, but I want to be included. I throw an angry look back at the table as I reluctantly walk towards the house. The grown-ups don't even notice. My Mutti is so deep in the pleasure of being together with her friend, so engrossed in talking and listening, that she pays no further attention to me. She doesn't care, she wishes I weren't there. I'm mad at her.

Just as I am getting even angrier, like a flash of lightning, like a blow to my body, I suddenly sense that my Mutti must have lived before me, that she didn't start when I was born, that we haven't always been together. Have I not always been the center of her universe? I don't understand at all how I know, but I am sure of it. I try to think, but nothing comes. I can't visualize my mother without me. Maybe it's not true? Still, I can't shake this new idea. Who was she before I was there? Perhaps even now I am not the center of her life. Are others more important than me? I wish we were home again, where everything seems so much simpler. Perhaps she lies when she tells me that I am the most important person in her life. She always tells me that, she says she had wanted to have me more than anything else. Instead of the twelve children she had planned, she says. So I'm twelve times as important to her. I believed her. Now I'm not so sure. I don't know what to think. It makes me dizzy.

The sudden realization that my mother and I were indeed two separate people instead of a unit, that I was not an integral part of her person, and that the cord that held us tied together was not permanent and immutable, made me feel very sad and very lonely. That she could think and feel without me, and that there were parts of her life that I would never share, was such a loss to me that it made me start to draw into myself, so that nothing would touch me deeply enough to hurt me the way my new knowledge was hurting me now. I must have decided right then and there to act as if I were no longer dependent on her. I was not aware then that the gulf I was creating between her and me on that sunny afternoon in the garden in Bremen would last until long into my adulthood.

"Who needs them anyway?" I say to myself, trying to be brave. And so, with determined steps I leave the terrace and march into the sunroom and over to the aquarium. It's bigger than our bathtub at home and takes up one whole wall of the room. There are lots of fish of all sizes and colors and for a while I watch them swim around, but my heart is still pounding with a feeling of anger and disappointment, my head hurts, and even though the fish are unusual and colorful, I hardly see them. "Boring" I say out loud, hoping they can hear me out there. "Really boring, boring," I say even louder. Maybe later I'll be allowed to feed them. At least that will be something to do.

I like the cats alright, but they too seem not to need me. I throw a little red ball, "Here kitty kitty" I say, but they don't want to play, they are much too dignified to play with a child like me. The new kittens are snuggled against their mother on an old brown cushion in the corner of the living room and the old "Onkel Katze" as he is called, is hovering nearby, in case he is needed. They all seem very content.

Everything is in its place in this house, everyone knows their place. Except me. It is very quiet and so I wander into the big kitchen. There are many plates and bowls behind the glass doors of the tall white painted cabinets, but I don't see anything to eat. I don't dare open drawers and cabinets, even though I would like to. In my head I hear my mother's voice reminding me to always be *bescheiden,* not to be too bold, not to want too much, not to push oneself ahead, especially if you are a child. She doesn't approve of anyone who is forward. It's a black mark on one's character, even blacker than making spots on the tablecloth or on one's clothes. Even though right now I feel like really being bad and disobeying. I don't quite dare, and so I go without anything to eat. There is cake on the table on the terrace; I had a piece before, and could probably have some more if I asked, but I don't want to go out there.

What else can I do? I remember that I have never been up to the third floor of the house, where the oldest sister, Lotte, has her rooms. Her name is the same as my mother's, but it's like a different name to me because she is so different. She is very thin and bent over and she much prefers books to people, and her eyes behind their thick glasses always look angry. Even so, I go back to the table on the terrace and ask Lotte whether I can go up and look at her books. I keep my head down; I don't want to look at anyone, especially at the Lotte who is my mother.

"Yes," she says, "there are some books with beautiful pictures of interesting places right on the table. Be careful though," she adds. "Yes, be careful," Mother-Lotte repeats out of habit. I wish she hadn't spoken. I heard it the first time.

I run through the house, up the two flights of stairs, trying to make as much noise as possible. On the top landing I yank open the door to Lotte's room. There in front of me, her rocking chair. I throw myself into it and rock myself back and forth as fast as I can. Suddenly I see a small dog bound out of the corner of the room towards me as I swing back and forth and before I can pull my leg up, he has hold of it with his teeth and won't let go. I shriek, I howl, and the women come racing up the stairs. Lotte-friend grabs her dog, and Lotte-mother grabs me. Blood is gushing from the wound, and tears of pain and anger are gushing from my eyes. The iodine stings terribly and I shriek some more, and when the wound is all bandaged up, I put my arms around my mother's neck and let her carry me downstairs.

Later my mother says, "The dog couldn't help it. You see, he is like Lotte's child and was jealous. So don't be mad at him." But I don't forgive the dog, and I don't forgive the grown-ups either for a long time after.

❧

THE APARTMENT HOUSE at 43 Gneisenaustrasse in Hamburg in which I lived until I was ten years old is no longer standing. Allied bombs in World War II destroyed it, together with the rest of the buildings in the working class neighborhood in which it stood. Our apartment was on the third floor: a parlor with heavy dark furniture was almost never used, the narrow hallway led to three bedrooms, a small kitchen and a tiny bathroom. The room my mother, my Mutti, and I shared looked out on the street and had a small balcony. The icebox stood outside on the back balcony, and each room had its own tall *Kachelofen* a tiled coal stove. Once a week the boiler in the bathroom produced enough hot water for the four or us to take our bath; grandmother, Tante Bertha, my mother and I. It did not seem to be a tenement to me; I did not know that we were poor.

The white lace curtain covering the single window is billowing gently back and forth. Mutti likes the window open, in spite of the damp air outside. It is not often sunny where we live, and even though the apartment buildings on our street are no more than three or four stories high, the pale north European sun does not often penetrate into the narrow treeless street below.

In our small room the hand-me-down upright piano takes up the space where the old bookcase used to stand. Everything had to be pushed around for the piano. I am taking piano lessons at last. How old am I? Perhaps seven. The table with my mother's typewriter, covered now since she no longer types envelopes at home but works out of the house, stands against the wall, squeezed between my small bed and the bookcase with its glass doors behind which, along with Mutti's books, I keep my favorite reading: Anderson's fairy tales. My mother's bed, covered by a blue and red patterned throw, serves as a couch during the day. There is a straight chair, now pulled over to the piano and a small chest of drawers. The middle drawer is mine.

My favorite spot in the room is in front of the narrow glass door in the corner of the room which opens to the balcony which is just big enough for two chairs and a small round table. I often stand in front of that door, lean my head against the pane, and look out at the street below, daydreaming.

Saturday afternoon. As so often, it is raining outside, and there is little to see, even less than on clear days. Now and then a black umbrella, carried by a pair of quickly moving legs, passes in the street below. It disappears into the greengrocer up the street or moves up to the broad main street, where there are more shops. I stand there sucking my left thumb, as I watch the raindrops run down the pane. I am ashamed to still be such a baby who needs her thumb. I tried, but I have not been able to give it up, in spite of all sorts of heroic efforts on the part of the adults. As long as I am not seen by others I don't mind; on the contrary, with my thumb in my mouth and the other hand stroking my upper lip I am quite content.

It is very quiet in the apartment. I think that it must soon be time for Mutti to return from the office. Tante Bertha? She's not home either. Oma is there, I know, because she takes care of me when Mutti is out working and besides she very seldom goes out anyway. She wouldn't leave me alone, I know that too. It's just that she is so quiet that it feels almost as if I were alone.

Is she in the parlor, reading? She loves reading. We don't have a radio or a telephone and few visitors; maybe that's why. She often sits at the little table near the window until the light dims and it is time to prepare the evening meal. She never turns on the lamp. I sometimes see her books lying on the table, and I try to read what it says: Joan of Arc, Catherine the Great. When I ask her who these people with their strange names are, she tells me she likes to read about famous people who lived long ago.

Maybe she is doing things in the kitchen? It's still raining, a steady monotonous veil of water between me and the dim out-line of houses across the street. There is no one out there, now that it is getting darker. The streetlight at the corner must have been turned on. Standing on tip-toe I can just make out the semicircle of its yellow aura at the corner of our street reflected on the wet pavement. A small shiver is slowly running down my spine. Maybe I'll go where Oma is.

She is in the kitchen, ironing a tablecloth.

"Are you hungry?" she smiles down at me. "We'll have sup-per when Mutti comes home," she says.

I shake my head, no. I never like to admit that I need any-thing.

"I'm almost done ironing," she says. "Why don't you bring your book? You can read here, while I finish." But I don't want to read just now. Instead I sit on a kitchen chair in the corner and watch her. Neither one of us says anything as the iron glides back and forth on the cloth. Now and then she puts the iron back on the gas burner to reheat it.

I see that she is wearing the big brown and tan clasp in her hair today. It's pretty. She has told me that it's made of the shell of a big turtle; tortoiseshell, she said. Her hair is gray with some black in it, like the little cat that I see in the street sometimes. It's always the same, always put up neatly with many pins and a clasp. I wonder why she always wears that beaded ribbon circled around her neck. Mutti and Tante Bertha don't and I don't either. But Tante Lina does. Maybe all old people do? Will I wear one when I am old? Will Mutti? Anyway, I like it on her, because the little beads sparkle and that makes her look pretty. She sees me watching her and smiles, "Well, what do you see?"

"Oh nothing," I say and keep looking as she goes back to her ironing. There is something about her eyes that's very beautiful, I think. They are gray with a little bit of blue when the light is just right. It's the way she looks at me that makes me feel important and really good. I continue studying her. I don't know why I do this. It's comfortable here in the kitchen with her, and I don't feel any longer so alone. She is wearing her gray everyday dress with a big blue apron over it. I don't understand why she needs an apron; she never gets dirty or spills things, or runs and knocks things over the way I do sometimes. I look down at my own dress; sure, there is a spot on the skirt where I spilled soup at lunch. Mutti will scold me when she sees it for having been careless. Being careless, I know, is almost as bad as being lazy.

Oma has finished her ironing. She takes off her apron and hangs it on a nail near the back door. "It's almost time for Mutti to come home," she says as she leaves the kitchen and heads for her room. "I'm going to lie down for a while."

"OK," I say, but I am still thinking about her dress. I know she has another one, for Sundays and special occasions. It is black and white, with zig-zag stripes. I wonder if she has any other dresses. Maybe not. I've never seen her wear any others. Mutti has more dresses than just two, and so do I.

13

I hear the key in the front door. Tante Bertha has come home. I go to greet her but she only says a quick hello and asks, "Where is Oma?"

"She's lying down," I say, and she disappears into her room. She must be in a bad mood, I think, or maybe she is tired. I'm disappointed, because I like it when she comes home and tells me stories about the people in whose houses she sews. She tells me how they live and how fussy the ladies are sometimes and how she then has to rip all the seams open again and start over. I think about the rhyme she taught me last week; she said it was funny: "*Trennen unser Unglück, Wiedernähen unsere Hoffnung.*" It's a play on a German saying which sounds almost the same and means: to separate (rip open a seam) is our misfortune; to see each other again (to re-sew), our hope. Then I feel sorry for her, because I don't like to do things over either, especially if I think it is OK to begin with.

Since now there is no one to keep me company, I return to our room, wondering what I might do next. It's getting late and Mutti should really be coming home. Just as I think that I hear her open the front door, and before I can say hello, I hear Tante Bertha shouting something in an angry voice.

"Leave me alone," I hear Mutti's voice, annoyed. "Can't you see, I just got home!"

I am straining to hear through the closed door, even though I hate it when they argue. Why are they fighting again?

I've thought about that before and I can't understand. Aren't they sisters? Aren't sisters supposed to like each other? That's what Jenny told me her Mutti says when she and her sister argue. Maybe it's different for grown-ups.

"You think you're her favorite!" Bertha's voice, bitter.

"Don't start that again; you know that's not true."

What's going on? Her favorite? Oma's favorite? I know that I'm Oma's favorite, Mutti and Tante Bertha come next..

Mutti moves towards our room and opens the door, but Tante Bertha pushes her away. She stands in the doorway like a policeman with her hands on her hips and blocks Mutti's way .

"I can say whatever I want, even though you never want to hear it."

She is shouting angrily now. I can only see the back of her head which is bobbing up and down with each word, but I imagine her face looking ugly.

"This is my home too, don't forget. Even though I am only one person and you are two."

Mutti pushes past her through the door, and Bertha turns around and looks at me. I can see tears in her eyes. Maybe she is no longer angry? Is she sad?

"You know I love the child, so why can't I come into your room?"

Her voice is harsh and angry again. Mutti doesn't answer and walks over to where I sit on her bed.

"What's so special about the room of a fancy office worker? Better than a seamstress? I pay my way too."

She takes three big steps towards where I sit, puts her hand on my head and strokes my hair, but it doesn't feel good.

She moves towards the door to leave. "Your new blouse is almost finished," she says to me, almost in the doorway.

I hear the door to her room slam shut.

"What's the matter with her?" Mutti says to no one in particular "I'm tired," she says. "Come, give me a hello hug."

I give her a quick cursory hug. I am bewildered, I don't understand what's going on, but I know I didn't like what just happened. Oma hates their arguments too. She and I are alike in that, and since she is the most important person in the family maybe I am second. I love her.

That evening in bed I start to wonder why Mutti and Tante Bertha always have to get so excited and yell at each other. Why can't they be friends the way they used to be when they were little? On a picture Mutti showed me a while ago, taken when she and Bertha were little girls, they really looked like sisters. When I asked Mutti, she told me that they got along OK and played with each other and didn't argue. I wonder what happened to change that. They don't look so much alike now, because Mutti is smaller and I think prettier. She has dark hair, while Tante Bertha's is lighter, almost blond. But I love her too, although in a different way than I love my Oma and Mutti. I love her, even though she and Mutti don't get along.

What if I had a sister? Would I like that? It had never occurred to me before to ask that. Maybe I like it just the way it is: no fighting.

I know Tante Bertha loves me because she always talks to me and sews for me, a new blouse or a skirt from left-over fabric, and sometimes she brings me little presents. Except of course when she is in a bad mood like today. I often wish she had more time to play with me, but she is always busy sewing. Usually I can go into her room and watch her sew, but today I better not, because of her bad mood.

I like her room a lot. It's different from ours, not so neat. There are colorful scraps of material all over the floor, and fashion magazines strewn all over the bed, and a big ironing board in the middle of the room and spools of thread and pins and bright buttons all over the place. She always stops her sewing when I come into the room, but sometimes she asks me to wait a minute while she finishes a seam. Then I watch her feet move the treadle on the machine up and down and I listen to the melody the machine sings. It goes up and down depending on how fast Tante Bertha's feet are going. Usually her feet are going fast and the song is high and a little shrill.

Near the door Dora the dummy stands on her one iron leg. She gets to try on all the dresses Tante Bertha sews. Her body is covered with gray cloth and she doesn't have a head or any arms. When I was very little I used to imagine that she would come to life at night when everyone was sleeping and would hop all over the apartment on her one leg.

I wish I could go there now, because Mutti isn't in a good mood either and it's no fun to be with her. Maybe tomorrow. We usually don't talk much when I am there. I just like to watch her, but I don't like it when she coughs and has to spit into her handkerchief.

At supper it's only Mutti and me. Oma is still resting and Tante Bertha is probably still mad and won't come out of her room. I like having Mutti all to myself once in a while. She is always so busy away at the office, or typing, or washing clothes or ironing or cleaning our room that she seldom sits down with me. I have started to wash my own socks and I help her dust, but still, there is so much for her to do.

I think about how when I was little, Mutti was home more than now. That was really nice. She would sit all day at the little table in the center of our room, typing envelopes. The roller made a grinding sound as she put an envelope into the machine, then the keys went clickety-click ,and then again the roller grrred, as she removed the finished envelope with one hand and slapped it on the pile of finished work, while with the other hand she took a fresh envelope to start all over. It was like a little song. At first I would only watch her, but after a while I knew the sequence of the sounds and the song became familiar, over and over, day after day, even on Sundays.

17

We spent a lot of time together then, and I was able to show her my drawings, or how much longer the multicolored wool braid which snaked out of the bottom of the old wooden sewing thread spool was getting, as I looped the yarn over the four protruding nails on top. Later she would help me sew the braid together to make a pot holder for Oma. That was a nice, cozy time.

⚬

THERE WAS A STORY from that time which my mother would tell now and then. How I had been sitting on the floor with cardboard and scissors and crayons while she was typing at the card table in the center of the room. "Do you know what you said to me when you were barely four years old? 'Mutti,' you said, 'you don't have to buy me any toys, I can make them myself'—that's what you said, as little as you were. You wanted to save me money. Was it because you saw how hard I had to work and how tired I was?" I liked that story, even as I thought that maybe she made some of it up.

What I remembered was that I had some minor sickness and that I sat on the floor while my mother was busy typing and snipped and pasted to make a simple board game, my slightly feverish body warm and a little trembly there on the floor next to her feet, content and filled with such a feeling of belonging together, mother and child, that I had to use all my usual self imposed restraint not to get up, throw my arms around her neck and kiss her. Instead I decided to first finish my project, before I would allow myself that outburst of emotion. Strangely, when I was satisfied with what I had produced, I no longer wanted to hug and kiss her as I had wanted to just minutes before. Was it the joy that comes with creating something one self, a joy independent of the opinion of others that held me back? Or was it a sudden fear that if I let myself be carried away by the ecstasy of loving closeness to my mother I would somehow be swallowed up by her? I think that already then I was aware of her great need for me, already then I found myself in the push-pull state of wanting to love her while at the same time needing to guard myself against her overpowering possessiveness of me.

I got up slowly from the floor, walked over to where she was sitting, and showed her my new game. She stopped typing for a minute, stretched out her arms for a hug, smiled, and said, "I'm really proud to have such a clever little girl of my own."

CHAPTER TWO

SEPTEMBER 1933. I am starting first grade. The school is just down our street and a little to the right. I am excited and skip along as my mother walks me there the first day. Beginning tomorrow I can walk by myself, she says, because she doesn't have time to take me. Today is special, so she has taken the day off. I only have to cross two small streets where there are almost no cars and she knows that I am careful. It's exciting to finally be able to go to school, to learn to read and write and do sums and learn to do other things, as Mutti has told me. I can read a little already, and do sums up to ten. Still, I'm eager to go. The big brick building has two entrances, I notice. All the girls with their mothers are going into one, and the boys are going into the other one. In the street I play with the boys, but school is different. We have to be separated.

I've never seen so many little girls all in the same place. The first grade classroom is big with lots of tall windows and light green walls. The teacher stands in front of a giant blackboard that covers the whole front wall, smiles at each little girl as she enters and tells us to sit down at one of the little desks. I don't mind that Mutti has to leave. She bends down for a kiss; I wave her a cheery good-bye, and find a desk in the front row. A few of the girls are crying. They are still babies who can't leave their mothers, I think. Not me, I'm glad I'm here, and as I look around the classroom at the other little girls, and the teacher, and the alphabet letters posted along the top of the blackboard, I can hardly sit still with the happiness of fulfilled expectations.

I don't remember anything more about that morning except that at dismissal time Mutti and Oma are waiting for me at the school door. Mutti hands me a big bright blue cardboard cone, decorated with gold and silver trim. It's filled with apples and oranges and cookies and candy. *"Für das neue Schulmädchen"* —for the new schoolgirl—she says smiling. All the other little girls are carrying paper cones as well, many of them much bigger than mine, I notice. There are many mothers and older brothers and sisters and everyone is chattering happily. I like my cone, and I'm happy too. Happy for finally being able to go to school, happy in the expectation of the treats in my paper cone, and happy that Oma came with Mutti to pick me up. The three of us hurry home together for a festive meal of my favorite foods: buttered noodles with green peas and vanilla pudding topped with stewed black cherries.

It must have been a little while later that I overheard my mother answer Bertha's question, "Why aren't you sending her to the Jewish school?" by saying that she didn't believe in "sectarian education"—big words that I didn't understand, although I understood the "didn't"—and "I don't belong to a Jewish congregation and we don't observe Jewish traditions."

"But we are Jewish," Bertha had said. "Our mother, you and I, and by Jewish law, the child too. Why do you deny it?"

I had listened with interest because never before had I heard anyone in my family talk about being Jewish. I didn't know what that meant, I didn't know yet that we were different from

21

our neighbors. I knew that Oma didn't eat anything on a certain day in the fall, and that every autumn we all visited Cousin Alfred for a New Year's dinner. "For Oma's sake," my mother would say to me, somewhat apologetically. But I didn't know why we did that, nor could I figure out why there were two New Years to celebrate in one year. She didn't explain and I hadn't asked.

Gradually over the course of time I was made painfully aware, not only that we were a Jewish family, but also that I was different from them because, according to Nazi laws, I was a *Mischling*.

But on that first day in first grade in 1933 I didn't know any of that, and I was just happy to finally be going to school.

BY NOW I AM a full fledged first grader, walking proudly by myself to and from school every day. On this Monday when I come home from school, Oma is there as usual to greet me and to give me my glass of milk and a slice of bread with jam. It's to keep me from getting too hungry until supper time when Mutti comes home. I show her the picture I have made in school. It's of her and me in the kitchen. She takes it and smiles. "That's beautiful. Will you give it to me?"

"But it's not very good." I hesitate. Drawing is hard.

"I like it. You and me in the kitchen. What a nice idea! Thank you." She gives me a little hug.

"I don't know how to draw well," I object. "Mutti knows how." She probably won't like my picture, so I won't show it to her. I know how critical she gets, especially when she comes home tired. She gets irritated and scolds me for the slightest thing, like having disobeyed one of her many rules of good behavior. Yesterday she got really annoyed with me and slapped my cheek, gave me an *Ohrfeige*. It didn't hurt very much, but I felt insulted. I must have said something she didn't like . . . I can't remember what; maybe it was the way I said it? When I told Oma about the *Ohrfeige* she tried to calm Mutti down. "It's not so important, Lotte," she said. Then Mutti felt sorry and wanted to hug me, but I didn't let her. And then Mutti cried a little. I know Oma wants to protect me. I feel safe with Oma.

Back in our room I think about how Oma needs my protection too. I am sure of that, although I really don't know what she needs to be protected from. There is a dream I have, over and over, which convinces me. In it our doorbell rings several times and I go to open the door. A huge hairy man, dressed in strange, colorful rags, wearing a scary mask and wig like the figures in the House of Horrors at the November fair, tries to push himself into the apartment. His words, raucous and insistent, ask: "Where's your grandmother? Go get her. Quick!"

She has appeared behind me at the door. "Who is there?" she asks in her soft voice. I am terrified and try to shield her with my body by making myself very big in front of her. I can't say anything, I am mute. I can't warn her. He must not see her. I know he wants to do her harm, take her away, kill her, and I know she doesn't know that. I wake up screaming. I can't tell Mutti when she asks what the dream was about.

The last time I had the dream I hit the monster with a broom over and over to kill him, but he kept coming and coming. Until my scream.

I stand there at the window, thinking about that dream. It feels so real to me and I am so afraid, that I have to run and check on Oma. Perhaps he came, found the door open and took her away? But there she is in the kitchen peeling potatoes for the evening meal. I throw my arms around her waist and hold her tight, nuzzling my face into her apron for a long time.

"What's the matter?" she asks, astonished by my sudden out-burst of affection. She looks at me and puts her hand lovingly on my head. I can't answer. I am so relieved that she is still there.

"You know what?" she says smiling. "Tomorrow we'll make noodles and I'll need your help. Just like last time, remember? Don't forget now. Do you want to help me now with the potatoes?" She sees that I am still upset, that something is still bothering me, but she doesn't insist that I tell her what it is about, the way Mutti always does. She just tries to make me feel better, to feel happy again. She knows that noodles are my favorite dish, especially the kind she makes, served plain with just butter. She knows that I don't like most foods the grown-ups eat. I once tasted ice-cream and that was delicious, but it is expensive and we don't have any place to keep it. The small ice-box on the back balcony isn't cold enough, especially when the ice man hasn't been around for a few days. We don't eat meat very often and I abhor any kind of fish. Noodles now, there's something I could eat every day! Mutti tells me that she is worried about me because I am so skinny. Maybe Oma worries too, but she doesn't say anything. How I love my Oma!

I am now ashamed of my sudden outburst, and so I tell her I don't want to peel potatoes; that I'd rather play piano.

"All right," she says, smiling, "I like to hear you play."

I go back to our room, pull the chair closer to the piano, take a cushion from my mother's bed, put it on the chair and sit down. First I want to practice for my lesson on Wednesday afternoon. I like to practice the assigned pieces, but I don't like finger exercises. What I like best of all is to play from the two books of piano arrangements of Mozart operas: *Figaro* and *The Magic Flute*. I play only the melody line with one hand, one finger at the time; the accompaniment is much too hard for

24

me. The words are there and I sing along as I play. The music is so beautiful that I forget about everything else, my dream, my loneliness, the rain outside.

I sit at the piano a long time, losing track of time, as I play the tunes and daydream in turn. This spot in front of the piano is my second favorite place in the apartment.

I hear the key turn in the apartment door and my mother is there. She seems tired and she hardly greets me. In a way I don't mind, because I am not ready to emerge out of my private space and I also know that when she is tired like that it is had to please her. She goes into the kitchen to find Oma. I return to the piano, but the interruption has spoiled it for me and I bang the lid down.

It's the next day and I am ready to help Oma. Making noodles is a long drawn out procedure; that's why Oma doesn't do it very often. I am proud to be allowed to help my. She has cleared the table which stands in the middle of the kitchen and scrubbed the plaid oilcloth really clean. I climb on one of the wooden kitchen chairs to watch. She is wearing her blue apron over her dark weekday dress. Her hands become white as she spreads flour all over the oilcloth. Little by little the stripes of the oilcloth disappear under the flour-snow. I am tempted to etch a little drawing there, but now she brings the already mixed lump of dough to the table, places it in the center and passes the wooden rolling pin back and forth over the flattening dough. Now she turns the pancake of dough over and rolls the other way.

"Look child," she says, "it's getting flatter Come and help me roll it some more." I pull the chair close, lean over the table and take hold of the rolling pin. Back and forth I push it, roll and push, roll and push. It's hard work, but I am determined. I like to be Oma's helper, I want to do it right.

"Very good," she says smiling. "Look, it's almost thin

enough." The dough has become like a tablecloth, a noodle tablecloth that covers almost the whole table. Not quite thin enough though, so she cuts it in half, folds one half carefully into quarters and lays it aside. I look down at the front of my dress, it's covered with fine white dust. "Never mind," Oma says, seeing the worried look on my face, "you look like a real noodle-maker now. Thank you for helping, it's almost done." She moves the rolling pin smoothly over the dough in all directions until the dough is almost paper thin.

As the rolling pin passes back and forth, I imagine that my grandmother is a character in one of my stories, who is making noodles for her favorite princess: me Suddenly, for only a brief instant, the ogre appears, but I chase him away with my rolling pin, to never appear again.

She takes a special long knife with a narrow thin blade and quickly cuts the dough into long strips, and I get to pick up one strip at a time to hang carefully over the backs of the kitchen chairs to dry. When we are done, the kitchen is draped with noodles everywhere: a noodle paradise.

SOMETIMES I GET an uneasy feeling that I cannot explain. Am I picking up something unspoken from the adults around me? Something held back, that the adults know but keep me from knowing? Something that worries them, something threatening, something that wasn't there before? They often stop talking when I enter the room, but I can see their worries in their faces. I'm not supposed to know, I don't know what questions to ask, or what answers I expect. I sense that somehow things have changed in many ways, but at home life is pretty much as before. Still that uneasy feeling remains.

I hardly ever have that feeling when I am at school. I like

school, I like to learn, it comes easy to me, and I am happy when Fräulein Schrader, our teacher praises me. Sometimes she reprimands me for shouting out the answers before anyone else has had a chance. I try to control my eagerness and I try to raise my hand, index finger extended the way we are supposed to and wait my turn. Still, often I jump up from my seat and wave my arm high in the air. I can't help it. It's hard to be patient, even though Mutti tells me over and over that I mustn't be a show-off, that it is enough that she knows that I am smart.

I guess Fräulein Schrader knows it too. Why else would she ask me, later on in first grade, to help others in my class, who are falling behind? Maybe it's because I know how to read easily and to write and do sums? Maybe because she has noticed that after I am finished with the routine exercises I always become fidgety while sitting and waiting, trying to keep my hands primly folded on the desk in front of me the way we were taught, waiting for the other twenty-nine little girls to finish? Whatever the reason, she noticed, and so I become Marie's tutor.

I think about Marie all the time; I think she is beautiful and I want to invite her home with me. Does she want to come? She is so unlike the other children I know in school and in the street. She is so unlike me. I know that she is the poorest student in the class; she can't even remember how to read the simplest words, like *Haus* and *Hund*. Only *Mama* and her own name, even with all my help; but that doesn't count. I think she doesn't even understand what school is all about. At first I was so proud when Fräulein Schrader asked me whether I'd like to be little Marie's helper. "Oh, yes" I had said, eager to start my new job. Now I still want to help her learn, but that's not all. I want to look at her all the time. She is so beautiful, so little, so delicate, so . . . I don't know what. Mutti says she is a miserable little thing, so skinny and obviously neglected.

27

"Maybe she is very poor," I say, not thinking that we are poor too. I hardly notice how dirty her little face is, and how her fingernails need cutting. She is much smaller than I am, just to my armpits; she is the smallest girl in the class. Her long, stringy brown hair needs washing and combing; even I can see that, but still I find her beautiful. Mutti says that even if you are poor, you can still be neat and clean. "Doesn't anyone wash and iron her clothes? Besides they are much too big for her, and even have holes!" She shakes her head. But I don't care. I only see two huge dark blue eyes that look with puzzlement from a pallid little face at the confusing world around her. My heart has gone out to Marie.

"Isn't she beautiful?" I say to Mutti when I bring her to our apartment for the first time. "Like a little princess." Mutti looks at me quizzically. "Like a fairy tale princess," I repeat earnestly.

My mother is aghast, shakes her head at such absurdity. She doesn't understand why I have chosen Marie to be my friend, when there are so many other, nicer girls in my class. But I insist I love her and she reconsiders and even praises me for taking care of little Marie. I do want to take care of her, always; I know that. I am the fairy-tale prince, in love with the beautiful fairy-tale princess. She is Cinderella and only I can rescue her, only I can see past the ashes on her face and the rags on her body. Only I can take her away from her horrible family. I want to make her happy; I want to see her smile at me. I don't care if no one else likes her. I'll protect her and make her glad that I am her friend. I'll teach her things and take care of her, every day.

Marie still talks a little like a baby, she can't say some of the words right. I give her a banana. She calls it "nana." I say, "Not 'nana,' say *banana*," but she repeats, "Nana, nana" and takes a big bite out of that special treat. That little word *nana* touches my heart; she is my little sister, my baby and she can't do wrong. I am blind to the reality of her condition. She is like my shadow; she follows me around like a puppy dog wherever I go, on the playground at recess, when we line up to go to gym, everywhere. She follows me home every day after school too, trotting a few steps behind as she tries to keep up with me, until I slow down to let her walk next to me. I wonder why her mother doesn't care where she spends her time, that she doesn't want her home for supper

"I'm allowed," Marie says when I ask her. "I can stay as long as I want."

And she does. We play together and I set a place for her at the supper table. She loves all the food Oma serves her—how she gobbles it down! I wonder how she can eat so much when she is so little. She says she likes it here and wants to live here; can she sleep here? But there my mother draws the line.

"You know," she says to me quietly, so that Marie can't hear her, "we don't have a bed for her in our room. It's enough that she is with you every day."

I show Marie all my treasures, my books and the games I have made myself, my tin flute and my new doll with real hair that can be combed, eyes that move and eyelids that close and open. She doesn't care for books or games, only wants to play with the doll, to dress and undress her, to comb her hair and put her to bed. She loves that doll and wants one just like that.

"My Mama will buy me the exact same one for my birthday," she says. "Then we each have one. They'll be sisters, like us."

She gives me a big wet kiss and laughs. But I know that her birthday isn't for a long time, and the next day she tells me, that her Mama says it's too expensive, much too expensive. Her face falls as she says this and she is close to tears. I'm close to tears too and so I tell her that I'll give her my doll. "But only if you leave it here with me," I add, hoping that way she will always be with me.

As sometimes happens in such a lopsided relationship, my ardor cooled after a while. I became bored by Marie's constant presence, I was ready to move on, and even though I missed her, I was relieved when one day she was no longer in school. Her family had moved, the teacher said.

What was it that changed this unlovable little creature into a fairy tale princess for me? What was it that gave me the wish to rescue her, to love her, to take care of her? Perhaps I wanted a younger sister like my mother had; more likely that I wanted to love another person freely without feeling that it was somehow my responsibility to do so. As the main recipient of my mother's love I think I must have felt beleaguered by her expectations that I would love her equally in return. What kept me from loving her in ways she would have liked? Or in ways that I loved my grandmother? Or how in later life I gave myself freely to others? For a six-year old, loving little Marie was much easier than trying to sort out feelings towards her mother. Did I learn so early that love can be risky, can be scary?

ON THE DAY before Christmas, when I am almost six, Mutti brings a little fir tree home for the first time. She places it in the corner of our room and while we decorate it with candles and shiny glass ornaments and tinsel, she tells me why she decided that I too would have a Christmas tree.

"When I was a little girl, year after year I had wanted to have a tree like everyone else. My parents said no, Jews didn't do that. All my friends had a tree. I remember how it felt, being deprived of something beautiful without having had something else in exchange. I don't want you to feel the same way." She looks at me and adds almost as if to confirm her decision, "This is for you. Isn't it beautiful? Doesn't it smell good? There's no harm in having a tree, right?" I nod my head yes. I suspect that she wants the tree a little for herself as much as for me. From then on we have a tree every Christmas until I am eight years old.

To her mother and sister she explains that it is "for the child," and succeeds in persuading them that there is nothing wrong with keeping some of the secular traditions of Christmas for my sake.

"I don't want her to feel left out," she says.

The four of us sit around the table in our room on Christmas Eve, Oma, Tante Bertha, Mutti and I. The room looks festive, with the tree in the corner and a shiny white cloth on the table and on the window the colorful cardboard Advent calendar which Mutti had fastened there twenty-four days ago. This morning I have opened its last and largest door. Every morning I have waited expectantly to see what picture would be revealed: Snow White and the seven dwarfs or other fairy tale figures, little baby angels, pictures of toys or ice-cream cones and today the Nativity scene. All German children have the calendars, it's a German tradition, Mutti has explained, just as all German children put their shoes on the outside window sill every night until Christmas so that Santa Claus can put a treat into them if they had been good, or a piece of coal if they had been bad. Of course, I only got treats: an apple or orange, nuts or a few pieces of candy. Bertha is in a good mood, and she and Mutti seem for once to be sisters instead of enemies. Oma, who as always has done the cooking, wears her good dress under her apron. Somehow I know that she has done it reluctantly. Maybe just to please us.

I won't eat the traditional Christmas Eve carp, for I hate any kind of fish, but I eat everything else: mashed potatoes and peas and carrots in a special cream sauce and finally the dessert torte with whipped cream. Mutti and Bertha smack their lips and ooh and aah about the taste of such unusual delicacies.

The next day, Christmas Day, Mutti roasts a goose, and even though I will only take a little taste of the meat, I love the rendered fat from it which is saved in a brown earthenware jar and then spread thick and salted on hefty slices of dark rye bread for me. It's a special treat and is supposed to help fatten me up.

While the adults enjoy the meal, I have my eyes on the tree and the few packages in their bright wrappings under it. I think they are all for me, and I know that as soon as the meal is over, Oma goes back to her room, Tante Bertha goes out, and then Mutti lights the candles on the tree. Finally I am allowed to open my presents.

There is a blouse from Tante Bertha which she sewed for me. I lay it aside quickly; I've seen the material in her room before, so it is not too much of a surprise. But then I spot the dark blue plastic zipper closing at the neck. Now that's new and interesting! I've never had anything with a zipper before. I move it up and down, up and down, until Mutti warns me not to break it. I can hardly wait to wear the new blouse to school after vacation. This year Mutti has picked out a new wooden pencil case for me and the board game Halma which she promises to play with me some evening when she isn't working. I am glad she didn't get me a doll; I don't really like to play with dolls anymore. What I'd really like is a train set like Peter's next door, but that's too expensive I know, and it's only for boys anyhow.

Lili has sent me a wooden soprano recorder. What a surprise! A real instrument, not just a ten pfennig toy! Mutti must have told her that I liked to play my little tin flute. There is a new music book from her too with words and melodies of some of the songs I know. Oma? She doesn't give presents for Christmas; somehow I don't mind.

There is one other package under the tree. I am about to open it, but then I see the tag. "Lotte," it says; it's for Mutti from Lili, a silk scarf with long fringes. She drapes it carefully around her neck and smiles. Its beautiful greens and blues shimmer in the candle light on the tree. "Feel it," she hands it down to me, "feel how soft it is." She smiles again, and I can see the happiness on her face.

CHAPTER THREE

THIS SUNDAY is another one of the many days on which everyone is supposed to display the German Flag. The red flags with the white circle and black double hook in the center are waving from every apartment window and balcony. They come in all sizes, but I notice that there are very few small ones. From my place in front of the window it looks festive. Our balcony is the only one in the street without a flag. The law forbids it, Mutti told me. Besides we would not want to anyway. "We don't approve of what is going on; we don't approve of Hitler," she has told me. I don't ask her why and she doesn't volunteer more. I think she doesn't want me to know more, but once in a while I've overheard them talk in worried tones. I know about Hitler; his picture is everywhere, in stores and on huge billboards in the streets, his voice can be heard blaring from loudspeakers and the neighbors' radios. Today I avoid going into the street to play. I don't want the kids to ask questions.

I think back to two years ago, when I so much wanted us to have a flag too, and my Oma found her old flag, saved from the last war—black, white and red in three broad stripes—and we tied it to the balcony railing. I felt really proud. I am bigger now and I understand that the old German flag no longer counts, and that we are different too.

In a way I don't mind so much being different, as long as it means being better; like being smart in school or having piano lessons. Yet I feel very bad to be told that I don't measure up, that therefore I am not entitled to the same things others have.

I haven't forgotten how at the end of first-grade the teacher had written on my report card: "*Elisabeth ist eine richtige Führernatur,*"—she has the personality of a true leader. I thought that was something good; maybe I really had some special gifts? After all, didn't I help other girls with their work, and wasn't I the one who always finished her assignments first? Mutti, on the other hand, was puzzled and appalled. A *Führernatur*? Like our *Führer*, Adolf Hitler? She showed my report card to her friends and told everyone the big joke that the teacher thought that the child was a true leader, just like Hitler. They shook their heads in disbelief and laughed. A joke about me? About Hitler? I was confused. Did she think it was bad to be a leader? Was she a little proud of me too? I had been eager to show my mother my report card. I had taken that remark as praise, as my teacher's report about my accomplishments in school. Now I no longer knew what to think. In the end I had to agree with my mother that the teacher had made a mistake in judging me And yet . . . maybe in some ways it was true?

When all the other girls wear their uniforms to school on special assembly days, I make sure that I wear my almost out-grown *Berchtesgartner Jäckchen*—the black sweater with red and green borders and silver buttons—which is like a semi-official uniform if worn over a white blouse, so that in class at least, I can blend in. It's just that I am not allowed to attend the assembly without wearing the real Hitler Youth uniform. I have to stay in the classroom alone until the others return.

In class there are the twins, Kristina and Barbara. They arrived in the middle of the year and are almost as smart as I am. Their handwriting is always perfect and they are much praised. Their pictures are pretty: little girls wearing fancy dresses, houses with red roofs and many windows, fenced in gardens with graveled paths and colorful flowers, which everyone admires. They look exactly alike and are taller than I am. They have long blond braids with big ribbons and large blue eyes. I notice their expensive looking dresses. Even their uniforms seem to be made of finer materials. They are always together and don't seem to mind if some of the other girls are envious and whisper behind their backs. Hearing them being criticized like that makes me feel a kind of rare solidarity with the rest of the girls. Before they came I was the best in the class. I have decided that I don't like them.

Kristina asks me why I am not wearing my uniform the way I am supposed to.

"I forgot," I answer.

"Then you can't go to assembly," Barbara sneers.

"I know," I snap back. I want to add, "I don't care," but I can't say it, because I do care. At that moment I care very much; that lie doesn't seem like a real lie to me, and I worry about what I can say next time and whether they'll know I lied.

I sit alone in the classroom and hear the German anthem, "*Deutschland, Deutschland über alles*," and the "*Horst Wessel Lied*" being sung in the gymnasium. The melody of the anthem is so beautiful that it makes me feel all shivery inside and suddenly very lonely. Quietly I sing along. I don't sing the other, new song .The melody is not as nice, and I can't remember the words: something about the flag and dying for glory and the fatherland.

For some reason nobody asks me the next time why I don't

wear my uniform. The twins seem not to care, they dismiss me; I think they are glad they found me lacking in something. The other girls don't seem to give it a thought and remain as before.

The new girl Alice is small and has asthma and is often sick. She can't go to rallies and belong to the youth group because she is too sickly. I am drawn to her because she is different and like me doesn't quite measure up. I like to think of her as a friend. I wish she would invite me to her house some time, but she doesn't. She can't come to mine because she isn't supposed to walk that far. We are only friends in school. All the other girls like her too and I am only her special friend when we are excluded together. I like that part, and I try not to be jealous when she is friendly with the other girls. I think about how she is different in a way that makes everyone want to be kind to her and make allowances in order to protect her, and how I am just plain different no matter how much I try to be included.

At show-and-tell after Easter vacation Alice shows the class her souvenir: a shiny Italian coin embedded in a lump of black rock.

"We've been to Italy," she tells us, "and we saw a big volcano that spews fire and rock."

I look at that foreign penny and at the rough rock surrounding it. I am fascinated by that little piece of rock and my imagination soars to that foreign place in which such strange things happen. She shows us a picture of Mount Etna with its plume of fire and lava and I want to go there to see for myself. Suddenly I am no longer in the classroom, I am no longer in our small apartment on the narrow street; I am a world traveler, an adventurer, a famous explorer. The small restricted world in which I live has vanished, my family has vanished and I find myself in a world full of wonderful exotic places. I can't concentrate on school work, I am far away, and the teacher reprimands me for not paying attention. Gradually, on my way home, reality asserts itself, and my fantasy is replaced by my everyday world.

I had completely forgotten about that coin until recently, when suddenly the memory of it reappeared. It struck me, though not for the first time, how over the years that small girl's spirit and yearning for adventure gradually adjusted to the exigencies of survival and how there remained long into adulthood an empty place somewhere inside me in which that spirit of adventure had been.

After the summer vacation Alice doesn't return to school; the teacher tells us that she has moved away to the south somewhere, where she can get better. I imagine her sitting in a big chair on the terrace of a beautiful house with many windows. She is holding a book and is looking at a wide lawn that slopes down to a blue lake surrounded by snow peaked mountains. The grass is a very lush green, and there are huge trees. A white sailboat is floating on the lake and the sun makes the water sparkle. Just like the colored picture in one of my books, and a little like Heidi in the mountains. I wish I could be there with her. I miss her.

WHEN I WAS about four years old my mother rented a *Schrebergarten* from the city, a small plot of land on which working class people would grow vegetables and fruit for their own consumption or to sell to supplement their incomes. She cultivated it intensively, a few hours after work and every Sunday morning from early spring through late fall. We would take the streetcar to the end of the line and then walk a mile or so to the area where the plots of land were laid out. I remember that I was very small when I started helping, and old enough later to resent having to do so almost every Sunday.

My mother loved working that garden and she did not seem to tire of the many chores that needed to be done. There was a narrow path along one side, which led from the small green-painted entrance gate to the back of the plot, and several even narrower paths, just wide enough to get through, led here and there among the beds. The rest was fully planted.

It must have been hard work for her, the spading and hoeing, the weeding and later the harvesting. But I know that those were some of her happiest times. She would test the soil by rubbing it between her fingers or smelling it, even tasting it the way farmers did, to see what it needed to be productive. She was happy when her hands and knees were black from kneeling among the rows in which she planted seed potatoes. When she talked about her garden her face, which usually looked drawn with one worry or another, became calm and happy. When she spread the horse manure she had collected in buckets from a nearby field, she smiled. She taught me to love the soil too, the way she did.

In the spring the stems of last year's sunflowers, tall enough for that year's pole beans, had to be erected, the blackberry suckers which had escaped the hedge needed to be trimmed, and I helped to carefully place pea and bean seeds into the narrow furrows she had prepared.

A small wooden garden shed, painted green, stood at one end of the rectangular plot, in which she kept garden tools, clay pots, watering cans and a pair of rickety garden chairs. When it rained I would sit under the awning of the shed and play one of the games I had made myself, or read, while Mutti, wearing her olive-green poncho, kept working.

"Nature doesn't wait," she would explain. "Now is the time to put in the potatoes"—or prune the cherry tree, or pick raspberries.

In June I was allowed to pick strawberries, provided I would be very careful not to step on the plants.

"You can eat some, but not too many," she would say. The first time I squatted among the rows of strawberry plants she told me the story of how she and the other young people on the farm, where she had been apprenticed after the war, had to whistle while picking berries. "Do you know why?" she asked, and when I couldn't think of the reason, she told me to whistle and not stop. There were those luscious berries, and I couldn't eat any! Well, I didn't have to whistle after that, and many of those ripe strawberries, dirt and all would disappear into my mouth, always however with a little bit of guilt. Had I eaten too many? Should I have whistled?

At the beginning of August I helped pick peas and beans, and later I helped dig up potatoes. There seemed to be rows and rows of them; too many, I thought. It was hard work. When as sometimes happened, the harvest yielded mostly potatoes that were small, she would remind me of the folk-saying: "The dumbest farmers always grow the biggest potatoes." And I would laugh with her, even though I didn't really understand what was funny.

Occasionally on summer Sundays my mother would persuade my grandmother to come with us to *Das Land,* as we called it. Oma would then sit under the apple tree in her dark Sunday dress, a book on her lap and would watch my mother work. I would sit near her on the grass, also with a book, and we would read when we got tired of watching. On those Sundays I did not have to help; those Sundays were special. Now and then we would look up from our reading to see whether Mutti was finished working, but we could never persuade her to sit down with us and rest. The demands of the garden drove her on; growing things to eat was both practical—it supplemented our

40

otherwise limited larder—and at the same time it was what she liked to do best.

One Sunday afternoon my mother's uncle Leopold and his wife Lina came out for a visit. They, being well-to-do city people looked around the garden, shook their heads in wonder and admiration at my mother's work and then asked her why she didn't grow any flowers. She answered something about there not being enough room for such luxuries, that growing things to eat was more important. Strangely, I was ashamed; I am not sure why. Did I realize that we were so much poorer than they and was I ashamed of that? Or was it that I too had missed flowers? In any case, the next year Mutti put in a flower bed. I was happy and proud when on our return on the streetcar the other passengers admired the big bunches of dahlias I carried in my arms.

The products of all this work were put up in jars or canned. I would go with my mother to the cannery, where an area was set aside for people to bring their own beans or peas or other vegetables, already ladled into tin-plated iron cans. The cans were transferred to big kettles and boiled under pressure, and before they could cool, someone would bring them over to a machine which put on the lids. I was fascinated. I especially liked the machine that dropped lids on the cans, turned them around while crimping the rim of the cans over the lid, thus sealing them. An iron arm then descended from above, pressed down on the lid and embossed a few letters and numbers on the can, a code for the contents and the year of harvest. I remember how the air was hot and steamy and smelled like vegetables, how the clanking noises of the big machines assaulted my ears. I never liked all the waiting around, before it was our turn; but of course, everyone's beans were ripe at the same time, Mutti explained. "Don't be so impatient," she would say, but I would continue to fidget. Finally our name would be called, and after she had placed our cans on a long table and given instructions to a woman in a white smock and cap, we were able to leave. I could tell Mutti was happy by the way she smiled and walked swinging our arms, my hand in hers. The year's harvest was safely in. The next day we would come back with large baskets to carry the sealed cans home.

Grandma helped with the fruit, which were put up in Mason jars or made into jams and jellies in our small kitchen. The first couple of years I found all this activity interesting, but later, harvest time lost its charm for me, and seemed just a lot of work.

Finally, because she was Jewish, my mother was no longer entitled to till that little piece of German soil and there were no more harvests for us.

The loss of her beloved garden was a tremendous blow for my mother. I noticed how on Sundays, for many months to come, she would be restless, trying to do busy herself with other activities. We now took more walks in the suburbs, or took the streetcar to visit friends. We spent many Sunday afternoons at the house of one of her German friends in whose large garden she would work while I played with one of the neighbor children. But it wasn't the same for her. She liked to help her friend and enjoyed the work; still it made her very sad. It remained a loss not easily made up.

Years later, during the war, there still remained on the shelf some cans of peas and jars of strawberry jam she had put up. As she served them judiciously, so they would last, as I savored the precious taste of berries on my slice of dark bread, or as I mixed peas into the potatoes on my plate, I thought of my mother's hard work which at the time I had not always appreciated. It had been worth while; I appreciated it now.

How did my mother come to know so much about growing things? How had she learned about planting and pruning and fertilizing and all the many things one has to know to be a successful gardener? Like most small children I assumed that my mother would succeed in anything she undertook; it never occurred to me to ask her then how she had learned so much about plants. Only much later when I was in my early teens and we had just returned from helping an old friend plant some small apple trees in her yard did I finally ask her how she came to know and care so much about gardening.

"It was great sadness that drove me to learn about plants," she said. "I must have had what we now call a nervous breakdown. I felt sick and weak and I couldn't stand being indoors working in an office six days a week."

"Why? What was that sadness?" I asked, wondering what that must have been like.

"I guess I never told you that I had been engaged to be married just before the War started in '14. He was sent to the front for four years and then in 1918 he died in the influenza epidemic. We had waited for the end of the war to get married. Too long, because now he was dead."

"Why didn't you get married before?" I asked her, not understanding.

"Well, maybe we should have. But you know, in those days one waited until one had saved enough money to set up housekeeping. That had been our plan." She became quiet and I didn't know whether she would go on. "Well, that's a long time ago," she finally said. After another long pause she continued.

"I went to see a doctor who suggested that I get out of the office and find work outdoors in the fresh air. I apprenticed in a horticultural school in the country to learn the nursery trade.

It was hard work, I learned a lot, and I got better. That's the story, now you know." That seemed to be all she was willing to say, and I didn't ask about anything else that day.

Funny, I thought, she didn't tell me his name or what he was like, or how they met or what they saw in each other. It must be a closed door for her behind which only pain resides, I concluded.

CHAPTER FOUR

This sunday afternoon, as every other Sunday, Mutti and I visit Tante Lina, my grandmother's oldest sister. It is a duty call that is always the same, and not a fun way to spend a Sunday. Mutti insists that I put on my Sunday dress and polish my shoes before we go. It is quite a long walk through the streets where the flags are waving.

I wanted to take my blue scooter, but Mutti said no. It's a special scooter, a new invention. You don't have to push with your foot on the pavement like on an ordinary scooter, because it has an extra board attached to the footboard which makes the wheels turn. You stand on it, pump up and down with your legs like on a sewing machine treadle. It can go very fast and feels almost as if I were going on a bicycle, or even a motorcycle. I feel very powerful when I ride it, and I am proud of it, even though it is not new and only a hand-me-down. I wonder how someone could have let such a great thing go.

Tante Lina is very old and wrinkled, much older than Oma I imagine. She is short and very fat and usually sits at her little table in front of the window drinking coffee out of a cup, whose flower design is almost totally faded. It must be very old too, like her. I have never seen her standing up or walking around

45

her room. Maybe she is too old, maybe she sits there even at night. But no, there is a bed covered by a dark red patterned quilt, and a counter with some kitchen things, and a couple of straight chairs. This is her domain, that room. It has a balcony like ours, but even in the summer she never sits on it when we visit and the window is always closed. I hate the smell in the room, a little like the bathroom smell at school, but also like something else, something very old, something specifically Tante Lina.

Mutti knocks "Come in." She is expecting us. As we enter, she turns around and gives us a big smile. But then, as the corners of her mouth turn down, she says: "What took you so long? I thought you would never come."

At every visit she says the same thing, even though the clock next to her bed says two o'clock. We've been punctual as usual. I know it's her way of saying hello. Mutti plants a kiss on her upturned cheek; I do too. Her smell assaults my nostrils, like rancid fat and old perfume mixed with dust under the bed. We pull up chairs to the table and sit with her. She pushes away the Jewish newspaper she had been reading and asks Mutti to pour her some more coffee.

"The upper half, please," she says, smiling. It's her only joke, repeated every visit. Tante Lina loves coffee. It's one of the pleasures of her life, of which there are not too many; her only luxury. She offers some to Mutti, opens the round biscuit tin, and asks me whether I want one. I love biscuits, but these don't look so good. So we both decline. Suddenly she pulls me over to her, and as I see the food spots on the front of her dress come closer and closer, it occurs to me in a flash that maybe it is not such a sin for old people to have spots on their clothes the way it is for children. I can feel her big soft breast against my cheek. She hugs me and tells me that I have gotten even taller since last time. I can hardly breathe. The pin with the red stones she always wears on the front of her dress starts to scratch my face. I turn my head away and she lets me go.

She and Mutti talk a while. I hardly listen to what they say; it is not very interesting and is always the same. It's about her worries: whether as a Jew she will be allowed to keep her small government pension, whether the apartment owners will ask her to leave, about a former neighbor who is now afraid to visit her old Jewish friend, about how long it has been since her sisters visited her. An hour has passed and we get up to leave. "Already?" she says, as always. She is indignant. Such a short visit!

"We have to go, but we'll be back soon," Mutti says. A goodbye kiss, and out the door we go. "She is lonely," Mutti says. She becomes silent and seems sad as always when we leave Tante Lina. I am skipping along, glad the visit is over, and after a while she seems happier too.

THE FOLLOWING SUNDAY we visit Tante Emma, my other great aunt. Our biweekly visits to my grandmother's sisters are part of our routine. Even though those visits are boring and I never want to go, especially to Tante Emma, I have to. She too has never been married and I don't think she likes children, but Mutti reminds me that her aunts Emma and Lina are the only relatives we have, except for her cousin Alfred and Oma's brother-in-law, Leopold, and his wife. She says that since I am the only child in the whole family, I am very important to them. I don't really believe her, but then perhaps I don't understand old people. I wonder sometimes why Oma doesn't come with us like she used to. Maybe it's because she doesn't like to go out much any more, or maybe because she doesn't like the way her sisters always complain?

I put on my Sunday dress and polish my shoes and off we go by streetcar to Cousin Alfred's apartment where Emma lives. I remain silent and look out of the window. I am mad that we have to waste such a beautiful afternoon visiting.

Mutti bends down to me and says, by way of further explanation, "You know, she is old and lonely and that's why we have to cheer her up a little. We won't stay long."

I can tell that she doesn't want to go either. We're in this together, so I've decided to make the best of it. At least I get to see a different, nicer part of the city, and maybe there'll be cake or cookies.

I look around at her large sunny room. It doesn't smell bad the way it does at Tante Lina's, and it has a large window overlooking the broad tree lined street. She is thin and elegantly dressed; her wavy gray hair is neatly arranged. The corners of her mouth are permanently turned down, which gives her face a sour expression, and her voice is whiney as she complains to us about the food the maid prepares for her, and how her nephew Alfred is never home to keep her company. Usually when we visit she sits in her chair near the window embroidering a handkerchief or crocheting an antimacassar or a doily. Mutti has told me that she used to be one of the finest embroiderers in the city, and that she had worked for very expensive dress shops when she was young. Sometimes she gives Mutti a finished piece: *"Für Elisabeth,"* she says, "for when she gets married." Mutti holds it up admiringly and tells her how beautiful it is. She nudges me to thank Tante Emma with a kiss. I plant a quick one on her wrinkled cheek. Neither one of us likes it.

It's one of those grown-up things that are difficult to remember, thanking someone for a gift that you don't even like. But I also see that she is giving me something she is proud of because I am her grandniece. Besides, I am supposed to always be polite and think of the other person's feelings.

Today she is involved in something different. She is slowly and carefully moving a handle mounted on a small wooden box so that its needle-like pointed end rubs against a shiny translucent rock on a metal stand. The box emits soft swooshing noises that rise and fall, squeak and rumble as Emma pokes the crystal with the needle and every now and then a human voice can be heard. She pokes some more: music. Not very clear, sometimes loud, sometimes hardly audible, still, a radio! I am fascinated and would like to try to make that music appear myself. Tante Emma says no, the apparatus is too delicate and I might break it. "I won't," I say defiantly and stretch out my hand to touch it. She turns off the switch. No more radio. It's hers, she won't share. I am disappointed and angry at her. At last something to make the visit interesting and she won't share! And she's a grown-up, not a girl on the playground with whom I could argue or whom I could pay back by not sharing either. I like her even less than usual and maybe next visit I won't come along!

Mutti notices my disappointment. "Come," she says on our way home. "I'll tell you a little about her and then maybe you'll understand. You see, Tante Emma, and Tante Lina, too, never got married the way Oma did. They had no one to take care of them and no one to take care of. The way I take care of you."

"Hm, hm," I nod my head.

"They worked hard all their lives, but they didn't earn much money. So they were always poor.

"Why didn't they do something else?" I ask.

"Well you see, in those days, in the little town in Poland where they lived, girls didn't go to school very long, maybe to twelve or thirteen, and then they were apprenticed to an embroiderer or a dressmaker and got jobs in dress shops. That kind of work paid only very little. Oma too did that for a while, but then she married your grandfather and had us, and no longer needed to work. Look, here's our stop. We're almost home."

⤫

ONKEL LEOPOLD and Lina, my other Tante Lina, my mother's uncle and his wife, have come for afternoon coffee and cake. There on the white embroidered tablecloth lies the big open box of chocolates they have brought. No one seems to be paying any attention to it, but I do. I open my eyes wide with wonder as I peruse the luscious treat before me. This is not something that happens often in our home: a giant box of chocolates! Secretly I select the one I will pick when it becomes my turn, a big mound of light brown chocolate with a half hazelnut on top. "Mutti likes dark chocolate best, she won't want that one," I think, "and probably the other grown-ups will feel the same way." Maybe I'll be allowed two; what'll I chose next? But the grown-ups keep talking and talking, and no one seems to care about the candy. I get up from my chair and surreptitiously my hand creeps over the tablecloth towards the center where the gold paper covered box is. I would never take a piece on my own (oh the delicious naughtiness that suggests!) until it is offered, but maybe my fingers can be very near my choice, just in case. Maybe the grown-ups won't notice. Mutti notices of course, and her eyes say, "What are you doing??" Quickly I withdraw my hand, pretending it is there only by accident.

"It's time to dig in," Onkel Leopold says suddenly. Maybe he has seen my hand too? "Which one do you want, Little One?" He and Lina never call me by my name; they have no children of their own. I point.

50

"Wait till the adults have chosen," Mutti says. I withdraw my hand.

"This is how you choose," Onkel Leopold says with a twinkle in his eyes. He proceeds to bite into one piece, looks at it, shakes his head, and says, "Not this one," and puts it back in the box, with the bitten side down. He peruses the box, chooses another one with a flourish, and does the same thing. Now all the adults are laughing, but I don't see what's so funny. How can he do that? Because he's not a child? Doesn't he believe in having to be *bescheiden*, the way I was taught?

Laughing and shaking her head, Mutti asks "What are you teaching the child?" And then I finally get my piece of candy. And a second one too.

The German expression *Bescheiden sein* was written large in my mother's moral vocabulary. It was a dictum which she drummed into me, to which she insisted I adhere, even though my spirit rebelled—for I would have preferred to stand out, to be looked up to, as proud and self assured as a small child could be. I tried to be modest and diffident and not take pride in anything I did.

"It was nothing, it was easy," I would tell her when I brought home a good mark from school. I think my mother liked that. It was alright for her to praise me, but her message was that I must never praise myself. That she made clear.

As I grew up, History conspired to embed my mother's belief in the value of not standing out firmly in my psyche. If I didn't call attention to myself in school, the other girls wouldn't mind that I was missing at their rallies and marches and celebrations, that I was different. After first grade I stopped waving my hand enthusiastically in the air, or calling out the answer to a teacher's question before anyone else. I learned to wait a decent minute before I would raise my hand demurely, trying

51

with all my might to push down my spirited self, which was stuck like a heavy lump in the upper part of my chest. That I was not expected to have any ambitions beyond doing the best I could in whatever task was set for me, made it a little easier to learn not to stand out, though deep inside me there remained that nugget of desire that wanted to be recognized as someone outstanding.

That I did not expect much was perhaps also the reason that I never knew how poor we were. I don't remember ever asking for a treat or a present; when one was produced I was happy and grateful. I grew up in that genteel poverty that doesn't seem to care about who is rich and who is poor. I never heard my mother or grandmother talk about who had what and who didn't. My grandmother had a dignity which seemed independent of social position, and my mother was much too busy holding this or that job to keep food on the table to express a longing for more possessions. I was aware that Onkel Leopold and Tante Lina had a bigger apartment than ours and had fancier furniture and gave big parties, and that Cousin Alfred had a maid and lived in a nice neighborhood with a yard in the back with beautiful trees. Maybe the fact that they didn't have any children kept them from being a measure of affluence for me. Even Lili's big house in Bremen didn't count, for there too were no children. I just did not think of them as being like us.

TANTE BERTHA has left. Oma says she is away in the mountains to cure the illness which makes her cough so much and makes her irritable. I don't miss the arguments she and Mutti had almost every day. I would usually try to shut the door to our room when they got started, so that I wouldn't hear anything. But I really miss her now, going into her room to watch her sew. When she made me my new blouse and the skirt a while ago from her ladies' left-over fabric, I had to stand still for only a few minutes while she measured me. Later, when she finished sewing, I tried them on and admired myself in her mirror. I like her big wall mirror where I can see myself full length as I stand among the fabric scraps and ribbons and pins on the floor as if I were standing in a meadow full of flowers. Our own room is very neat, everything always in its place, and the small mirror over the chest of drawers is much too high for me. When I stand on a chair and look at myself, all I can see is my head and neck and those ugly round glasses with the metal rims which are supposed to help my wandering right eye find its proper place again. I don't like my short straight brownish hair either; I'd like to be blond like the twins. It is better to look at my whole self in Bertha's mirror, especially when I have something new to wear.

She has sent us a postcard of the place where she is staying, and I try to imagine how it must be to be in a place that is so beautiful. She says that she is beginning to feel better and that she hopes she can be home soon. She misses us and sends me a special hug.

The door to Bertha's room is locked; Mutti does not want me to go in there. "Why?" I ask.

"Because it is *her* room, we have *ours*," she says.

I don't understand. I think about that locked door and about *our* room and *her* room and how Tante Bertha almost never comes into ours, nor Mutti into hers. I also know that for a while now Mutti had discouraged me from going into that room. Just a week ago she got very upset and yelled at her sister for letting me sprawl on her bed. Tante Bertha got excited too and yelled back, about not being a leper, or something like that—I don't know what a "leper" is, must be something bad—but Mutti pointed at the crumpled handkerchiefs lying on the night table. "What about those?" I looked up from the magazine with the pictures of ladies in beautiful clothes, looked from one to the other and wished they would stop yelling; instead Mutti made me get up and leave the room in a hurry. There were some more angry words between them; I couldn't understand what all the fuss was about. I think that perhaps my mother didn't want me to see the beautiful clothes in the pictures, or that she disapproved of the disorder in the room. No, I think it's more that she wants me all to herself. She doesn't want to share me with her sister with whom she is always arguing. Now the door is locked and it's even more quiet than usual in the apartment. I miss Tante Bertha.

I AM STANDING on a chair in my slip, ready for the first fitting of the new skirt my mother is making for me out of the good parts of Oma's old spring coat. Usually Tante Bertha does the sewing for me, but now she is gone, and Mutti has to do it. It makes her nervous, she says, it's not something she likes to do, but I've outgrown my old navy-blue pleated one. The double hem has been let out twice, the suspenders that cross in the back are too short and so it is time for something new.

I hate to stand still, I am already getting impatient, and we haven't even begun.

"I like my old skirt, it still fits. Why do I need a new one?" I try to stave off a confrontation. I know how exacting Mutti can be, how everything has to be perfect for her, especially when she does something for me. We are both on edge, but Mutti is determined to proceed.

"When can I go?" I ask, looking down at her head. Standing

like this I am taller than she. Her scalp shows white through the dark brown hair where the part is.

"Just stand still and be patient; it won't take long," she says. I know better; it always takes a long time with her. Too long. I despise *anpassen*.

She adjusts the new skirt on me. Its many pleats are fastened down with white basting stitches.

"It's much too long," I complain, looking down. As I bend the skirt seem to get even longer.

My mother, with pins in her mouth and the yellow tape measure in her hand doesn't answer.

"I don't like it this way!" I stamp my right foot and almost slip off the chair.

"Hold still," she says, irritation in her voice. "Now turn."

"I want to get down," I say. I've had enough. The soles of my feet tingle and I wiggle my toes. I don't care if I don't get new clothes ever again.

Mutti is beginning to lose her patience. "I'm doing the best I can. Stop wiggling so much!"

Relentlessly she measures, pins, gives me a little push to turn, measure, pin, turn, measure, pin, turn . . . a little bit at a time. It's taking an eternity. We are both angry; she at me for being once again ungrateful for the effort she is making on my behalf, and I because I feel trapped up on that chair, like a prisoner, with my mother being the prison guard.

"It never takes that long with Tante Bertha. She's much faster than you." My voice is snappy and I jump off the chair. I've upset the pin box, and pins are rolling all over the floor.

Suddenly my cheek is burning. I hardly heard the single slap of hand on cheek before it was done.

"Ungrateful child," she says, her voice petulant. Then in a gruff voice: "Pick up those pins. Now!"

I crawl around on the floor, still wearing the unfinished skirt. Its pins prickle my knees as I dutifully pick up each spilled pin and put it in the box. My mother leaves the room, and I take off the unfinished skirt and put on my old one. It's just her nerves again, I think, rubbing my cheek, that's why the slap, the *Ohrfeige*. I have overheard her talk about her nerves, of how nervous she is, how high-strung, how sensitive, how easily overwrought. I'm not ungrateful, and I know she knows too. Maybe I was a little bit bad, but even so, I didn't deserve to be slapped like that. I wish she wouldn't let things out on me. That's not fair, and I hate her today.

CHAPTER FIVE

LIKE THE GIANT stones erected by ancient peoples in open fields which one visits once, admires and forever remembers, but about whose significance one can only make conjectures, or like an abstract sculpture in a public place that we think about, whose meaning eludes us, I have occasionally met individuals who, though never close to me, have stood out above the plateau of all the others who remain in my memory. My mother's old teacher, Fräulein Kuhn, is one of those.

Fräulein Kuhn lives in Cuxhaven, a small town at the mouth of the Elbe River. Mutti and I are on our way to spend a few days with her. She reminds me that only a half hour bus ride away is the beach

"We were there once with your Papa," she reminds me. "Remember?"

I try to, but I can't picture how that was when we were there together.

I let Mutti hold me by the hand as we walk along the platform in the station because I am a little scared by the noise and smoky, oily smell and by the many people hurrying. The hands on the huge station clock point to ten and eight; I know that is only a few minutes until our train is due to leave and I start to pull my mother along. I am getting excited about the train ride; it's not often that we go away like that; only once a year in the summer to be with my father at the beach or in the mountains. This is extra and so doubly exciting.

From my window seat in the third class compartment where I am kneeling, I watch as the train pulls out of the station. I watch the backs of tenements pass by, I see women hanging clothes out to dry and children playing on tiny back balconies, like the one in our apartment, where I don't like to play because it is dark and there is nothing to see except the backs of other tenements. The train speeds up as it follows the bank of the river and we can see the embankment where we would sometimes go for a walk, *spazieren gehen*, on Sundays. There Mutti wouldn't let me walk by myself, I had to hold her hand, "too many people," she would say. I like our occasional Sunday walks in the big cemetery on the outskirts of the city better, because there are wide avenues and beautiful big trees and flowers among the grave stones. There I can run ahead alone and even bounce a ball as long as it doesn't bounce on the graves. We don't know anyone who is buried there; we go there because it is one of the few parks to which one can take a short streetcar ride from our apartment.

Where the river becomes wider, Mutti points to Hamburg's famous shipyards. Its huge cranes stand like giant birds on long legs, bending their necks towards the water. She points out the different kinds of boats we pass, ferries and tugboats with barges, and fishing boats, excursion boats, a big ocean liner and in the distance on the other bank many strange looking gray ships. Warships, she says, and then becomes quiet.

She doesn't say much for the rest of the journey, even as she hands me the sandwich she has prepared for the train trip. There are now very few houses, only an occasional farmhouse surrounded by big trees. The train crosses a long bridge which seems to rise barely above the river and then there are meadows and cows, and more meadows and cows, until even that stops and the flat land becomes a grayish brown bog and I become sleepy and close my eyes.

It is beginning to get dark when we arrive in Cuxhaven. Mutti's old teacher meets us at the station and they shake hands warmly and smile. She calls Mutti by her first name, Lotte, but my mother calls her formally Fräulein Kuhn as if she were still her high school teacher instead of a friend. I am a little miffed because Fräulein Kuhn hardly acknowledges my presence. I watch the two women as I walk behind them the few blocks to her house. They are already deep in conversation. What can they be talking about? I'm not sure I will like this friend.

After we climb the steep stairs to her apartment, Fräulein Kuhn points to the living room couch. "This is where you'll sleep," she says to Mutti. "It's pretty comfortable."

Now I wonder where I will sleep. The apartment is very small; two tiny rooms and a kitchen where the wooden table takes up almost the whole space.

"I'll make up the child's bed later," she says. She points to the table. "Under there," she adds. "It's big enough for a little one like her."

Luckily just then I spot the cake in the center of the table and the cups and plates. There are two cups and a glass or milk for me, but only two plates. She pours the coffee and then puts a piece of cake on each of the plates and hands one to my mother and one to me. There is none for her. Maybe she made a mistake and my piece was really meant for her? I hold onto my plate with both hands.

"Where is yours?" Mutti asks.

"Cake is for my special guests only," she replies in a matter of fact tone. We both look at her. "As long as there are children in the world who don't have enough bread to eat, I won't have cake," she adds without any further explanation. I dig into my piece of cake. Delicious!

I like my bed under the kitchen table. It is like a little cave of my own. As I lie there under a warm blanket I can hear the two women talk in muted tones until I get sleepy and my eyes close. I am not even mad at them any more.

The next morning Mutti and I take the bus to the beach. It is only a short ride, but half way there I begin to feel sick and throw up all over the bus. I'm embarrassed and the bus driver is mad. On the way back, the same thing happens. From then on we get off half way and walk the rest of the way. It's a long walk and my feet are beginning to hurt in my almost outgrown shoes.

"Why does Fräulein Kuhn wear those funny big shoes?" I ask Mutti .

She smiles, "They are men's shoes."

"Why?" I don't understand.

"Men's shoes are bigger, so she can wear them first on one foot and then on the other. That way they don't wear out so fast and last a lot longer."

I look down at my too-small, scuffed shoes that are almost worn out. "Can't she buy new ones?"

"Yes, she can, but she doesn't want to spend money on herself. She gives all the money she gets for having been a teacher to poor people."

I think about that some. "Why?" I ask.

She hesitates before answering. "Promise you won't tell anyone. Not anyone, promise?" I promise. "Because she believes in something called Communism. She says that everybody should share what they have with those who have less, so that everyone is equal."

Over the many years since that visit to my mother's old teacher I have held on to that image of Fräulein Kuhn's big brown misshapen shoes, not as something odd and ugly, but as a reminder of the power to act nobly that true conviction can bestow.

↔

I WAS FOUR the first time my mother took me to the annual November Fair. I remember that we went twice more until I refused to go again. It was always the same: I went with great anticipation and ended up feeling bad. My mother couldn't quite understand why. Now that I was older, didn't I enjoy it more? Didn't all children love fairs? She thought it would be a special treat for me.

November in Hamburg means rain and a cold wind. I am almost six. I am wearing my blue slicker and rubbers as Mutti and I step off the streetcar. It's been a long ride, too long and it is already quite dark. She holds my hand as I skip along beside her to the fairground. Calliope music is getting louder and multicolored lights are blinking through the lightly falling rain, and there are lots of families hurrying just as we are. The two of us are just by ourselves, while everyone else seems to be many, parents and children and often grandparents too. The older kids are running too fast for their parents to keep up, and there is a lot of shouting ("Wait, wait for us, Willie") and yelling of threats and words that I don't hear at home. I have stopped skipping, my steps slow down, and as I now walk a bit behind my mother down the main fairway, no longer holding her hand, the sounds of the fair surge over me in waves; louder and louder they engulf me, they press into me, I am drowning: the barkers' staccato shouts, meant to entice, the carousel's calliope playing the same melody over and over, the Ferris wheels' whoosh, the bumps of the Dodgem cars, the crack of air rifles. I squint against the rain, and all the lights blur into multicolored streaks. I try to jump over the puddles that have formed on the dirt paths, but sometimes I miss and black mud splashes up my legs. I am excited and anxious at the same time.

No, I don't want to go on the merry-go-round. We stop a moment and Mutti points out how much fun it is to ride one of the colorful horses that go up and down as they go round and round, but I remember that last year it made me dizzy. No, I don't want to. Maybe the Dodgem cars, but not by myself. Mutti doesn't like them, and thinks they are dangerous. The House of Horrors: I look at the monsters painted on the outside of the tent. They are just like the monster in my nightmare, and I look away. Mutti wants me to have fun. I think she wants me to be like the other children here. That's why we came and that's why I tell her that I want some cotton candy, even though it's too sweet for my taste.

There is a big crowd gathered in front of the freak tent. We stop and listen to the barker's spiel. This is something to watch, and I want to stay. When the man comes around to collect money, Mutti pays and we are allowed into the tent to see the show.

First, the ten-foot man. He is wearing strange clothes, a red and black checkered jacket and a tall black hat and pants patched with pieces of cloth of many colors. He makes loud noises that are not words, more like an animal's grunts as he tries to sing a song. He stomps up and down on the little stage with his long legs. I don't like his crooked smile as he looks at the audience. It's not very friendly, but I clap anyway when everyone else claps. His upper body bows to the audience and he disappears behind the curtain.

Next are the tiny people; dwarfs, the barker says. They are

world famous entertainers he tells us and we are lucky to see them. I wonder about them, they are no taller than me but their heads are much too big, and their faces are old and get all scrunched up when they smile. I don't think they like to smile. They mostly look angry, even when they dance a little dance together on the stage and talk to the audience in squeaky voices. Are they looking at me? What do they want? I take hold of Mutti's hand. They disappear behind the curtain.

Loud drum rolls—the barker's voice gets louder. Two ladies' heads with long blond braids peek out from behind the curtain. Look, they are coming on the stage! One body in a blue dress, with two arms. I almost don't want to look. But I do. Four feet in fancy shoes that dance to the music. I hold my breath. Mutti looks at me sideways. Does she like this? More drum rolls and more applause, and a baby buggy appears from behind the curtain. In it sits a man with tiny stumps for arms and no legs. The two headed lady pushes him back and forth on the stage. Both heads coo and smile at him. Clapping and hollering. I turn my head away.

"I want to go home" I whine. Mutti looks down at me.

"I want to go home now!" I insist. The show isn't over and we have to squeeze through the audience to the exit.

"There's much more, ladies and gentlemen, the best is yet to come! Don't miss the best parts!" The barker seems to be talking directly to us, he is taking our leaving personally. I am embarrassed, but I don't want to stay.

It has stopped raining and now there are even more people than before. They are laughing and pushing each other and the music and the lights seem even more intense than when we came. I run ahead towards the exit, and I throw away what is left of my cotton candy. I feel like crying I am so sad, but I don't know why. I panic and slip in the mud in the path, but Mutti catches me just in time. When we are finally safely in the almost empty streetcar that will take us home, I feel forlorn and I try to stop crying so Mutti won't ask me what's the matter. I promise myself that I will never ever go to the November fair again in my whole life.

❧

THE CHRISTMAS I am almost eight Mutti suggests that I take out the children's Bible she gave me the year before so that we can read the Christmas story together.

"You need to know some of these stories," she says and hesitating a little she adds, "Your father would like that."

She smiles. It makes me nervous that our reading the Christmas story in this book has to be kept a secret from Oma. I know that there are secrets in our house; secrets from me, from Bertha, maybe from my mother. And now even from Oma. I'm used to secrets in our house.

I walk to the bookcase and take the book with the dull green cover and the black and white illustration from the back of the top shelf where I had put it last year. I remember how the stories are written two columns to a page, not like an ordinary book. Last year after Christmas I read the Old Testament stories about Abraham and Isaac, and how the father almost killed his own son, and about Jacob and that long, long ladder up to the sky. About the women at the well and how the Red Sea parted to let Moses and his people get away. After that it got boring. The New Testament part began to bore me after the first few pages, when Jesus grew up to be a man and started to tell people what to do. I didn't finish reading that part, but I didn't tell Mutti.

This year I say to her that I don't think that there is really a God who is everybody's father who runs things the way it tells in the book, who can grant your wishes if you only pray enough to him, as the girls in school have told me.

My mother tries to explain.

"Not an old man with a long white beard up there in the sky," she says. "Of course not. That's just something people made up to be able to see. To be able to draw pictures, to paint and decorate churches. I don't see God that way."

I nod my head. OK, that makes sense.

"But I know that there is someone or something," she continues, "some higher power, something we humans don't understand, something mysterious. I believe that."

I look doubtful.

"When you get older you'll understand."

She has decided for me. I shake my head vigorously. I don't like her to decide things for me

"I really like some of the stories though," I add to placate her.

She tries another approach.

"Then how do you think the world began? What keeps it going? Our earth, the moon and the stars, everything around us, flowers and trees, all the beautiful things that grow? Animals and people and the rivers and mountains?" She is serious; she tries to persuade me. "Yes," she continues. "There has to be someone in charge. I believe in that," she says emphatically and a little sadly. "You should too."

I shake my head again. Someone in charge? Why? I don't understand.

"I think the stories in the green book are just like fairy tales, and I don't believe those are real either. Just good stories," I say.

She bends closer to me, as if she were going to tell me a secret.

"I don't go to church or temple, but still I believe. You don't have to do that to believe in God. You don't have to believe that

Jesus was the son of God, the way it says in the New Testament. Jews don't believe that. Jesus was a real man who lived almost two thousand years ago. That's true."

I don't know why I don't let myself be persuaded by her.

"There has to be," she says again, almost as if my denial made her doubt a little too. "There has to be." I look away from her. I want to change the subject, but she persists in trying to persuade me.

"How can you be that way?" she says finally, sadly. I see how disappointed she is in me. "How can you be so *nüchtern*—so prosaic?" she says. So unfeeling, is what I hear.

I look at our little tree and watch the candles burn slowly down; the magic in those flickering lights makes me feel better. I try to forget our conversation about believing and I shyly turn my head to look at her, to see how she feels. She smiles at me in a conciliatory way. Maybe she has forgiven me my stubborn unfeeling stance, maybe she too tries to forget? Maybe she is even a little proud of me because I've tried to think for myself? I start to feel again that rare closeness between us, as if our daring to enjoy Christmas in a Jewish household and our conversation about God were a special bond between us, not shared by anyone else. Even so, we don't hug or even touch out of that feeling of closeness. Perhaps she has become accustomed to that stubborn insistence for self-sufficiency in me that keeps us physically apart. Or is she still too disappointed in me to draw me to her for a hug?

AS EVERY YEAR I am the only child at Tante Lina and Onkel Leopold's large New Year's Eve costume party. I sense that Mutti is a little afraid of Lina who likes to give un-asked-for advice in an imperative tone of voice. She was trained as a drama coach and prides herself on her poetry recitations, which take place at the drop of a hat whenever there are a few people assembled. Her deep loud voice becomes dramatic as she moves her arms in sweeping gestures through the air in front of her, especially when she recites her favorite poem, "The Song of the Bell," by Schiller:

> *Fest gemauert in der Erde*
> *Steht die Form aus Lehm gebrannt....*

She goes on and on, the poem seems endless, and after a few lines I no longer hear words but only the rhythm of the lines accompanied by her sweeping arm movements, like a song without words. She had suggested not long ago that she give me elocution lessons to improve my speech, but Mutti had declined politely. She thinks that there's nothing wrong with the way I speak, and besides why sound like Lina?

In their elegant apartment full of thick oriental carpets and overstuffed chairs I am not allowed to touch the keys on the grand piano or the leather-bound books in the bookcases which look as if they were never read. They have no children and Mutti says they don't understand children. Still, they seem fond of her, and so they tolerate me.

I like Onkel Leopold better than his wife. He has a bushy white mustache and a bald spot on the top of his head, and he seldom gives his own opinions but just nods his head agreeing with his wife. When I was very little I had pointed at his mustache and then at his head, saying," Onkel Leopold, the hair you have here you should have had up there." I've heard the story many times; by now I don't find it amusing any longer. However his taking bites out of the chocolates to see which one he liked had impressed me. I still remember the twinkle in his eyes.

Today he wears a tall white chef's hat and a white apron over a red checked shirt. He has dyed his mustache black. Almost like Hitler's. Mutti is dressed like a water nymph with her loose hair held back by an embroidered ribbon. She looks pretty. Oma thinks dressing up is undignified, so she just wears her good dress and a black velvet beaded ribbon around her neck. There are pirates and princesses and gypsies. Someone takes a picture with everyone arranged in rows near the potted palms. I squat on the floor in front. I am not wearing a costume; just like Oma.

On one of the little tables I spot the thick photo album with pictures of all former parties. A lot more people then, I notice, and more elaborate costumes the further back I flip the pages. No children at all. The sheiks and goddesses are smiling and seem to be having fun.

No one seems to be having much fun today. The grown-ups are all talking in small groups with each other, their voices subdued.

I overhear someone say, "Do you know what happened yesterday on Bismarckstrasse?" They put their heads together and whisper.

"Cuba is supposed to be easy," someone else is saying.

"They won't let it go on," from another group.

No one is laughing at all. Not much of a party, I think.

I don't understand what they are talking about, and so I wander in the direction of the kitchen from which emanates a delicious smell. Onkel Leopold is there, preparing his favorite dish. Prunes and raisins and carrots bubble in the big kettle on the stove.

"Come," he beckons me closer "Watch." He puts his hand into a bucket on the floor . . . the eel squirms and snakes its long black body around his arm.

"Look," he says, "watch me put it in." Head first into the boiling broth . . . it's still slithering around . . . sinks to the bottom . . . I wonder why I don't run out of the kitchen. I'm rooted to the spot. He puts another one in and another. It's looking at me . . .

"Mm-mm, that's going to be delicious," he says gleefully, his eyes twinkling. I feel queasy . . . I'm getting sick to my stomach . . . one last look in the direction of the kettle . . . my hands clenched over my quivering lips . . . throat tight . . . I'm out of the kitchen to the bathroom, in the nick of time.

CHAPTER SIX

T ANTE BERTHA has come back. Her face is rosy and she has a different hairdo with many curls surrounding her face. I like the way she looks and I am happy that she is back. She is still coughing a lot, and I notice that she doesn't go out to her sewing jobs much any more and spends most of the day in her room with the door closed. I have become more hesitant to visit in her room, and so I see her only at mealtimes. But it is not the same as before. Mutti hardly talks to her, and since Oma usually doesn't say much, mealtime is very quiet and heavy-feeling. It's not how it was before she left, and not how it was when she was away. I don't like it this way at all, it makes me feel bad. I leave the dinner table as soon as I am finished and go to our room to read. I'm reading *Heidi* for the third time, and I can't wait until I get to the part where she is in the city and misses the mountains and her grandfather and is so sad. I don't like the last part much, because when she returns to the mountains it is not as sunny and happy as before she left. I can't explain why the end of the book makes me feel sad too—sad and good at the same time. Like when Mutti and I return from our vacations with my father.

Suddenly I hear a burst of banging and shouting from the kitchen. Mutti and Tante Bertha must be having one of their arguments, and I try to shut it out as usual. But this time the yelling doesn't stop and I hear Bertha's voice shrieking, "I hate you, I hate you," then a crash and my mother crying out. I run towards the kitchen just as Mutti, blood streaming from the top of her head down her face, opens the kitchen door. In a flash I see broken dishes on the floor, and the ceiling lamp with its heavy pointy counterweight swinging violently back and forth above the overturned kitchen table. Mutti, with her hand on the top of her head, dashes into the bathroom, and closes the door behind her. I run after her but she has locked the door. I can hear her crying inside, and water running.

"Let me in, let me in." I am in a panic. I've never heard her cry like that before.

"It's all right, it's all right," her voice weakly from the other side of the door.

From my post outside the bathroom door I see my grandmother standing stock still in the kitchen. Tante Bertha has gone to her room, and I can hear her sobbing from behind the closed door. When Mutti comes out of the bathroom she is very pale and she has a large plaster on top of her head. She sits down on her bed and as I approach she pulls me over to her and hugs me hard. My panic subsides gradually as I feel her warm body next to mine. I hug her back. I am so relieved that she is no longer crying.

From that day on something happens between Tante Bertha and me, something that crept in quietly, a distancing that neither of us has sought nor wished for. Nevertheless, it is a turning point in our household. Bertha keeps more and more to herself; even at meals she is seldom there. For a while a friend of hers stays in her room with her and I am no longer invited in. She no longer offers to sew for me. I seldom hear the familiar whirr of the sewing machine. It seems that now my mother and I belong together more than ever, while my grandmother

71

moves about the apartment almost like a shadow. Tante Bertha has become a virtual stranger.

⤙

IT IS fall 1935. Today, as I do every Saturday afternoon, I am riding my red bike along the streets to my piano lesson. It's the highlight of my week. My teacher Fräulein Herbert expects me to be always prepared for my lesson. I like Fräulein Herbert and I don't want to disappoint her. Everyone is pleased about my progress: Mutti, the teacher, and even me. The piano is my best friend. I don't mind having to practice playing scales. Fräulein Herbert says that scales are the backbone of all music, and she makes them more interesting by playing matching chords with me. Sometimes we play duets, and that's really special. I'm getting pretty good at arpeggios too. Mostly I still love Mozart best. I want to practice a lot to make good progress. Fräulein Herbert thinks I might become a good piano player provided I work a lot, and don't skip any lessons.

My legs pump to the rhythm of the Clementi sonatina in my head, the fast movement, the one I have practiced. Now and then I hum along and the fingers of my left hand stretch out and pull together, press down and lift, as if the handlebar were the piano keyboard. My right hand rests lightly on the old brown music bag clipped to the back of the saddle. This time I am especially well prepared; I've practiced a lot and I think Fräulein Herbert will praise me. On Sunday I'll have to play for Onkel Leopold and Tante Lina. I better play well because Lina is very critical and even though Leopold won't really listen, they both want to see whether I have made progress since the last time. After all, they were the ones who had asked my teacher to take me on for free. I secretly think that they are probably paying her something. Even so . . .

I have left the narrow streets of my neighborhood behind. Now the streets are wider and tree-lined and there are bushes and flowers in the front yards of large elegant apartment buildings. I know the way without paying a lot of attention.

I mustn't be late to my lesson and so I pedal faster until I come to my favorite tree where I slow down. Most of the leaves on the big chestnut have turned yellow, their fat fingers still spread out, but already curling at the edges. On the ground hundreds and hundreds of chestnuts, glossy brown, smooth and round, each with its contrasting tan spot, less shiny, each a slightly different shape. There are more now than last week, and they are more beautiful even. I stop the bike and look for the "twins" that together make one whole, many still attached to their prickly green mother husks. Good luck they are, like finding a four-leaf clover. The palms of my hands itch to pick them up, but it's late and I only have time to gather up a few of them. I promise myself that later on my way home I'll find the most beautiful ones to keep. I'll put them in my saddle bag and if there are too many, I'll fill my pockets too.

I'm a little late after all, but the teacher doesn't seem to notice. I play for her what I have practiced. "Good, good" she says. She seems distracted; she corrects me hardly at all. Usually she notices everything—a wrong note here, the rhythm not quite right, the Czerny exercises not fluent enough. Today she is satisfied with it all. I'm surprised. Maybe she is tired. At the end of the lesson, already at the door, she plants a light kiss on the top of my head. She doesn't say as usual, "See you next week. Practice well." As I run down the stairs I wonder why she did that. Oh well, grown-ups. As I pass the chestnut tree, still thinking about my lesson and Fräulein Herbert's kiss, I forget to stop and pick up the rest of the chestnuts as I had planned.

The next day, voice flat and eyes looking at nothing in particular, my mother informs me that yesterday was my last lesson. Just like that.

"Why?" I ask. I don't understand. "Did I do something wrong? Was it because I was late?" I thought she liked me, she even told me I had talent. "Why?"

Mutti hems and haws but finally tells me that Fräulein Herbert doesn't want the neighbors to see a Jewish child enter her apartment any longer; that she is afraid.

"And so," she continues, her words crowding together to take up less space, as if to squeeze out their importance, "we have to understand that. She said she was sorry, really sorry, but under the circumstances . . . we have to understand . . . she likes you a lot, you've made so much progress, she has enjoyed teaching you . . . but she doesn't want to take a chance." Her words fall down on me like hailstones.

I stop practicing, and for quite a while I don't go near the piano, its lid remains closed and I pretend that it is just another piece of furniture and that it doesn't have anything to do with me. Once or twice Mutti asks me to play the Clementi for her again, but I refuse angrily. "I don't know how any more," I say shaking my head, and she stops asking.

One rainy afternoon after I finish my homework and there is nothing else I want to do, I look at the piano and without thinking, just as I had done in the past, I walk over to it, open the lid, and take the maroon *Magic Flute* piano arrangement book from the shelf, turn to my favorite melody, "*In diesen heil'gen Hallen*," and it is so beautiful that I can hardly see the music for the tears that are forming in my eyes. It is as if someone I love has returned to me after a long absence, and I sing along in my best and lowest voice to imitate Sarastro's voice. Even though the chestnuts I had gathered are rotting in my drawer and I finally throw them out, and even though my bike continues to stand in the downstairs hallway unused, and even though I am not making any progress the way I did when I had to practice scales and arpeggios and new pieces, the spell has been broken and the piano and I are friends again.

~&~

MY FIRST musical friend had not been the piano, but a little ten penny tin whistle. In my memory early childhood events are often telescoped, so that I do not remember exactly how old I was nor what time of year it was, whether the sun shone or gray rain filled the street, as I crossed to spend my five pennies in the little neighborhood bakery and candy store opposite our apartment house. I must have been about four or five. Probably I skipped across the street happily, for it was not often that I had money to spend on candy. What I do remember is the feel of the pennies in my hand, round and flat and jingly and warm, as I clutched them firmly to make sure I didn't drop any.

The shop, even in the eyes of a little girl, seemed small, the counter was very high, and the woman behind the counter enormous. She knew all the children on the street as they came in with their pennies, pointing to their favorite kinds of candy, which were kept in large glass jars on the shelf behind her, saying, "I want those, please," holding out their coins in an outstretched hand. That day I knew what I wanted. "*Salmiak Pastillen,* please," small thin, black diamond-shaped licorice shapes with a hint of ammonia flavor, which the proprietor scooped out of the jar with a spoon. One penny would buy one spoonful, enough to paste on the back of one's spit-moistened hand in the design of a star or a little man, to be gradually licked off, until only a faint dark shape would remain, and one's tongue would be black for many hours.

Today, lucky me, I have five glorious pennies. She will put

the candies in a little cone-shaped paper bag, and I will have enough for a firmament of black stars to lick.

As I stand in the shop waiting for my turn and looking around, my eyes land on an uncovered jar full of silvery tin penny whistles, and suddenly I know that is what I want.

"How much?"

"Ten *Pfennig* each."

"But I only have five!"

"Maybe your Mutti will give you another five," the shop-keeper suggests.

I am hang-dog disappointed as I trudge up the three flights of stairs to our apartment. I don't have much hope, but I try to explain. Mutti opens her coin purse and gives me the other five, puzzled and pleased about my choice and about my insistence that I want that flute and nothing else.

That is what I now do, hours on end: I teach myself to cover the holes with my fingers and work out some tunes for myself. It makes me really happy to do that and I spend a lot of time on it. When for Christmas that year Lili sends me a wooden soprano recorder, I am thrilled, and even though my hands are still too small to cover the holes properly and I am disappointed in the sounds I am able to coax out of it, I am very proud to have a real musical instrument of my own.

Once Mutti realizes that I enjoy music, she hunts around for some musical activity I can join. And so I find myself with several other small children standing in a circle in a brightly lit room. The teacher gives us small colored balls which we throw to one another as we sing their colors: blue for do, mi is green, sol is red, la, purple, ti bright yellow which points up to do again which this time is light blue, up and down the scale, or in different intervals. We sing and then throw the balls or we color as we sing the notes of each color. We make special hand signals for each note, up and down an imaginary note ladder, or we walk around the room to different rhythms the teacher produces on her drum. It is so much fun, serious fun in a way, for I am learning something that makes me happy, the connection of colors and sounds and movement. Once a week that little group of children meet and now and then the teacher plays her guitar and we sing songs together. Suddenly it is over: the teacher has left for Palestine, Mutti tells me, and there is no one else to teach us.

Many years later while taking a course in music education at a university, suddenly something from long ago stood vividly before me: the circle of children, our red-haired teacher with drum and guitar, and the colored balls and hand signals by which we learned to sing in tune. I thought of the fun of that activity, but also how at that time good things had to stop suddenly, again and again.

After Tante Bertha leaves again for the sanatorium and my piano lessons have stopped, the house is even quieter than before. Most days now, Mutti works late somewhere, so Oma and I sit at two sides of the kitchen table and eat supper by ourselves. More and more, I notice that she eats very little. "Aren't you hungry?" I ask. Maybe she doesn't like the food, the way I dislike so many things, but then, why doesn't she make something else?

Sometimes now the door to the seldom used dark front parlor is open and I see her sitting at the little table near the window, a book in her hand, not reading the way she usually does, but just looking into space. I wonder whether she is too tired or whether she is thinking about Tante Bertha, missing her.

"Why aren't you reading your book, Oma?" I ask as I peek at the book cover.

"I will," she answers wearily, and opens the book at her bookmark. I like to read too, but the books she reads are very big, too big for me. I just read the titles sometimes when I see them on the table.

I have read *Heidi* over and over; I think five times, and I know that is not the last time. Heidi is a real little girl and I pretend that she is my cousin. She doesn't know it, and I suspect that she would not want me as her cousin anyway. We are so very different; I am sure she would not like me the way I like her. She lives in the mountains in the south the way my father does, and I imagine that when he goes hiking with his friends he goes to places that are just like the pictures in my book.

I also like fairy tales, Hans Christian Andersen's fairy tales especially. Even though the two blue volumes of his stories have very small print and no pictures, I have read almost all of them. I like "The Little Match Girl"; it's my favorite story. It is very sad at the end when she dies from the cold but is happy none-the-less, because when she strikes the last match she sees her grandmother who carries her in her arms up to where there is light and joy and no hunger or cold. I like them all; I like them much better than the stories in my big Grimm's fairy tales book, even though it has colored pictures. Some of them give me nightmares; I don't like the dark woods and I don't really believe in witches and goblins and such.

I still have my copy of *Der Struwelpeter*. It's an old book with old-fashioned pictures that most German children have. Mutti read it to me a long time ago. Once in a while I take it out and remind myself of all the terrible things that can happen to children if they don't obey their parents. The little girl Paulinchen, who goes up in flames because she plays with matches, and the boy Peter, whose long hair gets caught in a fan, the thumb sucker who has his finger cut off by a giant pair of scissors, and the picky eater who wastes away and dies, and other such lurid tales. The stories are supposed to teach children to be good.

Oma doesn't approve of the book, she doesn't think that fear is a good teacher. She doesn't believe that I can learn to be good without those stories. And of course, good I am when I am with her, although I am not always that way with Mutti. I don't know what she thinks; maybe she got the book just because everybody does. I am not really like the children in the book, except of course for the thumb and being a picky eater. But I'm trying and getting a little better.

Today Oma is sitting again on the straight-backed chair at the window. I have entered very quietly because I feel a little lonely and want company. Her face is in profile; her upswept hair and fine thin nose are beautiful to me. She hasn't noticed me yet, and so I look around the room before I approach her: the heavy dark china closet on whose top shelf the bronze statue of Mercury the messenger stands poised to take off; the picture of "Isle of the Dead," in tones of gray and black on the opposite wall, the two maroon upholstered chairs around the table covered with a tapestry cloth, all so dark and gloomy. Why does she want to be here? No wonder we hardly ever use this room. Mutti avoids it and I have been in it only a few times.

She turns her head, sees me and smiles. It's such a beautiful sad smile, that I run to her and throw my arms around her. I want to be with her always.

PART TWO

CHAPTER SEVEN

I AM SITTING ON the floor of my study, taking old photos one by one out of the big cardboard box where they are jumbled together with letters and old postcards and children's drawings saved over the years.

I sort the old photos into piles: My mother and her sister, their parents, two sets of their grandparents, even a faded early photograph of my mother's great-great-grandmother. I lay them out in chronological order. There are also assorted pictures of their cousins and aunts and uncles, friends and distant relatives. A postcard shows the house where my mother's great-grandfather was born. It is the usual orderly procession of a family through the generations, and so I look for family resemblances to me and to those I knew: My grandmother, my aunt, my mother.

First the pile of photos of my mother, taken over the years: a baby picture, several snapshots of a little girl who resembles the woman I remember: a beautiful young woman in profile, my mother among a group of other young women circle-dancing on a meadow in loose Eleanore Duse gowns, and many more from later years. They remind me of what I remember: her brown hair, very fine and rather thin lying close to her head, parted on the right side. When I was small she usually wore it loosely pulled back, the ends rolled around a stiff wire sausage at the nape of her neck. I don't remember ever seeing her hair hanging free or uncombed.

Later, in San Francisco when she could afford to have her hair done, she would get a permanent, and artificial looking waves would lie, still close to her head, with the ends still curled up into a roll in the back. Very slowly, when she was already in her seventies, it turned gray. She then had it dyed her natural color, with the result that I remember her only with the same brown hair she had when I was a child. It was frugal hair, something that was just there as a head covering, and I could never imagine anyone wanting to stroke it or pass their fingers through it lovingly.

She was small, barely five feet tall, and as she grew older she became smaller still, her back became bent and leaned to one side, so that her left shoulder blade seemed to protrude a little, no matter how much she tried to compensate by bending slightly to the right. She took great care to make sure that the seamstress who altered her dresses and coats put special pads in the right places to minimize her deformity. She never spoke about it as a flaw, but rather that clothes just weren't made to fit her. So many images of my mother!

I move on to the small pile of pictures of my father. I pick up four of them, one by one, and look at them carefully. In one he is sitting at a desk in his office writing in a ledger with papers lying about in orderly piles and a print of leafy plants on the wall. On top of a cabinet behind him are five ornate beer steins. The picture, in sepia tones, is faded. He looks middle-aged with broad shoulders, his face thoughtful and serious. Another small oval portrait is formal. Hair cut short, beard and mustache neatly trimmed, somber suit jacket and tie. He looks straight at the camera: a family man, maybe a minor government official.

In another photo he is sitting on a boulder in the mountains surrounded by four elderly gentlemen, his hiking partners. He wears short hiking pants and a jacket with a velvet collar. Deep lines run from his strong straight nose to the corners of his mouth. He is smiling and looks relaxed and happy, but also not like someone I once knew.

The last picture was taken in a park in the little town where he, my mother and I had vacationed together. It shows him standing tall and straight, a big man. He wears a fedora, rumpled shorts and knee socks, a Tyrolean jacket, a short tie. His face, in profile, is shaded by the hat.He looks tired and a little sad. He looks familiar. That is my father. Is that all there is? I try to remember, I try to bring to life hidden memories of him.

WHEN I WAS SMALL my father was no more real to me than the fathers in the fairy tales I read so avidly over and over; he appeared in my life less often than they did. I did not see him any more clearly than I saw Hänsel and Gretel's father. I imagined that the old shoemaker for whom the elves worked at night had a beard that looked like my father's beard and eyes that looked with wonder at the finished shoes in his shop the way my father looked at me, the product he had helped to create.

I didn't understand about fathers. I knew in a vague sort of way that the children on the street in the working-class neighborhood where we lived all had fathers. One of the children might say something about not being allowed to go here or there, because her papa might get mad, or sometimes I heard male voices shouting. There was also that legendary figure, Herr Gerstenmaier, the house painter, whom I had actually never seen, the father of one of my classmates, to whom I was supposed to bring the stem of the pear I had just eaten, core and all. "Take that brush to Herr Gerstenmaier, he can use it," my mother would say and we would both laugh.

If I were to have a real father like other children, though I hardly ever had that thought, I would have wanted a father like the husband of one of my mother's friends, whose effect on his children I coveted. He often brought home toys for his children, wonderful toys: antique train sets for his son, who was a year younger than I was, and for his daughter dollhouses with furniture and tea sets, porcelain dolls with beautiful golden hair and old-fashioned clothes, sleds, bicycles and roller skates, and all sorts of other unheard of luxuries, all of which, to my astonishment, were barely appreciated by his children. He himself was a shadowy figure to me, for I never saw him when we visited their large apartment.

WHO WAS THAT PERSON, my father? I try to pull together the little I know about him. It is now, as I see my own sons being fathers, who come home from work in the evenings, who delight in their children day in and day out, who are there to encourage, to scold when necessary, to help with homework, to read bedtime stories, that I wonder why, as a child, I never asked my mother the questions that needed to be asked: Why did that tall bearded stranger who she said was my father, appear once a year for two weeks in the summer and then disappear again until the next summer? Where did he go when he was not with us?

"My papa travels a lot," was my answer when my playmates on the street asked about him. That seemed a good enough explanation for them. Was it for me? Was that what my mother had told me? Or was that my own idea of the mystery of his whereabouts? She did not tell me that he had a wife and children somewhere in the south of Germany. She did not tell me and I did not ask. After all, my family, if I thought of it as a family at all, seemed complete with Oma, Tante Bertha, Mutti and myself.

I never questioned whether perhaps he wasn't really my father, that perhaps it was just a story my mother chose to tell me. I did not then know the specifics of how a man and a woman made a child together. I wonder now why I never did ask.

MY MOTHER BELIEVED in eugenics. She thought that the fact that I had a non-Jewish father had made me a healthier, if not a superior child in every way: mentally, emotionally as well as physically. I don't remember what the occasion was, except that I was still quite young, when looking at me proudly, she said, as much to her as to me, "You are a good mixture, being half German. We Jews are too sensitive, too neurotic. We are not very strong, not very healthy, but you, you have the advantage of also having good, strong, healthy German blood from your father."

How could there be two kinds of blood in my body, one kind Jewish, and one kind German? I wondered about that for a while. Were the two kinds of blood also two different shades of red? Did they mix; did they race each other as they coursed through my veins? Did they go through different parts of my body? Which one came out when I fell and skinned my knee? Maybe she is wrong I thought; maybe my blood is just like everyone else's blood, just one kind of red? Pretty confusing, that.

The matter of my birth was something that I didn't like to think about. I don't recall ever asking, "Where did I come from, Mutti?" It seemed to be her secret; it seemed to be something that did not really concern me, a story that I was not supposed to know. Whenever my mother told me that she had so much wanted to have me, that I represented the many children that she had wanted to have, I would always feel very uncomfortable. Perhaps she said this to reassure me, perhaps to reassure herself. She never elaborated and I didn't ask any questions. I didn't like having to be many children.

Every summer until I was seven my father would join my mother and me for two weeks at a resort on the North Sea or on an island in the Baltic. Later when I was eight and nine, we spent those two weeks at the house of my mother's friends, Hans and Elsie, in the town of Bad Godesberg on the river Rhein. Only much later did I realize that of course, under the Nazi anti-miscegenation laws it would not have been safe for an unmarried couple, my mother a Jew and my father a Gentile, to vacation together at a hotel, even if their child, the illegitimate half-Jew, was with them.

Among my photos there is a small one from a time when I must have been about four years old, which shows the three of us sitting together on a sandy stretch of beach. I am leaning against my mother who is wearing a dark bathing suit; my father, sitting next to her, is wearing a plaid beach robe. He is smiling. The picture triggers no memories about that time in me, no matter how hard I try.

Many years later when my mother and I looked at that photo together, she reminded me how he had built a big sand castle for us and how we had decorated it with stones and shells, and how he had said that I was the princess who lived in that castle. Even then it still remained only a story for me.

As she reminisced, her head tilted slightly to one side, and a far-away look came into her eyes.

"Do you know what he would sometimes say about you?" she asked. I shook my head. She turned to me. "*Das ist mein bestes*

Product," she quoted his words in German, imitating his dialect. "'She's my best product'; that's what he said about you."

"Yes, he was proud of you," she added looking at me. Maybe, I thought, he said it more as a compliment to her than to me, the product he had praised as the best he had produced. "It's a part of *her* story," I said to myself, "not mine. It has little to do with me." Still, I was pleased by what she had said.

At other times, when my mother referred to those vacations we spent together she would say, "Do you remember when?" or "When we were here, we went together for a ride over the tidal flats in a horse-drawn wagon with huge wheels. Don't you remember?" I would always draw a total blank.

It must have been that once our annual two weeks together were over and we were back home and he had gone, they became of no consequence to me; as if, perhaps in order not to have to think about these appearances and disappearances of the man who claimed me as his child, I would push every memory of our being together into the farthest recesses of my mind, where they remained. Except for the memory of the two weeks we spent together in August 1936 when I was nine.

⤵

MOTHER AND I have taken the train to Bad Godesberg, a small town on the Rhein.

It is almost dark when the taxi takes us to Hans and Elsie's house. I can see the lights on the river appear and disappear as the taxi winds its way through the hilly streets of the town. Sleepily I try to picture how the river had looked the summer before, and how big their house was and how nice Elsie had been to me, what her garden looked like, and how I had my own room way up under the roof, really my own for those two weeks. I don't think about my father having been there too and that he would arrive late that night when I would be asleep.

The next morning I wake up early. The sun, streaming into the dormer window of my room on the third floor, makes a warm puddle of light on my bed. It is a beautiful room, big and light and airy. I pretend that the flowered wallpaper is part of the garden and that I have been asleep in that garden all night.

It's now time to get up and see what the others are doing. I dress quickly and run downstairs to the dining room where the table is already set for breakfast. Tante Elsie and Onkel Hans are just starting to drink their coffee. Tante Elsie gives me a little hug.

"After you eat you can go to the dairy to get milk," she suggests. I wonder why my mother isn't at breakfast. Usually she is up before me. Maybe she is sleeping late because it's her vacation.

Swinging the empty white-enameled milk pail back and forth I hurry on my way to the dairy. Suddenly I remember my father. Had he arrived last night? I try hard to think about him, to remember what we had done together the year before, but I can't remember, and so I stop trying. At the dairy a big smiling woman fills my milk pail to the brim from an oversized pitcher and writes Elsie's name in her ledger. I wonder about the cows that had given the milk; whether they are black and white like the ones I had seen near home or whether they are a different color, the way everything else here is different.

When I return, Elsie is picking peas in the garden.

"Come help," she says.

I know how to pick peas; I have done that in the garden plot Mutti used to rent. Next we get some lettuce from the back along the fence, and then I sit in the living room and look at books with pictures by famous artists.

Finally I go up to my mother's room. It's time she got up, I decide. The door is closed. I turn the handle, but the door is locked. I knock, loud.

"Let me in!"

I don't remember ever having been locked out of her room before and so I try the handle again. It doesn't give. I bang on the door with both fists: rat-tat-tat, rat-tat-tat, but to no avail. After a while my mother, wearing her dressing gown, opens the door slightly. Her face is flushed.

"Your papa and I are very tired. You mustn't bother us. It's rude to wake people up!"

My father must have arrived when I was asleep. I see the big unmade bed through the crack in the door. My mother lets the door swing open wider. Sunlight is streaming through the open window. I look around curiously, from the window with its background of trees and hills, to the little table with its two wicker chairs and the lamp with its multicolored glass shade, to the big bed from which a blue blanket is dangling precariously. I can't see my father anywhere, but his shirt and trousers are draped over the chair at the side of the bed. Two large brown boots lie on their sides under the chair, as if they had been taken off in a big hurry and carelessly thrown down. I always stand my shoes up neatly side by side under the bed, I remind myself. His clothes. I have never seen my papa's clothes without him in them. I don't recognize the two tan leather straps which are hanging from the back of the chair as suspenders.

Suddenly a door at the back of the room opens and my father's voice calls:

"*Puppchen, komm her, Puppchen!*"—little doll, come here. He is wearing pajama bottoms, his chest bare. With two giant steps he is at the door, lifts me in a huge arc through the air and puts me gently on the bed next to him. I can feel the hair

91

on his chest prickle through the thin material of my blouse as he snuggles me close.

"Come," he says to my mother. "Let's have the family together."

The expression on her face softens. I lie between them, my father's right arm around us both. I feel both of them looking at me, and then I hear his soft southern dialect say something which I don't understand. But I understand that it is something good and that it is about me. "She's my best product," is what he said.

The next days passed pleasantly sunny, and in my memory uneventfully. I don't remember what we did, whether we went sightseeing or stayed around Elsie's house and garden, how I spent my time when the adults were talking, whether my father paid special attention to me, or whether he gave his attention only to my mother. I seemed to have been reconciled to my father's presence as something that happened and then would go away as in previous years, leaving us just as we had been before.

OUR LAST EXCURSION was a special treat and stands out vividly in my memory. The day was beautiful, clear and sunny. My mother had put on her white dress with the navy blue stripe and belt. She wore her new white shoes and her hair was done up in a new way. I too wore my favorite dress; small white flowers sprinkled all over the red background, the white peter-pan collar framed in red rick-rack. My father, in tan hiking pants and Tyrolean jacket, carried his mountain climbing stick with many embossed metal emblems nailed along its length, which depicted all the mountains he had climbed. We were taking the big excursion boat up the Rhein and back down for an all-day trip.

The steep mountain scenery, with its soft green vineyards winding in wide ribbons up the mountainside, alternating with dark woods and rocky cliffs passed by as we three sat together on the foredeck. My mother pointed out the Dragon Rock which loomed ominously above the vineyards and told me about the old legends that named it. When the boat passed the rock overhanging the river from which the Lorelei was supposed to have lured the fishermen to their doom with her song, Mother hummed the familiar melody very softly:

> "Ich weiss nicht was soll es bedeuten,
> daß ich so traurig bin . . ."

My father looked at her and then at me. I could see he was happy.

"Shall we go to the shop to see what they have?" he broke the spell. He took my hand and we went below decks to the little shop where they sold postcards and souvenirs and candy.

"Can I have those?" I pointed at the rack of emblems.

"But you don't have a stick to nail them to. Never mind . . . I'll carve you a beautiful one some day . . ."

He bought me two; the Lorelei and the Dragon Rock.

During the evening meal in the dining salon the band played popular tunes and everyone gave a toast to "Father Rhein," pointing to my father. My mother looked very proud as he stood there very tall, very large, short gray beard, dark-brown, graying hair, feet apart. He lifted his glass, looked way down to where she and I sat, smiled at us, emptied his glass in one huge gulp, sat down again between us, and put one arm around each of us as the band resumed playing. I can still taste the slightly acrid "children's wine," white wine half diluted with water, which I was allowed to drink on this special occasion. I remember feeling slightly tipsy, then very sleepy, my body resting against "Father Rhein," secure and protected by his bulk and by the approving looks the other passengers threw our way.

Two days later on the patio in the back of Tante Elsie's garden the table was set for seven. It was our farewell party; my mother and father and I sat in the middle, the others around us, Elsie and Hans, and her two sisters, Katie and Irmi. There were three kinds of cake, whipped cream and lump sugar. The grown-ups drank coffee out of thin gold-rimmed cups; I too drank my milk out of a cup, because it was a special day and I was allowed "upside-down" coffee, milk with a large dash of coffee for color and grown-up flavor. The sun shone through the foliage of the tall Linden tree above us. There was much conversation, and some laughter. Later my father drank a large stein of beer and laughed more, and the women clustered around him as if drawn to a magnet. His brown eyes twinkled, and the laugh lines around his eyes deepened.

I leaned against his knee; and as he held me there I felt for a fleeting moment that I belonged to this strange giant, who appeared once every summer for two weeks to claim my mother and me, and who then disappeared again until the following year, and that he belonged also to me. Onkel Hans got his camera and the three of us posed in front of the grape arbor. I stood between my father's knees for the picture taking and looked at my mother's face while she looked at him.

The party was coming to an end. One by one the others disappeared into the house. Only the three of us were left at the table.

"And now you must help Elsie with the washing up," my mother said firmly.

Very reluctantly and slowly I walked to the kitchen, kicking up the gravel on the path. In the kitchen Elsie handed me a dish towel and complimented me on being such a good little helper. Through the window I saw my mother and father still sitting at the table in the garden in serious conversation. My chest constricted as if the air in the kitchen were too heavy to enter my lungs. I wanted to run out there and be there and have my father hug me to his big bear chest. I dried the dishes and silverware in silence. Tante Elsie said something to me which I did not understand. I felt the loving cadence of her voice, but the tightness in my chest did not disappear.

The dishes done, I threw one more longing glance into the garden where my parents were still sitting and off I went into the parlor, where the piano stood open and where the walls were covered with large paintings of flowers and mountain landscapes done in greens and browns. The piece of music on the piano did not look too hard. I tried it, first one hand, then the other, and then I walked over to the French doors that led into the garden. My mother and father were alone, no longer talking. She was leaning against him, eyes closed, his arm around her. How little she is, I thought. I wanted to run out and be there between them.

"I don't care if they don't want me!" I tossed my head, yanked the drapes closed, sat down on the piano stool, gave two enormous bangs on the keys with both hands, and immediately started to race through all the pieces I knew by heart.

THE NEXT DAY, on the platform of the railway station, my father picked me up, held me very close for a moment, and said, "*Sei brav.*" I knew that in his dialect it meant "be good"; be good and obey your mother is what he meant. I saw how serious he looked and I wondered why he did not kiss my mother goodbye. From the window of the train as it moved slowly out of the station, we watched his huge white handkerchief waving for a long time until we could no longer see it.

I secretly studied my mother's face as she sat looking out of the train window and wondered what she was thinking. The tops of the mountains we passed were bathed in the red glow of the setting sun, beautiful even as they became lower on the way north. I thought she looked sad. She hardly spoke for much of the journey, and as she handed me my supper sandwich I noticed that her eyes were red.

It had started to get dark outside; there was not much to see any longer. After riding in silence for a while I got restless and decided on a walk down the train corridor. My mother seemed deep in her own thoughts, her eyes closed.

"Don't be long," she pleaded. "Go to the toilet and come right back."

I was surprised. I looked at her. It seemed that just then she hadn't cared whether I was there or not.

When I returned from my excursion, her mood had changed. She seemed more cheerful and was telling one of the women in our compartment what a beautiful city Hamburg was. I too started to think about home, and about Oma, and how long it had been since I saw her. I briefly wondered why I had not missed her more these last two weeks. About school too I thought; how there were only two more days of vacation, how this would be the last year before the new school and the last year with Fraulein Schrader, my teacher since first grade. It seemed that both Mother and I were leaving all that had happened in the last two weeks behind and were indeed coming home.

CHAPTER EIGHT

THE CLOSER WE GET to home, the more excited I become. I can't wait to see Oma, our room, my piano, and all the familiar things of my everyday life. We take the streetcar from the station and when we get out at our stop, I jump down quickly and run ahead of Mother with my knapsack bouncing up and down on my back. I bound up the three flights of stairs to our apartment and lean on the bell. What takes her so long? Wasn't she waiting for us? Wasn't she anxious to see us too? Finally she opens the door. I run to her, look up into her face and put my arms around her middle. She smiles down at me and gently removes my arms. "I'm so happy you are back," her voice, even softer than usual. "Come, how about some cocoa, yes?"

Why won't she let me hug her? Is she angry that we went away? No, that's not it. Then suddenly I remember that she had been a little sick before we went away, that my mother had cooked, instead of her. I wonder whether she is still sick. I don't ask her, I am just too happy to see her, and so I follow her into the kitchen for my cocoa.

The next day, Sunday, as I let myself become reacquainted with life at home, I realize that my grandmother is indeed not the same. Mutti tells me to be really quiet.

"Oma is not feeling well and has to stay in bed. We mustn't make any noise; maybe you shouldn't play the piano for a few days." She sees that I look worried. "She'll be better soon," she adds, "and then you can play again." I am relieved, maybe everything will be the same as before our vacation.

I am happy to be back at school. Everything is very familiar: the teacher Fräulein Schrader, all the other girls, even our classroom is just like last year's, with its light green walls and high ceiling. Only the flag in front of the room next to the blackboard is different. There used to be two, the old German flag and the one with the swastika. Now there is only the one with the *Hakenkreutz*, the black hooked cross in its white circle in a red field, big and brand new. There are now also two pictures of the Führer, the official one and the new one. On it a little girl with blond pigtails is holding a bunch of flowers which she is about to give to the *Führer*, who looks kindly down at her. They are standing on the lawn in front of a school building, while the sun is shining on beautiful snow capped mountains in the background. It doesn't at all look like my school, which is a dark brick building surrounded by asphalt; but then I think that Heidi, if she were alive, might go to such a school. Schools must look like that in the place where my father lives, I think.

Our desks are bigger than last year and have ink wells set into them. This is the year we are going to use pens for the first time. I have five steel nibs and a brand new pen holder in my pencil case together with a soft piece of leather to wipe the extra ink off. In my composition notebook a pink blotter is waiting. I am ready.

On Monday, after school dismissal, I have just slung my satchel over my shoulders, ready to walk home, when to my surprise I see my mother's friend Irmi waiting for me at the door. Why is she there? I haven't forgotten the way home and I certainly don't need anyone to pick me up. Besides, Tante Irmi, (I called all my mother's women friends *Tante*) doesn't live in our neighborhood. Why does she walk so far, when she is so fat? Maybe I have forgotten something at her sister's house in Bad Godesberg? No, I don't think so. If only none of my classmates will see me, a big fourth-grader being picked up! Too embarrassing.

"*Deine liebe Mutter*—your dear mother—is staying with me." Why do adults always refer to my mother as "dear"? I wonder briefly. "She's not feeling well. Come, I'm taking you to her."

I trudge along beside her, not knowing what to make of this.

After a while Tante Irmi says, "You have to be very nice and very quiet when you see her and not upset her."

The walk to her apartment seems endless. Why can't Mutti be at home when she is only a little sick, not as sick as Oma? Why does she need to be in someone else's house?

Arrived at the apartment, I stand on the threshold between the front hall and the parlor. The door is partly open. The heavy drapes are drawn shut. I can barely see my mother who is lying on the chaise lounge that juts diagonally into the room. In the dim light I am aware of the intricate design of the carpet, of the heavy dark furniture, of the richness and strangeness of the room. I start to run to my mother who has a white washcloth covering her forehead.

"Shhh—she's sleeping." A gentle hand on my shoulder holds me back. My mother opens her eyes, moves her head slowly and heavily in the direction of the open door. She is wearing all her clothes under the shawl covering her. Limply she motions me to her.

I cannot remember ever seeing my mother lying like this. I don't recognize the expression on her face. What happened?

Quickly I start to catalogue possibilities. But just as quickly I put all speculation away. I am good at clearing my mind of disturbing thoughts. Slowly I move closer to her and with an almost inaudible sob my mother clutches my right hand, pulls me down next to her on the chaise and starts to cry. My knees press against the frame of the chaise, my body is twisted and I feel awkward and embarrassed. I don't know what to do. I sense that she is not sick, that something else, something serious, has happened.

"Your papa is dead" is all she says, drops my hand, gives me one long look and turns her head away to hide the tears streaming down her face.

I don't know what to do, what to think. I look at the back of her head, and when I hear her sob, I put my arm around her and lay my head on the pillow next to hers and kiss the back of her neck. Suddenly my mother's grief infects me and I too start to cry. Her grief has become my grief too. At that moment I feel very close to her.

After a few minutes the door opens soundlessly. Ashamed of my tears I jump up, my eyes still on my mother's prone form. Irmi puts her arm on my shoulder and I let myself be guided out of the room. The door closes behind me.

My papa dead . . . my papa dead . . . As I walk home through the darkening streets, the words ricochet in my mind as I put one foot in front of the other . . . left-papa, right-dead, left-papa, right-dead . . . a refrain, over and over. I try to imagine how that is, being dead. No one I know has ever been dead, no person, no dog, no cat, not even a bird. The walk home seems endless. My satchel is getting heavier, but I speed up my walking almost to a run. The refrain has changed to "Dead, dead . . . papa dead . . . dead, dead, papa dead . . ." I am out of breath now and as I slow down I try to think how his being dead will make things different from other times when we have come home after our vacations together. Why is my mother lying there so helplessly in someone else's parlor? . . . Will she die too? What does his being dead have to do with me, with my going to school, with my Oma, my piano? Will my life change? Will his now being dead feel different from his disappearance every year? All that is very confusing. I can't think about it any longer. In any case, there is our street. Soon I'll be home and Oma will be there.

I run up the narrow staircase, taking two steps at a time, up to the first landing, where I stop for an instant, take in the cabbage smell emanating from the Schmitt's apartment, and listen to the scales their son is practicing on his violin. I wonder whether he ever wants to skip notes the way I like to skip steps. I am taking three at a time now. The hallway is beginning to get lighter as I get higher up. As always, just before opening the door to our apartment, I take one look up toward the skylight where the attic floor is. I would choose to live there in that bright space, if I could.

Grandma is in bed sleeping, her head propped up by a mountain of white pillows. I want to hug her and stroke her thin face. I wish that she would open her eyes, because I can never get enough of looking at her eyes, and because I like to be looked at in that special calm way those eyes have. But lately there has been a translucent film drawn over her eyes, and I remember how the day before, she seemed not to be looking at me at all, even when she spoke to me. I bend down to lift the heavy porcelain bedpan out from under the bed. Some of the urine sloshes to the floor, but I can't stop to clean it up. Carefully I carry the bedpan to the bathroom down the hall to empty it, return it, wipe up the spill with paper and go into the front room. The house is totally still. My mother's typewriter is standing open on the table in the middle of the room, with the beginning of a letter in it:

101

My dearest Ernst,
The child and I arrived safely home last night. . . .

I walk slowly over to the window and look out at the street below. The late afternoon scene down there is the same as always. A few housewives are entering and leaving the greengrocer and the delicatessen to buy something they had forgotten during their morning shopping; the older children are sitting on the stoop in front of the candy store, Frau Muller across the street is hanging out of their window on the second floor yelling at Karl to come in the house right away. I lean my head against the window pane and put my thumb in my mouth.

Footsteps, and the front door opens, then slams shut.

"Is that you, Bertha?" My grandmother's voice asks.

Tante Bertha waves to me as she passes the open door and disappears into Oma's room. The door closes behind her. I go to the bookcase and take out the dark green volume of Oscar Wilde's *Fairy Tales* my favorite reading at the moment. I choose "The Happy Prince," and when at the end the statue cries real tears, I too cry.

In the kitchen the wooden table is set for two. Tante Bertha is arranging a tray. She puts a hand embroidered linen mat on it, a plate, a soup bowl and a cup of the blue and white patterned company china. She adds grandmother's rolled up napkin in the old-fashioned silver napkin ring and two water glasses. I watch her ladle broth into the bowl and lay two zwiebacks on the plate, pour boiling water into the teapot and carry the whole tray out of the kitchen. Looking at the table in front of me, I see the two empty spaces where my mother and grandmother usually sit, and it seems to me that I am only visiting here in this kitchen, in this place.

Tante Bertha sits down at the table after putting a piece of meat and some fried potatoes on each of our plates. I don't like the meat, but love the potatoes, which I eat first. Mutti always makes me clean my plate and wants me to learn to eat everything and not be picky, but Bertha doesn't think that is so important. I put the meat back in the pan and drink a glass of milk instead.

"I am sorry your father has died." She looks down at me. "It will be hard for Mutti." She coughs, can't stop coughing, gets up to go into her own room down the hall and closes the door behind her. From the kitchen where I am still drinking my milk, I hear her continue to cough.

In bed that night, I can't fall asleep. I am used to my mother being there at bedtime and I don't know why she has to be away. I am jealous of Tante Irmi and angry at my now dead father who made Mutti sick so she can't be with me.

My father's being dead has no substance, no reality for me. I think of a line in one of my stories: "And when the old king died, everyone cried." The queen and the princess and all the people in the kingdom cried. Everyone understood that the king was dead and that nothing would ever be the same. But my father's death was not real to me, and nothing would change. Only that his dying is keeping Mutti away from me. I am excluded from what is going on, from this something that is so very important to her. That's real. Maybe after all, I don't count for much, and my mother belongs more to others than to me. Oh well, I think defiantly, if she doesn't want me, I won't want her either. But I wish she'd come home anyway. Soon. I don't like it when I wake up in the morning and she isn't there, I don't like it one bit.

Suddenly a scene stored deep in my memory: I am three and I am left alone without my mother for the first time.

She and I are standing on the gravel path in front of a big gray house, a Kinderheim, *a place in the country where children can be cared for*

temporarily. I am holding on to my Mutti's hand. I don't know why we are there. Are we visiting? She leads me towards a woman dressed all in white who is rapidly walking towards us. Mutti looks down at me, loosens my hand from hers and tells me that just for a little while this nice lady will take care of me.

"I have to go some place where I can't take you," she says, "but I'll be back very soon to take you home. You'll have a good time here. It's a beautiful place."

I look at her, not understanding.

"Where I have to go there are no children for you to play with. There are lots of children here. Isn't that right?" The white woman nods yes. I look from one to the other. The white woman smiles down at me. I don't like her smile.

I stand close to my mother leaning against her leg while she and the white woman talk about something that I don't understand. They seem to be making arrangements and I hear them saying "she" and "das Kind." I look down at the ground and twist my feet into the gravel until I have made two little holes.

"Don't do that," Mutti says and takes hold of my arm.

No, I don't want to be here. Why can't I go with her? She can't leave me here.

Mutti is in a hurry.

"I have to go now," she says and bends down to kiss me. "No," I say, and I turn my head away. I am so angry at her that I start to stomp away towards the big gray house at the end of the garden, even as the white woman runs after me.

"Come, say good bye to your Mama," she says. I shake my head no, but then I take one glance back at my mother, who is standing in the same spot, tears running down her cheek. "I don't really need her, I'll never come home again," I think.

❧

I REMEMBER HOW in order to cure me of thumb sucking, my hand had been tied with a ribbon to the side of my little bed every night the whole time I was there. I remember also that when my mother came to pick me up after what had seemed an eternity for me, she had cried when I wouldn't kiss her because I was still so angry, and how I hadn't felt even a little bit sorry for her.

Instinctively I now put my thumb in my mouth again, even though I have given up that old habit.

The next day I go to school as usual, but when I come home and am about to enter our apartment, Mutti opens the door. She pulls me into her arms, holds me tight and kisses me over and over with long, hard kisses. Her cheeks are wet. "Now it is only you and me," she says. "You have to be very grown up and especially good from now on. You are the only thing I have left." I want to put my school bag down but she is still holding me tightly pressed to her body. I don't know why she says that. Wasn't I always good? And I always feel quite grown up anyway. What's so different now? I don't know what to do next, so I tilt my head up and kiss her neck just under the chin.

I wriggle away from her and run into my grandmothers' room and throw myself on her bed. "Oma, Oma I love you!" My head is sinking deep into the huge feather bed. She is too weak to sit up, but she reaches over and lays her hand on my hair.

Mutti enters the room. "Let the child stay here for a while," my grandmother says almost inaudibly. "She doesn't bother me."

CHAPTER NINE

ON SATURDAY AFTERNOON I go out to play. Max and Jenny and Willie are just about to start a game of Territories in the street in front of our apartment house.

"You want to play?" Jenny asks.

"Sure," I say. The game is best with four players, I know. Each of us has to have a knife, so I run quickly upstairs to borrow Oma's old paring knife, because I don't have a pocketknife of my own like the others. It's a good knife, with a heavy handle and a sharp point. If I plan well and have some luck, maybe I might win today, even if I haven't played for a while. Of course, it depends on the others too.

Territories is our favorite game just now. It's the game for late summer, the way marbles is for spring. We draw lines with our knives to lay out our territories adjacent to each other on the strip of hard packed dirt between the sidewalk and the curb. The boys have the advantage because their territories are on the outside, less vulnerable to attack. Jenny doesn't think that's fair. I agree, but we are anxious to play, and so we don't argue much. Max, who usually wins because he is older and more skilled at throwing his knife, chooses to be Germany. Willie wants to be Austria; Jenny wants Russia. I've told her that Russia is bigger than all the other countries together. I call my territory Uruguay; I like the sound. We take turns throwing our knives into the ground, draw lines in the direction of the blade to carve up our opponents' territories and join them to our own, wiping out the previous borders.

Uruguay, attacked from two sides, is eliminated first. I sit down on the curb safely away from the flipping knives, and watch the continuation of the game. Willie now owns most of my previous territory, Jenny the rest, but Max is making inroads. I want Jenny to win, or maybe Willie.

I like this game because it makes me think of other countries, other places. Of course, I haven't been to places that are really different, like Russia or Africa. I haven't seen any high mountains or jungles or places where there are different kinds of people. It's hard for me to picture those places, even when there are illustrations in our school geography book. I sometimes try to picture the place to which my father disappears every year after our two weeks together. He said that he goes somewhere with mountains, where people all talk the way he does. Boys probably wear short leather pants like he sometimes does.

Every year I used to forget what he looked like a little while after we returned from our vacation, but not today. Today I remember how he looked on the riverboat and in the garden; I also remember how he looked on the platform of the railway station waving good-bye as we waved back from the window of the carriage. But he is dead, I suddenly think. It's where he used to go, it's how he used to talk, I correct myself. I don't know how he died or where he died, only that "he didn't suffer." I don't ask questions. We never talk much about him anyway, and besides I don't really want to know.

The game is finished. Max has won after all. I help erase all traces of the game from the dirt. Time to go in, but I don't want to yet. The doctor is with Oma and I don't want to be there while he is. So I sit on the curb again and wait. Finally the door opens and the doctor comes out of the house. He passes me by without seeing me and walks to his car.

Slowly I climb the three flights of stairs to our apartment. The door is standing ajar. The doctor must have left it open, I think. Suddenly I see the ogre, who had threatened my grandmother a long time ago, sneaking in through the open door, into her room. Has he harmed her already? And I'm not there to protect her! My heart pounding, I run to her room. The door is closed and all is quiet. I am about to burst in. Is she dead? My heart is in my throat. What must I do? My hand is on the doorknob when suddenly I know that there is no ogre, that no one wants to kill her, that it is only that old nightmare from a long time ago, and that she is alive. Still, my heart continues to pound and as I stand in the narrow, dark hallway all those closed doors, all that silence, frightens me. Only the kitchen door stands open. In the late afternoon light I can barely make out the white enamel tea kettle on the stove and a tray with a cup and saucer on the kitchen table. That must be for Oma's afternoon tea.

The door to her room opens quietly and Mutti tiptoes out.

"Can I go in?" I ask.

I am still wondering whether she is really alright, in spite of it only having been a nightmare. I want to make sure. But Mutti tells me that Oma needs to rest.

"She'll have her tea and then we'll have supper," she assures me, looking at me strangely. "You look upset," she adds. "What's the matter?"

"I'm OK," I insist, but clearly, I am not yet OK. I hate it when Mutti seems to be able to guess my state of mind. It's as if a bit of my fiercely held independence were taken away every time she does that. Just to show her, I tell her I'll play piano while I wait for supper, "or should I help you?" I ask.

"No, you play. But softly. And close the door. I can manage." She too seems to want to be alone.

"Just you and me now," she had said when she came back home, "now it's just you and me"

Had she forgotten about Oma, I had wondered at the time. Why did she say that? How could she forget? Somehow since then we seem to have avoided each other much of the time.

I pull the chair over to the piano, close the door and open the red piano music book of Mozart operas to Papageno's song, in which he wishes for a wife, and start to play the melody with my right hand. I don't sing along like I sometimes do; I don't feel like it today. After a while I hear a door opening and Tante Bertha's steps into the kitchen. I am through with Mozart; I am letting my fingers wander randomly over the keys to produce different combinations of sounds.

Just as I get more interested in this activity, I hear voices through the closed door. They are arguing. Again, I think. Why do they argue so much? Oma hates it, and I don't like it either. Didn't Mutti say that everyone has to be quiet because Oma is sick? Now their voices are getting louder, shriller, more insistent. What are they yelling about? I am curious. This time I want to hear what they are fighting about. Very quietly I get up and open the door a crack.

Now it is only Bertha's voice: "Give me that tray! I'm going to bring Mama the tray! I'm going in to see her!" Her voice is getting shriller and shriller. Mutti is saying something I can't quite hear.

The sounds of dishes rattling, shuffling of feet, a thump on the table. A chair falls. Footsteps, my grandmother's door opening, then closing. Mutti must be inside. Another door bangs shut with a crash. Bertha's door. What's going on? I sit at the edge of my bed, taut, hands clamped down on my knees.

Maybe their fight is over, may be Mutti will have supper ready soon. I am hungry. It is getting darker, but I don't turn on the light. I just sit there on my bed waiting, alert to every sound, like a rabbit ready to take off.

Through the crack in the door I see Tante Bertha's shadow walk towards the kitchen. Her footsteps are loud. Mutti comes out of Oma's room. Maybe now she'll make supper. But no, there's more. Slowly and softly Bertha starts to talk. At first I can't hear what she is saying, but as she goes on her voice becomes louder and more insistent, the words more and more distinct.

"She's my mother too. I never gave her any grief like you . . ." Her angry voice pierces. "She forgave you. I wouldn't have."

Forgive for what? I wonder. What did Mutti do that needed forgiving? What grief?

"The child . . . without a real father."

Her words shrill, "You . . . you . . . mistress to a man old enough to be your own father . . . shame . . . disgraced Mama . . . my mother . . . really . . . you knew he was already married . . . You knew he had his own family. My sister, a married man's mistress; hah!"

"Shsh." Mutti's voice. Then momentary silence. I hear coughing.

A faint voice from the sickroom, "Lotte, Bertha . . . please, please." I can hear the great effort it takes her to speak, and I am frightened.

Mistress? I don't know what that is, but I can tell it's not a good thing. I sit on the edge of my bed, erect, straining to hear, hardly breathing.

Choking noises, then, as if her words come out of a deep

dark hole: "You told me yourself he wouldn't leave his wife and children and marry you, a real family man, huh?"

"Stop it, stop it!" My mother's voice, entreating.

But Bertha isn't through. "Wouldn't marry you, didn't bother to get a divorce."

"Stop it, stop it, think of Mama."

But Bertha doesn't stop. She is shrieking. "Did his family know? Or did they forgive him, like good Christians, hm? A minister's son he was, too. You fool . . . well, he's dead now."

Forgive for what? I wonder briefly. It is suddenly quiet, maybe they're through?

But no. More deliberately, with biting tone, Bertha spits out, "You think the child is safe in Germany because her father wasn't Jewish . . . won't do her any good being half . . . you'll see."

I hear feet scuffling and then a slap. Mutti must have given Tante Bertha one, an *Ohrfeige* like she gives me when she is really upset. What now? I don't hear anything for a while, but through my brain, like jack hammers, some of what I heard: his own family . . . a real father . . . already married . . . his mistress . . . disgrace.

There's too much. I can't think what it all means, but the words I overheard won't go away. They go round and round in my brain, like a refrain of a song now: *his own family . . . real father . . . married . . . disgrace.*

My mother comes into the room. She closes the door behind her and walks over to where I am still sitting on the edge of my bed.

"Come, you must be hungry," she says, her voice unsteady. But I am no longer hungry, shake my head no, and remain as before, sitting stiffly on the edge of the bed, my hands folded, as if it were too dangerous to get up and move about. She looks at me and I can tell that she has been crying. I want to give her a hug; I almost feel like crying too. I want to tell her something to make her feel better, but instead I only glance at her out of the corner of my eye. She can always read my eyes and I don't want her to know that I listened. She makes a move towards me as if to embrace me, but I get up and wiggle away.

"I'm going down to Jenny's house," I say as I grab my jacket from the hook and turn towards the door. I feel her eyes on the back of my neck, but I don't turn around.

"Wait," she entreats. "Wait. You need to know something."

Is she going to tell me about what I overheard? Maybe she'll explain. I let myself be pulled down to sit close to her on the bed.

"You see," she says, "Tante Bertha has a sickness that makes her lose control. She gets very angry and yells and says bad things. But she doesn't mean it. She just can't help herself. Don't worry, she has calmed down now. You know how she loves you."

I'm disappointed. What about the words she used? "Real father"? "Mistress"? "Disgrace"? Apparently Mutti is through explaining.

"I'll just look in on Oma," she says as she leaves the room.

I run down the first flight of stairs. On the second floor landing I slow down, and letting my hand slide down the smooth banister I take one step at a time. "His own family . . . real father . . . married . . . disgrace . . ." The refrain over and over, until I reach the bottom, where I sit down. In the gathering darkness I reach into the pocket of my skirt and pull out the two metal emblems he had bought for me that day on the boat, the Lorelei and the Dragon Rock, and lay them carefully next to me on the step.

CHAPTER TEN

MY LIFE WENT ON almost as before the vacation. I walked to school in the mornings, walked home for the midday meal, read or sat at the piano a bit and then walked back to school for the afternoon session. I avoided thinking about what I had overheard; I avoided thinking about my father having died. I secreted the two emblems in the farthest corner of my drawer, where I never looked at them again and from where eventually they disappeared.

My mother did not bring up the subject of my father either. Did she talk about it with her mother? Perhaps not, for my grandmother was now really sick. She spent much of her time in her own room in bed with the door closed, and often when I came home from school at midday a cold meal my mother had prepared before she went to work would be waiting for me on the kitchen table and my grandmother would call me into her room to tell me that she was sorry she didn't feel well and that I should eat by myself. Once or twice she asked me to bring her a fresh glass of water, but usually her voice was barely audible and I knew that I should leave quietly to let her sleep.

"Please close the door behind you," she would say. I'd then gulp down my food as quickly as possible and leave for school.

With Oma getting sicker, our apartment became even quieter. Mutti and Tante Bertha avoided each other, even their arguments stopped. The doctor came more frequently, and I was told not to play the piano or make any noise, lest it wake my grandmother up. Now and then I was allowed to go into her room to visit her. The shades would be drawn and all I could see would be the big white feather bed pulled up to her chin her face very thin, very white too, and her hair lying on her white forehead in even whiter wisps. I hardly recognized her. It frightened me. At first she would open her eyes for a little while to look at me and ask me in a whisper how school was, but later that stopped and I would stand at her bedside waiting, not daring to touch the bed, not daring to touch her thin white hand whose blue veins stood out in deep relief. The two gold wedding bands she always wore, joined together many years ago after her husband's death, hung loosely on the ring finger of her right hand. I kept wondering whether that was really my Oma, lying there so still, not moving, not responding to my "Oma, how are you?"

Usually now, when my mother came home from work in the late afternoon, she would go into her mother's room, and would only come out to have a quick supper with me; perhaps pea soup and bread and butter or little sausages and fried potatoes, and then go right back into the sickroom.

It was now 1937, and even though the 1936 Olympics in Berlin had passed with great fanfare and temporarily less persecution of Jews, I don't remember any conversations about our "situation." My mother was much too preoccupied with her personal life—my father's death, her mother's illness, her ever changing job situation, to spend much time on the affairs of the Third Reich.

In early March, my mother said casually one morning: "Tante

Martha has invited you to spend a few days with them. I think you should go. You always have a good time there."

I looked at her. What's that all about? I thought. Why now? How will I get to school?

"It's been so quiet here since Oma has been sick," she continued. "You always like playing with Jutta, don't you? They like having you too."

I wanted to say no, I don't like to play with Jutta in her house, but I said nothing and just looked away.

"Remember the last time when you two built the playhouse in their living room? You had a really good time."

She seemed to be very insistent that I go. Why did she think I minded the quiet? It was usually quiet at home anyway.

"You'll go Wednesday, and Saturday I'll pick you up again. Tante Martha will show you the way to school, OK? You'll have fun," she repeated. But her sad face did not promise me fun.

I was puzzled. Four days? Why in the middle of the school year? Nevertheless it was tempting, since now I wasn't allowed to play the piano nor spend much time with my grandmother. I hesitated. No, I thought, four days is too long to be away, too long to be there. I remembered that sometimes Jutta would suddenly act mean, as if I were an intruder to get rid of. In back of my mind there also nagged the big question, why? Why now?

I tried to figure out what was up. My mother's mouth was set in a determined way, and even though her eyes were friendly, I could see that there was no point arguing, that she really wanted me to go. She had made up her mind.

"OK," I said. "But don't forget to pick me up."

As I had half expected, the first afternoon Jutta and I played together with her dollhouse and toy store quite harmoniously, but when on Thursday she didn't want my company any longer,

I dedicated myself to making her brother's electric trains go round and round. I built a large crane with his Mecchano set while the two of them took their roller skates out into the street. How I wished I had roller skates too! Tante Martha placed a mug of cocoa and cookies on the kitchen table. To console me, I felt. As I sat there in her warm kitchen and watched her leisurely way of preparing the evening meal, I felt quite content but at the same time also acutely sad. Perhaps it was the aura of ordinariness that I sensed there, of a kind of family life that was described in our schoolbooks: two parents, brother and sister with skates and dollhouses and electric trains; Mother baking cookies and Father at work. Later, when the children came in, they argued and yelled at each other and were finally sent to their rooms until supper. Still that feeling didn't leave me. That evening, lying in the extra bed in Jutta's room, we were again two little girls giggling together, but before falling asleep I thought of Oma and I wanted to be home right then and there.

On Friday afternoon it rained and neither Jutta nor her brother wanted me there. "Why don't you go home," they grumbled. "We're tired of having you here."

"I'm tired of being here too," I answered defiantly, and I wished that my mother would come for me. Cocoa and cookies and a warm kitchen were no longer a remedy, and so I spent the day looking through magazines in the living room and staring out of the window at the rainy, unfamiliar street below. On Saturday Jutta and her brother were invited to play at their cousin's house, while I went with Tante Martha to do errands and helped her prepare supper. I was now more than ready to go home. Why didn't Mutti come for me? She had promised four days!

Early on Sunday morning, she finally came. She was wearing her black dress and on the sleeve of her coat she had tied a black piece of cloth. When she saw me looking at it she spoke, trying to keep her voice steady.

"Your Oma died." I looked at her, not comprehending. What is she saying?

Mutti's voice broke. She was crying.

"She was buried Friday morning," she managed to say.

I looked at her but couldn't say anything; her words made no sense. Was there more?

"It was very sad," she continued. "That's why I didn't want you to come."

She looked at me and after a moment she said, "Besides, a funeral is not for children."

I stood there with my arms hanging straight down at my sides, feet apart, braced against whatever else she was going to say. She took a step forward, and folded me into her arms. There was a sudden cry that seemed to come from deep within her. I let her hold me and did not resist. She lifted a hand to stroke my hair, but I tilted my head and placed a small kiss on the side of her neck. She let me go then and wiped her eyes and I was there, trying to think about what she had told me. I tried to picture Oma dead, buried, a funeral. I could picture none of it. Except for the sadness in Mutti's face, and the black clothes she wore. Even her shoes and stockings were black, I noticed.

I wanted to go home immediately, I wanted to be at home to see; I didn't even know what I expected to see. We hurried through the empty Sunday streets, side by side, not talking, not touching. It was raining steadily. I kept my hands balled up in the pockets of my coat, my legs pressing me forward towards what I needed to see.

At the top of the stairs I rang our doorbell several times hard. Bertha opened the door, her face red and swollen and streaked with tears.

"She's gone," she sobbed, "She's gone." Over and over.

I ran to Oma's room. The door stood open. I stood in the doorway not daring to go in, but I looked everywhere to find some signs of my grandmother. The lace curtain at the half open window moved gently in and out, the bed was freshly made with clean white sheets and a white coverlet, as if ready for a guest. The flower vase that had always been filled stood empty on the night table. There were no glasses, no carafe with water, no bottles of medicines. Oma's slippers were gone from under the bed and so was the heavy porcelain chamber pot. Everything was neat, the room was empty. Yes, I realized, she was really gone. It was as if a shutter had slammed shut somewhere inside my ten year old self that did not let me take in more than what I had just seen.

I noticed the parlor door open, not shut as always before. On the little table near the window, where my grandmother used to sit reading, a candle in a glass container burned day and night.

During the next days a slow anger started to burn in me. Why wasn't I there? Why was I excluded? Why did Mutti decide for me? Who made the rule that funerals were not for children? All funerals? Even my Oma's whom I loved more than I loved anyone else? Not fair, not fair!

A few days later, as I came out of the bathroom in my pajamas to go to bed, Mutti was waiting for me in our room.

"Come, I'll tell you a little about it," she said softly.

Perhaps because I had been slinking around the apartment silently, or looking very busy reading or writing in my school notebook, even though I wasn't going to school for a whole week in honor of our mourning, or perhaps because I avoided my mother and hardly answered her questions, she must have decided to talk to me. I wasn't sure I wanted to know, not sure that I didn't prefer to nurture my anger at her, not sure that I didn't prefer the closed shutter in my mind.

"I know you miss her a lot," she began. "We all do. But you should know that Oma suffered much the last weeks, she was very sick, she had a lot of pain. I know you wouldn't have wanted her to suffer like that." I nodded my head.

"The doctor gave her shots to take away some of the pain." She paused. I could see that she tried to keep her voice steady, not to cry. "I think she had wanted to die," she continued.

Why would she have wanted to die? Didn't Oma love me? Didn't she know that I loved her? Didn't she know that I would miss her? Was wanting to die a little like my wanting to get away from the children's home that time long ago? When something hurts so much that all you want is that it stops hurting?

"She had wanted a plain pine box coffin, like Orthodox Jews do," my mother continued, "and to be buried in the Jewish cemetery." I looked down at my shoes.

Was that the cemetery where we used to take Sunday walks? Where there were big beautiful trees and gravel paths and many tombstones surrounded by flowering bushes and where I wasn't supposed to run ahead and bounce a ball on the graves? Out of respect for the dead, Mutti had said. Was that the Jewish cemetery? But no, there were many crosses on the stones, and that wasn't Jewish.

"I don't even know where that is!" I spat out.

"It's far from here," my mother answered. "The hearse took her coffin to the cemetery, where she was buried. Many people came. It was very sad and very beautiful." She stopped talking. Tears were streaming down her face. I noticed the embroidered initials in the corner of her handkerchief: *ABH,* Oma's initials.

I didn't say anything for a long time. Mutti kept looking at me waiting for my response, but I didn't want to talk to her. Finally she must have felt the silence unbearable.

"Would have been too far for you," she ventured as if in explanation of her decision not to include me.

Why was she telling me all that? It made me jealous, of her and of all the other people who had been included while I had been left out; jealous and angry too. Angry at being sent away. Angry at being considered too young. Angry that Oma had to die. Angry at every thing. Didn't they know that I loved my Oma more than anyone else? That I needed her? It didn't occur to me that my mother had wanted to protect me by not including me. I was mad at my mother, mad at everyone, disappointed and not really sad at all. That came later, as I realized that my grandmother really wasn't coming back.

That night as I lay in my bed trying to go to sleep, I couldn't stop thinking about Oma's funeral. I tried to picture what Mutti had told me: a hearse with the coffin in it and lots of people. What I saw was a black, old fashioned hearse with large wooden wheels that creaked as it slowly proceeded through the cobblestone streets carrying Oma's pine box to the cemetery. The coach, pulled by a team of four black horses with black plumes on their heads, swayed from side to side. The coachman wore a black top hat and a lot of people, dressed all in black, were walking slowly behind the coach in a long line carrying large black umbrellas. I didn't recognize any of them, because they didn't have any faces except for Mutti and Tante Bertha.

Custom decreed that for a whole year there was to be no music in our house of mourning. Even though I would no longer have disturbed her, the piano remained closed.

Like the layers of a rock formation we notice as we drive along a road cut out of a mountain, so my childhood memories, tilted by events, by the upheavals of history, compressed and stretched by the child's need to cope and the adult's search for the truth, present me with puzzles which ask to be solved. What

120

was it that the child then knew? What is it that the adult now infers? I dealt with my grandmother's death the way I always dealt with difficult and painful things, with losses and disappointments, by putting it away somewhere unreachable. As I grew up, even though my mother spoke often sadly about how she missed her mother, for me, my grandmother resided in a peaceful place in my memory, a place neither sad nor regretful, a place that I did not have to disturb in order to know how much I had loved her.

It was different with my father. I was left with so many unanswered questions, so many questions I hadn't wanted to ask, that my imagination had to fill in some of the void.

Many years later when I was married, I sometimes had fantasies in which my husband would die suddenly and unexpectedly in a hotel room away from home during a conference he was attending; or that he had died in a plane crash on his way to a distant city. I would see myself at the funeral, dressed in black, among a large crowd of mourners. I would wear dark glasses to hide my dry eyes, and I would pretend sorrow, when in fact I would feel nothing at all. I would wonder why I didn't mourn in that fantasy, why I wasn't devastated, why I couldn't cry. I understand now that in that fantasy I had substituted the figure of my husband for that of my father whom I had such difficulty picturing. It was my father who died. I could not grieve for my father. I could not grieve for the absent father who had remained a stranger.

AS I TRY to reconstruct images of my father, I try to think of presents from him for birthdays or Christmas or other occasions. I cannot think of any; there were no gifts from him that I remember, no birthday cards, no Christmas presents. I had nothing from him when he died except for the two souvenir emblems he had bought for me on our last vacation.

My mother had a beautiful leaf-shaped silver pin with a green stone which he had given her and which she wore proudly while she was with him, but which she put away wrapped in tissue paper at the back of the bottom drawer of the chest we shared at home. Occasionally when she was at work, I would take it out, unwrap it carefully so as not to tear the paper and pin it to my dress, in the same spot where I had seen it on her. There it glistened for a few minutes, but then I quickly wrapped it up again and put it away. I did not want her to know what I had done.

Every January around the time of my birthday, a small green fluted porcelain vase would be filled with lily-of-the-valley pips. My mother would place it on the window sill in the afternoon sun. "A present from your Papa," she would tell me. "To honor your birth." It's really her present, to honor her, not a present for me, I thought.

Many years later I learned from her that vase and flowers were presents from her friend Lili, and not from my father at all. Had she told me that small lie in order to make me feel good about him on my birthday? Had she wanted me to feel that he really cared? I had taken her at her word and then dismissed it.

I remember the only time he become angry with me. It was during our last time together when I said something fresh to my mother. His eyes glared down at me from his great height. "*Genug!*" (enough) was all he said. It frightened me; I was not used to anyone's anger standing between her and me.

I have one other memory of my father. It is a very strange memory, for it is not set in a place, not in time, nor does it include his image. It is a memory of the heart, a memory without physical dimensions. Perhaps it is only the memory of a wish I may have had; perhaps it is a wish I have placed only later in my memory as I thought about my father. In it I am still very small. I feel his arm around me, I am snuggled against his big warm chest, the smell of his pipe tobacco pungent and somehow familiar, and I can feel his heart beat steady and strong. I look at my mother to see whether the feeling of comfort and safety, the sense of being loved and protected, is something that I am allowed or whether it is just a holiday feeling that can not last, a temporary illusion that does not exist in the real world in which I live.

Sometimes now I wonder whether in the deep recesses of my heart I had not carried a palpable void of something missing that I did not recognize; of something that mother and grandmother could not fill, which in my acceptance of life as it was, I didn't dare explore. What understanding could I have had of his claiming me as his daughter once every summer, only to disappear until the next year?

IT WAS NOT UNTIL I was in my last year in high school in San Francisco that I finally learned a little about how she and my father had met. We were sitting in her little maid's room in the back of the kitchen in her employer's house, she on her bed and I on the only chair in the room. I don't remember what brought up the subject of my father at that particular moment, but it was during a period when my mother would sometimes want to talk to me about her early life in Germany. She must have felt displaced, rootless, not integrated into life in America, and needed to look back. I on the other hand adamantly avoided thinking about the past. I remained singularly unmoved by the war news from Germany, even when we saw pictures of Hamburg, the city in which we had lived, in ruins. I just wanted it to end. I only wanted to go forward, to start over to be new. I wanted to be American as quickly as possible, and most of all I wanted to shed everything German in me.

Usually when my mother wanted to talk, I would plead too much homework to be able to listen. This evening however, it was a Friday, I had no excuse, and as my mother talked, I became more and more interested in her story.

"After the war I learned horticulture and then worked in a nursery. I think I told you that before . . ." She stopped talking for a moment. "Those were hard times . . . at the end of the war we had very little food, turnips mostly . . ." She smiled wistfully. "Yes, turnips, boiled, mashed, fried in a little fat, ground and roasted for 'coffee,' milled into flour to bake a kind of hard chewy bread . . . but we survived. And then during the inflation of '22–'23 all our money became worthless." I suddenly remembered the coins we had used as play money when I was little: dull silvery aluminum coins with denominations of 50, 100, 10,000 and even 1,000,000 Marks.

"My boss at the nursery started to send me to horticultural conventions now and then, and there I met your father," she continued.

"When was that?" I asked, suddenly really interested.

"In the fall of '24." Her voice was very quiet.

"And then?"

"Nothing much. He wrote to me and I wrote back. We fell in love. And then you were born."

"But he was so much older than you. And married!" I couldn't help but add. My mother didn't respond and I could see that she didn't want to elaborate.

What did Oma think? How was she able to accept her daughter's situation? How was she able to accept me? How did she manage to reconcile her old-fashioned ideas about proper behavior with my illegitimacy? So many questions, but I didn't dare ask. She seemed to be very far away, deep in a private world of her own.

After a long silence during which neither one of us knew quite what to do, she suddenly said, "Do you remember your papa in the station in Godesberg, the way he waved to us for a long, long time?"

I nodded my head. "Hm, hm." I started to open my book bag and moved toward the door. Enough for today, I thought.

"He died the next day in that same spot. He was waiting for the train to take him home. Strange, the same spot . . ." Her voice trailed away. I knew of course that he had died then, but that was all I knew, that was all I remembered.

"How did he die?"

"Don't you remember? I told you."

"No, I don't."

"The police found Hans and Elsie's address on him and no-tified them, and they wrote me that he had a heart attack and died." She looked at me sideways. "They said he collapsed on the platform and never revived." She continues looking at me waiting for my reaction, expecting a demonstration of my feel-ings. I listened carefully to her story. If I had any feelings, and I don't remember, I would not have wanted to show her. By now I was too far removed from any feelings of love or regret, and so again I moved towards the door, my school bag in hand.

"I really have to work now."

"You know," she said with some urgency, to hold me with her a little longer, "you know, I never told you that he carried a gun whenever we were together. He had sworn an oath that he would kill if anyone tried to harm you."

"Or me," she added almost as an afterthought. "Lucky he did not have to prove himself," she continued, trying to sound casual, as if nothing of importance had been said.

And then I asked her finally why he hadn't divorced his wife whom he didn't love, and married her whom he did. She hesitated and then answered, taken aback by my question, that he had been brought up in a religious Lutheran household, that his father had been a pastor, and so he had felt duty bound to stay married. After all, he had three children already whom he needed to support. No, it hadn't been possible.

"Later," she continued sadly, "when his children were grown, we could no longer marry. The Nazi laws, as you know, forbade marriages between Jews and Gentiles right from the beginning."

Maybe he was too conventional, I suggested, and I thought angrily that he had been cowardly. I was an adolescent who, struggling with the concepts of courage and moral responsibility was very ready to judge others. But secretly believing in the power of romantic love I thought that probably, if he had loved my mother enough, he would have acted differently. I did not say that to her.

Suddenly another thought: Had she really wanted to have a child? Was I an accident that she had to accept? She had told me over and over that she had wanted me, that she had chosen me and I think she was happy once I was born. But before?

I held onto the explanation of how he had died for many years. It seemed so simple, so acceptable, so conclusive. After all, he was so much older than my mother; an old man, really.

And then one day it occurred to me, as I remembered so vividly the image of him standing forlorn and sad on the station platform, waving that huge white handkerchief as our train pulled away, that perhaps he had killed himself on that same platform. Had he used the gun, which he told her he carried to protect us, on himself, because he knew that he would never be able to see us again? That they were both in terrible danger if they were discovered or if someone denounced them? This was after all Germany, 1936. The miscegenation laws, which prohibited contact between Aryan and Jewish men and women on the penalty of prison or death, were being carried out more and more thoroughly; my parents' meetings had become more and more dangerous. Even my mother's friends, our hosts, were at risk. Did they decide that this must be the last time? Did he despair of losing my mother forever, her, who had made his life worth living, as he had written my grandmother in a long letter which I found among my mother's papers after her death? Did he know that after all, he really could not protect us, as he had promised? What did they say to each other when on that last day I saw them talking together so seriously in the garden after our farewell feast? Did they make a decision then? Had my mother known and told me the heart attack story to protect me?

If in fact my father died a quick, natural death, was it because Fate knew what he wanted? Did the God, in whose power and caring my father believed, know how he felt and knowing his despair allowed his heart to stop when he felt that it must? I like to think that death came quickly and gently to my father, that he did not take his own life. I shall never know.

PART THREE

CHAPTER ELEVEN

M Y MOTHER and I move away from the old neighborhood almost immediately after my grandmother's death. We now live in the big apartment of Mutti's friend Irmi and her sister Katie. I know it a little, for less than a year ago Mutti lay there on the couch sick with the news that my father had died. I don't think about him much any more. I don't like to think about my grandmother either because it makes me sad. I'm not told the real reason why we are going to move; only that it would be better for us to live with her good friends and that Bertha would live somewhere else. It makes sense to me that the sisters would not want to live together now that their mother is dead. In spite of everything, I will miss Tante Bertha, but I won't miss their arguments; that's for sure! Mutti says she won't be able to live with her mother's empty room and the empty seat at the kitchen table. I agree, neither will I. Since Oma's death the apartment no longer feels like home to me; I think it's the same for all of us. All three of us feel lonely and lost without her.

What I don't know is that the new Nazi laws require that Jews live only in designated "Jew houses" and are allowed only one room per person.

Once, just before we move, Mutti says: "I'm glad Oma no longer has to suffer." There are tears in her eyes t; I can see how sad she is. And then, after a moment of hesitation, as if she were talking to herself she adds, "It's a blessing she doesn't have to be around, now that things are getting ever more difficult."

As for me, I don't find life more difficult than before. On the contrary: now for the first time ever I have my own room. That is so glorious that I can't care about anything else at the moment, including Mutti's many new worries and concerns. Maybe that seems callous and unfeeling of me; I believe she thinks so, but then I've known for a long time from her reactions or from what she says, that she is disappointed in me for not being as loving and supportive as she would like me to be. I don't try to change her opinion, even though I know that I am not really that way. Of course I have doubts sometimes, and wonder whether she might be right after all. For now the new living arrangements engage all my interest and I look neither forward nor back.

I hardly miss the old neighborhood now that I no longer belong there. The days of wanting to be part of that group of playmates on my street are over, and my attachment to the familiar apartment in which I have always lived is gone, now that my grandmother is dead.

My room, the former maid's room, is very small and very narrow, with barely enough space for the fold-up bed along one wall and a narrow table and chest on the other. The wallpaper is bright yellow with small red and blue flowers and it is always cheerful, even when it rains. Every morning I fold my bed up against the wall, pull its orange and yellow striped curtain along the track which is fastened to the underside of the bookshelf above the bed to cover it, and move the chair from its corner to the table. That is my kingdom. The chest is just for me and there are two hooks on the door for hangers. I can close the door when I feel like it. That way I don't have to concern myself with whatever else is going on in the apartment. When the weather is clear, the sun streams into the tall window in front of which the windowsill is low and wide enough for sitting. Mutti sewed a cushion for it and I love to daydream or read there.

Mutti is very much a member of this new household and I almost defiantly say to myself, as if I were saying it to her, "Well, if you are now part of this new family, and I am not included, (for really, I don't want a new family), then I don't need you either." The sisters talk about people emigrating, who has left and who remains. I don't know any of the people they talk about, and Mutti is usually quiet. They talk about leaving too, only that they don't know where they can go, whether there is anywhere that they can go. A sense of temporariness reigns in the house; I feel it too; no, I don't need to build myself a new family here.

Mutti comes home from her office job very late and is very tired and distracted. Sometimes at the dinner table she talks about her job. She says that her job will end soon, because the Jewish lawyer for whom she works and who is still allowed to help other Jews with their emigration affairs is leaving himself. I see her only at mealtimes, and even then she talks more with her friends, Irmi and Katie than with me. I call them Tante Irmi and Tante Katie, and like good aunts they often take my side when Mother criticizes me for one thing or another. They only scold me when I leave food uneaten on my plate. I don't like what they cook, especially when it is fish. They have to go far to shop in the store set aside for Jews, and besides, fish is good for you they say. I am spoiled they say. That's a whole new idea, that I am spoiled. Mutti comes to my defense. "Let her be," she says wearily.

Their ancient mother, who sits at the head of the table in the dining room and whose dentures clatter and clank when she chews, picks up the topic of food and I get a lecture on how to be a good girl. I don't really listen because I know she only wants to see me nod assent and doesn't need her rhetorical questions answered. Sometimes, with a gleeful cackle she shoves a spoon on which swims a gelatinous fish eye into my face before eating it. "Mmmm, delicious," she bleats in her cracked voice. She opens her mouth wide to show me that disgusting mess lying on her pink tongue. With some fascination I watch her shriveled neck move as she swallows. I imagine her as a witch in one of the fairy tales I used to read. My new found dignity is wobbly. Back in my room I am restored.

The rooms in the apartment are spacious and furnished with large pieces of carved furniture, a little like a hotel, I think. Of course, I have never stayed at a hotel, so I don't really know, but I imagine that it must be like this place: full of expensive unfamiliar objects, inhabited by strangers whom one recognizes, but does not really know well and whom one meets at mealtimes in the dining room, after which everyone goes their own way.

There is a large black grand piano in one of the front rooms. I've seen it once through the slightly open door, and my heart leapt. Maybe . . . ? But then I remember that I am not supposed to play until a year has passed since my grandmother's death. On the other hand, I reason with myself, this is a different apartment and maybe the one-year rule doesn't hold?

I ask my mother, "The piano, can I use it sometime?"

She agrees to ask.

"You know," she reflects, "it's in the room where the old lady sleeps. It's her piano, so I don't know, but I would really like it if you could play a little."

I'm really happy that she says that, so I am hopeful. But of course the answer is a definite NO.

"It's my piano, and the child doesn't need to play on a beautiful Bechstein like this," is the old lady's response. Hope dashed. Well anyway, I think, maybe I am just visiting here and will be called home soon.

The way to my new school on Hansastrasse takes a half hour, much longer than before, but I don't mind. I love walking along the broad tree-lined streets of my new neighborhood, whose houses have bushes and flowers in their front yards and broad steps, carved front doors and elevators. Even on rainy days they seem cheerful. On one side of the street there is a small park with tall chestnut trees along its edge, just like the tree on the way to my piano lesson, so long ago. How different all this is from the narrow streets of my old neighborhood, which were really quite ugly I now realize. Instead of climbing up three narrow flights of stairs in a tenement house, I take the elevator to the second floor where I now live.

I am visiting in school as well, it seems. I am older now, ten years old, in 5th grade, in a new school where we have different teachers for different subjects, not just Fräulein Schrader who taught us everything. I now know that I am different in the eyes of the authorities, even though I don't think of myself as being so different from the other girls. But I am also the only girl not involved in activities arranged by the various branches of the Party. Some of my classmates complain about the many times they have to go to assemblies and to parades and meetings. Sometimes I feel almost privileged not to be allowed to participate, but even though the girls are friendly and don't seem to care that I am not one of them, still I know better.

Mutti still doesn't think I should attend the Jewish school, where all Jewish children now have to go, no exceptions. Does she think that I am better off going to the regular school? She never asks me how I feel about it.

The girls in my class all hate the math teacher. They say she is old and ugly and makes them work too hard and is too serious about math, which is really not so important for girls to know; but I like her and try to defend her. She is very strict and gives no quarter when it comes to not doing one's homework because there was yet another Party event. Of course I do my homework and since math comes easily to me, I excel. But there is something else: I can see that she looks at me in a certain way, as if she knew something about me that I haven't told her. Whenever there is an assembly right after math class and all the girls except me line up to go to the auditorium, she lingers a minute near my desk and asks me whether I am alright there or do I want to go out to the playground. Her face is stern when she says that, but her voice is soft and caring to let me know that she is concerned, that she likes me. I tell Mother about her, how she is my favorite teacher, even though she is so strict, and I mention that in the required salute at the beginning of class, she raises her arm in a perfunctory way only and says the "Heil Hitler: very softly, as if she didn't mean it.

After some hesitation Mutti says, "She knows Fraulein Kuhn, my old teacher, in Cuxhaven." I don't understand the connection. "Remember?" she adds, looking at me as if wondering whether she should say more.

"Oh yes," I interrupt, "the communist."

"Ah hm," Mutti nods, "but don't tell anyone ever. OK?" She looks worried for having told.

HERR VOLKERT teaches English. He marches in, wearing his tan SA uniform and high shiny black boots. He expects a snappy "Heil Hitler" as we rise to our feet when he enters. He is not happy with our performance and so we practice: stand, right arm raised, hand flat with fingers together, "Heil Hitler" in a loud clear voice, over and over until we get it right. He is very tall and stands up very straight and his reddish blond hair is short and slicked down on two sides of the part. An ugly red scar runs the length of his right cheek. I wonder whether he fought a duel as a student to get a scar like that. I can tell he is proud of it, for he often turns his head just so and puts his hand on the cheek just above it, stroking it lovingly

"Where did you get that scar, Herr Volkert?" one of the more daring girls asks him one day. He seems pleased she asked and launches into a long story about the glory of German student days, and how dueling is a German tradition we girls should be proud of.

Another time he tells us that he fought in World War I against the English, how he was taken prisoner and learned their language.

"The English are weak; they are ridiculous; they don't even know how to march. Like this," he says and starts marching up and down in front of the class with mincing steps, one two, one two. He laughs and is obviously enjoying himself. We laugh too of course, but I feel uncomfortable about his performance. I watch his mouth tighten as he predicts that some day Germany will wipe England off the face of the earth. He knows very little English and we learn almost nothing that whole year.

SOMEONE HAS a concert ticket for me. Just me. Mutti can't go because she is Jewish, but I can because I am only half. We have to get used to all the rules, new ones almost every day, one kind for her and another kind for me. They creep up on us little by little over time and they become part of our daily lives. My mother, like all the other Jewish women, has had to add a middle name: Sara It's a nice-sounding name I think, but it is supposed to sound ugly and make her look hideous like one of the caricatures of Jews on billboards all over the city. She looks the same as always to me of course, only more tired and drawn, and not at all like that. She must never be caught without her identification card: Charlotte Sara Heyn—Jew. "Jews are our misfortune, a menace to the German people" I've read on posters all over the neighborhood. The people on the posters have long curved noses with evil grins on their faces, their richly dressed bodies are deformed and they are clutching huge money bags, while families of starving blond Germans cower in the background. "Oppressors of the German people." There are other posters that show blond handsome Germans, knees raised, about to stamp once more with all their force on Israel's and Sara's bodies, hurling them downwards. Into a pit? Into hell?

I am sorry that Mutti can't go to the concert. On the other hand, the prospect of going alone is exciting, an adventure; it makes me feel very grown up. I wonder whether she would want to go, even if she were allowed. Maybe she isn't really interested in music the way I am? She is pleased that I can go, although she worries about my having to be alone in a crowd. She doesn't begrudge me my privilege, I can tell, but still it makes me a little sad. I want to go and I don't want to go.

The performance will start in the early evening when it won't be fully dark yet. Mutti feels sure that I can follow her directions as to what streetcar to take and where to get off. One of her gentile friends will bring me home after the performance; she isn't allowed, there is a curfew for Jews after dark.

IT'S STILL TWO WEEKS until the concert and I am getting more and more excited. They are going to play Mozart, "A Little

Night Music." Cousin Alfred, who knows something about music, thinks it is very suitable for a first concert experience.

The next Sunday he invites me and Mutti to hear the piece on his Victrola. He lives in a different world from ours; he is an architect and has a big elegant apartment with huge carpeted rooms, even though there is only his old aunt and his new wife Alice. Her two teenage children, who are somewhere else at school, count as residents also, which explains the big apartment. Alfred wears wireless glasses and always looks quite stern and never smiles, yet he calls me *Puppchen* just like my father used to do before he died. He is the one who gave me a miniature camera with which to take miniature pictures and showed me how to use it. I took a picture of him, right away. It is the only picture I have of him.

The Victrola sits in a big brown wooden box on a special table. Alfred takes a black shellac record out of its sleeve in the album and puts it on the turntable. "Look," he says, pointing at the album cover, "a picture of Mozart. A genius. Do you know that he composed music when he was only six years old?" He looks down at me and smiles just a little and I feel that he thinks that even though I am not a genius, and that I will never write beautiful music, still he likes me. He knows about my piano playing, and the recorder too, and that I will enjoy "*Eine Kleine Nachtmusik.*" There is now a bond between us three: the stern uncle, the genius Mozart and me. Mutti stands a little outside that magic triangle; but she looks pleased too.

I watch as he turns the handle on the Victrola to wind it up, and as the record starts to spin he slowly lifts the tone arm with its large round head and very carefully sets its tiny pointy nose down on the turning record. "Dum-di-dum-didum-didum-dadaa . . ." the music goes. It's almost more beautiful than the melody line of *The Magic Flute* which I play on the piano

139

while singing along. Its sound so rich and happy. I listen very carefully so that I will recognize some of the tunes at the concert. He turns the record over; more lilting sounds, and then another record which gets turned over too. My eyes, fixed past the fluttering curtains at the window, see the sky turning to night. Silhouettes of evening swallows swoop above the trees through the darkening sky, the first stars blink, and it is indeed an evening to be happy.

The music has finished and Alice serves tea with pound cake and cookies. Mother sends me to visit Tante Emma in her room. I don't particularly want to go, but Mutti insists saying, "Alfred and I have grown-up things to talk about." Of course, that makes me want to stay in the room even more, to hear what that grown-up talk is about. "She'll be hurt if you don't visit her," Mother insists, and so I go, reluctantly.

A CHILD ALONE in the large marble foyer of a concert hall. I stand up very straight, chin out, pretending that I am just one of them, the adults who are allowed to hear a symphony orchestra play. I am used to being among adults, but this is different, and I feel a sense rising up from the pit of my stomach that I don't belong here and shouldn't have come. As I join the throng of adults finding their seats, I pretend that I am an adult music lover like the others. That helps me to deflect the curious looks I get and even some questions, *"Bist Du allein hier?"*—Are you here alone? I disdain to answer "of course!"

Now the orchestra players arrive, and then the conductor walks in to much applause from the audience. Curious, I think, why applaud if he hasn't done anything yet? They are playing another piece before the Mozart. It is nice, but I am too impatient to hear much of it. Again applause, and now there it is:

dum-di-dum didum-didum-dadaaa . . . I am off somewhere. Not in this concert hall but in some town where all the houses have flower boxes and people are in the streets under the night sky to smile at one another and look at the stars.

Intermission. People are leaving their seats talking and laughing. I am suddenly no longer that pretend grown-up from before, and for an instant I am angry at my mother for not being here. She isn't allowed, I remind myself, she didn't really abandon me; she couldn't come. Why not? What makes me so different? As always, I don't want to think about it. I don't go back to my seat once the bell rings. I decide to sit in the foyer and wait to be picked up. The happy night music feeling is gone and I am suddenly very sleepy.

"How was it?" Mutti asks when I arrive home."How was the concert? Did you like it?" Yes, I answer sleepily. She seems disappointed at my too brief answer, but of course it is very late. Suddenly I want very much to be held by her, I want to be picked up and carried to bed like a baby. Almost.

"Come," she says, "it's late. Quick to bed."

CHAPTER TWELVE

N O ONE TALKS TO ME about what worries them, but I can feel increasing anxiety and uncertainty all around me. In fact, things start changing very rapidly.

In the fall of '38 the front room is rented to a young couple.

"Isn't it wonderful the way she stays with him? After all, she isn't Jewish," I hear.

I don't understand. Don't they belong together? Aren't they married? "Not like my parents," a little voice inside me wants to say. It feels good to have them there, for they are lively and pay attention to me, and talk to me as if I were a grown-up. They are both photographers and one day the young wife, Helge, takes her camera to take pictures of Mutti and me. Mutti is smiling the way one is supposed to, but I don't feel like it and Helge doesn't insist. I look very serious on the picture, even a little sad.

One night there is an insistent knocking on the door and men's voices shouting. They have come for Helge's husband. When, in nightgown and robe Kätie tells them that he isn't there and she doesn't know where he is, the men don't believe her and search the whole place, even my little room. Someone must have warned the young couple, for they aren't in their room. Kätie had guessed and taken a chance. Her sister Irmi and Mother cower in the background as the men stomp through the house. When the Gestapo finally leaves, everyone collapses. Irmi is hysterical, but Katie, at least outwardly, is pretty composed. How did she know? How did she dare? "What else could I do?" she says. It is as if she were astonished herself at what she had done.

Helge comes back once for some of their things, but we never see her husband again. Years later we find out that they escaped across the border, ended up in the Atlas Mountains in Africa and eventually found their way to England.

The old lady dies, and the sisters can now make serious plans to leave Germany. They think that perhaps they can go to England as domestics to a rich family. It is one way out for women who don't have any other place they can go. My mother doesn't know what to do, where to turn, so she does nothing. Assorted people come through the apartment now and then, stay a night or two on their way to somewhere or other and disappear.

EARLY ONE MORNING in November, long before the accustomed time, I hear voices in the kitchen next to my room. I get up and see my mother and Irmi talking in agitated tones about what they have just been told. A friend of Katie's had come to the apartment in a state of collapse. Her husband had been taken away by the Gestapo in the middle of the night, and when she went outside she could see flames and heard yelling and the sound of glass breaking. It was the morning after *Kristallnacht*, November 9, 1938.

I remember that my mother did not go out that day and the next, but Katie volunteered to find out what had happened.

When she came back from downtown, she took her sister Irmi and my mother into her room and closed the door behind them. I heard them talking, but I couldn't really hear what they were saying. Only later did I find out what had happened, including that cousin Alfred had been arrested and sent to a *KZ*, a concentration camp together with many other Jewish men.

Kristallnacht should have been a wake-up call for my mother, but again she seemed unable to pursue a way for us to leave Germany. I don't know to this day what her thoughts were, whether she truly felt that somehow she and I would not be in danger. Did she still feel so strongly more a German than a Jew, that she could not imagine living anywhere but Germany? I remember that once, many years later, I overheard her saying to someone who had asked her why she had waited so long to emigrate, "I think it was that I felt so alone, just the child and myself, so powerless to do anything, without money, without family. I just didn't know where to turn." And then she added in a softer voice, "Maybe I couldn't stand to be uprooted, maybe I was afraid to start again." Her voice trailed away. ". . . Starting over and over."

I know that from early on she had loved the German landscape, the earth which she dug and planted in her garden, the German hills which she had hiked and the German folk songs she liked to sing and taught me to sing. She was attached to German literature and art, the world of Goethe and Dürer, to its philosophers, Schopenhauer, Kant and Nietzsche, which she had read so avidly with her friends when I was little; she valued all that which to her was cultured and civilized and good in Germany. Jew or non-Jew, there was no difference for her. She knew little about Jewish history and culture and had not encountered any anti-Semitism in her personal life.

Perhaps I need to look no further as I search for an explanation of my mother's ostrich behavior during the Nazi-period.

All the Nazi government's laws and the stridency of German anti-Semitism must have seemed just an aberration which would soon be corrected, a bad dream from which she would soon wake up. Her feeling of being helpless to do anything alone in the world with only me, the half-Jewish child to protect, must have placed a scrim before her eyes, which prevented her from seeing what was really going on in Germany. She had never read Hitler's *Mein Kampf,* where the plans of the Nazi Party were clearly spelled out, nor had her friends. They considered the book too vulgar, too common, too un-German to pay attention to. They considered politics a dirty game which did not interest them. The life of the spirit, of friendships and beauty was their realm, that was what sustained life for them. For my mother, and thus for me, the increasingly enforced restrictions were conditions of life to which one just had to become accustomed.

Life went on. My mother did not share with me her thoughts and worries and I enfolded myself in the safety of my room and books her friends had in their library, books way beyond my eleven-year-old understanding: *War and Peace, The Brothers Karamazov, The Magic Mountain.* I was so removed into my private life that little remains in my memory of the terror surrounding us.

Even though more and more my mother and her friends had long talks of what to do, she did nothing.

There are no landmarks in my memory for those years that I can now point to as having been traumatic enough for me to make me aware of the danger we were in. It seems strange to me now, that in my eleven year old mind there was little connection between *Kristallnacht* or the Gestapo looking for Helge's husband, or the many new restrictions imposed on Jews and the possibility that my mother and I were in danger as well. Since no one explained things to me, undoubtedly out of wanting to keep me from worrying, my perspective remained that of a child who didn't think about why none of my mother's non-Jewish friends came to visit us, nor why we never went to see them. Nevertheless, I felt something desperate in the atmosphere in the apartment, and so on weekends I looked forward to Monday and school. The school routines, the new things I learned, the girls in my class with whom I talked about the teachers we liked and didn't like, and the gossip about other girls, all that was a relief from the tense atmosphere at home. I knew of course that I could not share anything that went on at home with my classmates, nor did I have any friends outside of school. At home the adults were becoming increasingly silent with each other, as if there was little that was worth talking about. Now and then I overheard a brief conversation about a new outrage perpetrated out there in the world, but I paid little attention to the details. I lived inside a menacing cloud so dense that there was no vision beyond it.

WHEN KATIE LEAVES for England in December 1938 we move out of the apartment on Hegestrasse. According to regulations, we are not entitled to such a large apartment, and so my mother, Irmi and I move to a small attic apartment in a two story house also designated a "Jew House."

"The apartment has become too expensive now that Katie has left," she explains. I say I understand, for she has lost her job and there are no longer any jobs for Jews. I suspect that she doesn't tell me the truth, but I don't know. Sometimes I wonder why we don't leave also. Maybe we are different because I am a *Mischling*? Maybe she is persuaded that there is nothing she can do to change our situation?

Our second floor attic apartment in that narrow two-story

house on Wrangelstrasse is only a few streets away from our old neighborhood. But at least here there are trees in the street, and the apartment has a balcony just large enough to hold a little table and chairs, surrounded by a trellis of grapevines.

"It will be nice to eat out there in the summer," my mother says, and in fact it becomes a haven for her, where now and then she can feel insulated from all life's uncertainties and dangers.

I am unhappy that I have lost my own room, my precious kingdom. Now Mutti and I again share one small bedroom. It has a low slanting ceiling and on one side a small dormer window. After a while I start to like the cozy feeling of it; it makes up a little my loss. Irmi moves into the other room and we share the living room where she puts a few old pieces of furniture from the other apartment; and so it begins to feel a little homey, a little as if I have regained a family. We three are that family.

On a warm Sunday morning in spring I set the table on the balcony for breakfast. There are little light green leaves on the grapevine which has climbed up the trellis surrounding the balcony. One of Mother's non-Jewish friends has sent her some precious coffee beans, no longer available to Jews, and I grind them in the old coffee grinder clamped between my knees. The sun has made one of its rare appearances, and Mutti serves an elaborate breakfast: eggs, bread with homemade jam, put up in jars in the years when she still had her garden at the edge of the city, and cups and cups of coffee. She and Irmi look so content together as they sit, safely vine-leaf enclosed, at the little round table sipping their precious coffee out of gold-rimmed cups, oohing and aahing at the delicious taste of such a rare treat, that all seems to be well. I ask them to sit together; they lay their arms on each other's shoulders and smile and I take their picture with my little camera.

Did I know, as we were settling into our little attic apartment, that many events were occurring in the world around us that impacted our lives? Probably not, or if I did, it would have been only in a vague sort of way. Germany had now annexed Austria and the Munich Pact had been signed. Czechoslovakia had been taken over. At home, more and more strident laws against Jews are in effect: Identity cards, more restricted movements, barred from many public places, a curfew . . . something new every day. Last year all assets, all jewelry, all valuables had to be registered. I wonder whether Mother has put her few assets in my name, if that was possible or whether she has made them over to one of her non-Jewish friends. She didn't tell me. Things that were illegal had to be kept strictly secret, and I am still astounded at the courage her non-Jewish friends showed in endangering their own lives by helping us. I must have overheard one of their conversations, for I remember how aghast these friends were at what was going on. Maybe their way of protest was to help their Jewish friends any way they could. Yet Mother was still unable to do anything that would help us to leave.

Cousin Alfred comes back from Buchenwald. The thousands of men who had been arrested the morning of *Kristallnacht* are being gradually released provided they leave the country immediately and leave all their possessions behind. He is not allowed to talk about what happened to him, under threat of re-arrest, and he is not in good enough condition to have any visitors, his wife Alice tells us. This time what is happening out there has finally a familiar face for me, this time I am forced to think seriously about what all the changes in our lives, all the restrictive and punitive laws of the government, all the anti-semitic propaganda might really mean for us, for Mother and me. I try to imagine what it must have been like for Cousin Alfred at Buchenwald, but I can't come up with much. Perhaps it was like prison; a locked cell with bread and thin soup and nothing to do but wait? Now he is back and maybe everything will be the same again. But something fearful surfaces in me that is not easy to put down.

A week later, Alice comes to visit. She and Mother go into the living room and close the door behind them, leaving me out. I forget my manners and listen with my ear to the door. Will she tell Mother what really happened to Alfred? Will she tell her other secrets? I want to know. Something has changed in me; now I want to know what the adults are talking about, whereas before I hadn't been very interested. Now I want to be included.

At first it is hard to make out what they are saying because they are whispering, but then Alice's voice gets loud and insistent.

"Take your head out of the sand, Lotte," she says. "You must do something about leaving Germany. You must. Can't you see what's happening? Let Alfred tell you!"

She nags enough so that finally Mother seems to understand and slowly sets the wheels in motion for our emigration to America. She writes to her cousins in New York for an affidavit, she applies for a visa at the American consulate. And waits.

In late May friend Irmi leaves for England. She too has found a job as a domestic with people who are willing to vouch for her. Mother is really sad at her leaving, and so am I.

"I'll miss you," Mother says. They hug. Neither one looks happy, but I know Mother is glad for her, because now she will be reunited with her sister and be safe. Maybe Mother is finally becoming convinced that there is no safety for us in Germany. I can only guess at how fully she accepts that, for she doesn't talk about it.

One day on my return from school, even before I can put my

book bag down, Mother greets me at the door and leads me to the living room.

"Come, I want to show you something." She is smiling mysteriously. She opens the door slowly with one hand as she ushers me into the room with a dramatic sweep of her other arm. There, against the opposite wall a china closet in blond wood has made its appearance, and in the center of the room there is a round table with four gracefully shaped matching chairs. The old bookcase has been moved into the corner and there is a new beige carpet on the floor. Our tiny quarters look very elegant. Mother has never had such beautiful furniture before, and whereas I am no expert at home decoration, I like it too and I can see how pleased she is.

"What do you think?" She smiles, looking at me expectantly.

"Beautiful," I say. "Yes, I really like it," I add, sensing that "Beautiful" was not quite enough. I wonder, did Mother buy those things? Did someone give them to her?

As I look around and see her push the Italian majolica bowl carefully to the center of the table and see the gold rimmed cups and saucers arranged behind the glass doors of the china closet, an image of the old apartment and its heavy dark Victorian parlor where Oma used to sit floats into my mind, and my pleasure at the new look in the room is tinged with a hint of nostalgic sadness.

When I think about it now, it seems ironic that at a time when life was collapsing around us, my mother had finally something to her own taste, something of her own that she had done without all her life. Was it out of her continuing denial of our situation or out of a sense, as a terminally ill person might feel, that if not now than perhaps never, that she performed this pretense of normalcy? I shall never know. Nor shall I ever know how she came into possession of those things.

Mutti still thinks that the fact that I am only half-Jewish, will continue to bring me safety. There are separate laws for Germans of "mixed blood," depending on the number of Jewish grandparents one has. She also thinks that since she is the mother of such a child, she might have special status as well. Therefore, to emphasize my non-Jewish half, Mother decides that I should be baptized. I am eleven years old.

She makes arrangements with the minister of a Lutheran church far from our neighborhood. She alters an old white dress of hers to fit me; white for a traditional baptism I hate the way the material feels, the way I look in it and the way the little stand-up collar scratches my neck. I hate it and I shed many tears of protest, but I have to wear it none the less. She and I stand in front of the minister, I in my white dress and she in her Sunday best. He sprinkles the customary drops of water on my forehead, and says some words which I decide not to listen to. I am terribly embarrassed to be treated just like the baby girl who, lying in her mother's arms is next. Friend Lili, designated as my godmother, sends a little gold ring, inscribed with the first words of the Lord's Prayer, but she doesn't come for the occasion. Mother says something about how my father would have been happy to know of my baptism.

In the streetcar on the way home, I suddenly hate her. hate my father, my godmother, my baptized self. Today I hate everybody.

❧

THAT WAS MORE than sixty years ago. Today I know that she was concerned to save me, even though she must have realized finally that she might not survive herself. After her death thirty years ago, I found among her papers a package of documents tracing back the Aryan blood of my father down to his great grandparents, as required by the authorities: birth certificates, baptismal documents, marriage licenses, and a statement claiming paternity for me. She had collected some of these documents while my father was alive, and others later on. Just in case.

One Sunday morning, as we two are just getting up she says, "What do you think about taking English lessons before we go to America?"

She had asked around for a teacher who would be willing to teach us. Frau Herrmann is a New Zealander, and thus not afraid to have Jews come to her apartment once a week for lessons. She is married to a German and speaks German and English. Right from the start she talks to us only in English. Of course we understand almost nothing, but it gets better as time goes on even though she is not a very good teacher and not very interested in whether or not we learn at all. She has bright red hair and freckles, and wears flowery dresses that are meant for a much younger woman and is loaded with a lot of bright jewelry. She loves to tell us about New Zealand, its beautiful mountains and how civilized and friendly everyone there is. She is homesick, but can't leave Germany, she says. Her husband, she indicates, is an enthusiastic Nazi Party member; she however thinks that the Germans are barbarians and have terrible manners. Mother cautiously doesn't say anything in reply, only now and then reminds her that we ought to get back to the Berlitz conversation book.

After a month the lessons end. Mother guesses that her husband has found out that we are Jewish and won't allow it. Frau Herrmann dismisses us without further ado, saying in a brusque way that she is tired and doesn't want to teach any longer. Of course we are disappointed that the lessons have ended. As to the manner of dismissal, Mother explains that Frau Hermann had probably reconsidered and become worried that she had been too friendly with Jews. "Of course," I thought with my new understanding.

ACCORDING TO LAW, since Irmi left, we now have one room too many, and so a new person is assigned to live with us. An elderly gentleman rings the doorbell one evening: The new roomer. He is wearing an old black coat and no hat. I notice the large shabby suitcase at his side. He smiles a sad, shy smile. "Mannheim," he says, extending his hand to my mother. "Richard Mannheim."

"Can I help you with your things?" Mother asks, but apparently he doesn't have anything else. I can see that Mother doesn't look forward to having this rather unkempt stranger living with us. There is something in his smile, in his slightly bent over posture that appeals to me. I'm going to like him, I decide; I will like having another person in the house to fill in the close space between Mother and myself.

He is gentle and self-effacing and he likes children he says. He is a widower and his own grown children have left Germany. I can tell that he is lonely. When he is in his room he reads the newspapers and the few books he brought with him, and eats sardine sandwiches. Sometimes he tells me about the family he lived with before, and how wonderful and talented their children were, and how he misses them now that they too have left.

"I'll never forget them," he says. I am jealous of those children and I wonder whether in time he might like me as much as he liked them; that I too might have a special place in his heart, even though I am not wonderful and not talented.

LIGHT AND SHADOW, closeness and distance; the mutual dependence of mother and daughter, how did I navigate through that time, the period after we moved to our little apartment in the Jew-house? I did not allow myself to feel the implications of events as they presented themselves. I must have laid aside doubts and fears and ruminations about what it all meant and what was in store for us. The shadow of the restrictive life we were forced to lead, the fate of other Jews which, acknowledged or not, also threatened us, and yet the gulf which set me apart by being a *Mischling*, all that was very confusing . In that small apartment in which Mother and I shared a tiny bedroom in which our beds were placed side by side, we were always together, but when I went out into the street to ride my bike or in school where I was the only half-Jewish student, I was alone, not really belonging anywhere. Back and forth like that, I lived only day by day, without thoughts of the future as events unfolded.

CHAPTER THIRTEEN

IT IS JUNE 1939. There are now ever more restrictions for Jews, more of Hitler's increasingly belligerent rhetoric, the clouds of war are very near. Our affidavits from America haven't been approved yet and we are still waiting for our visas, but expect that all will be settled soon. On that hope and with some financial help from others, my mother books passage on a Dutch ship out of Rotterdam. She has also decided that in the interim I should attend a boarding school in Holland run by Quakers.

"You will already be in Holland when we are ready to leave," she explains. "Besides, you are no longer learning much in school here. It's a very good school; Alice told me all about it. She thinks you should go there. Her children went there and loved it."

"But doesn't that cost a lot?" I ask.

"That's been arranged," she says. "Don't worry."

OK, I think, and ask no further questions.

I FELT TORN for a long while. I didn't want to abandon my mother, now that even she had admitted that things looked bad for us in Germany. Yet the prospect of doing something completely different, of going to boarding school where there would be boys and girls in classes together, where I would have others for company was enticing. Even the idea that boarding school was usually for the children of the rich, was a luxury for me. I finally decided to accept my mother's reasoning, and started to look forward to this new adventure. In any case, she assured me, it would only be a little while until we would leave for America.

Was I sad at leaving her that day in July at the Hamburg railroad station? I must have been moved, but maybe I was too excited to allow sadness to creep into our good-byes. I don't remember. We hugged and she assured me with tears in her eyes, that we would be separated for only a little while until our sailing day from Rotterdam. My eyes remained dry.

Ursel, a little older than I, who was going to the same school, sat next to me in the train. I had watched her family's tearful good-byes, how she couldn't tear herself out of her mother's arms and how she had to be pushed onto the train at the last minute. She must be really spoiled to be so afraid, I thought. Or maybe she was more attached to her mother than I was to mine? Well, we were off. Ursel cried during half the trip and was silent the rest of the way. I would have liked to talk to her. I would have liked to know what she knew about the school, why she too was going there, but she didn't want to talk and seemed unfriendly. I ate my salami sandwich and read my book and tried to think about what new experiences would be in store for me.

As the train traveled through the flat countryside, moving gently from side to side, singing its monotonous clickety-clack, I became sleepy, half-closed my eyes and was suddenly thrust backwards in my half awake state to the time when I had taken another train ride alone through the same kind of landscape.

❧

I am seven-and-a-half. It is the beginning of summer vacation. Mother tells me that she has heard of an eye clinic in the country that can help me get rid of the squint in my right eye, and that she has made arrangements for me there. I shake my head. An Eye Clinic?

"It's worth trying. They have helped others just like you," Mother's voice persuading.

"What will they do to me?" I'm afraid. "Is it going to hurt? Is it going to be like taking off the warts on my hand? If it is, I won't go!" I wish there were a magic cure but I am afraid of pain.

"Don't worry, they do nothing hurtful to your eyes, just some very special eye exercises and maybe some eye drops, that's all." She sees me still looking doubtful.

"We are lucky; they don't usually take children there, but they've made an exception for you. Don't you want to get rid of your glasses?"

"Oh yes," I say, emphatically. I hate wearing glasses; none of the kids I know do, and besides, when I look in the mirror my skinny little face looks back at me transformed into an emaciated little owl.

Mother averts her eyes and looks out the window. "There is only one thing," she says. "I can't go with you. You have to go alone."

"Why?" I ask, worried.

"I can't get away, I have to work," still looking out the window. "Sit down and I'll tell you about what you'll do."

Something does not feel right to me. I look at her waiting for more explanations, but my mother quickly starts to tell me in great detail how I am to take the train, and how I am going to stay on a farm with some really nice farm people who like children a lot, and how they are going to take care of me, and how every day I can take a nice walk to the clinic which isn't very far away, and how very quickly I'd be back home and on and on.

157

"OK," I interrupt. I don't want to know any more. I look at her quizzically, and she now looks at me too, hesitates and says, "Well, actually it's because I'm not welcome at the clinic. That's why I can't take you."

"Why?" I don't get it.

Another hesitation. Finally she says, "Because they don't allow Jews. It's the law. But they are very nice there and you should go."

A week later she puts me on a train by myself. I can see how nervous she is. She gives me many last minuet instructions about what to expect and what not to do, but I am anxious to get into the carriage. I hope I can get a window seat. A last minute hug, three high steps up, and yes, there is a seat free at the window. I feel very grown-up as I set my suitcase next to me on the floor and turn to wave to my mother on the platform. She waves back with a smile, but I see that her eyes are moist. The train engine gives three big huffs, the whistle blows and the train rolls slowly out of the station.

Gradually we leave the city behind. As it runs along the Elbe River, I see a huge ocean liner making its way slowly up to the Hamburg port. In school we have just finished a project about ports and ships and I am glad I can see it all close by.

The scenery changes to yellow fields bordered by dark green hedges; tall trees and farm houses with thatched roofs. After a while I get bored looking out the window and suddenly I feel very lonely and wish I were back at home. I unpack my lunch and eat the sandwich and the apple and the cookies Oma had baked for me. That makes me feel better and I become drowsy and fall asleep.

The next thing I know, someone is shaking my shoulder.

"Wake up, wake up. This is where you get off," the conductor says as the train jerks to a sudden stop. I have arrived. Groggily I move towards the open door and jump off, clutching my suitcase.

It's a very small station and I don't see anyone on the platform. The train moves on, and just as the stationmaster asks me who is *coming for me, I see a man and a woman run huffing and puffing towards me. They are big and a little fat and older, just as Mutti has told me.*

"We're sorry to be late," the big woman says and puts her arm around my shoulder. "You must be little Elisabeth from the big bad city," she says, smiling. Welcome."

The big man picks up my suitcase. "Here let me take this, little one. Wow, that's heavy," as he takes the bag out of my clutched hand pretending he can't lift it.

I pull myself up to my full height. "I can lift it," I say proudly.

"Sure you can," he says mock-earnestly, and heaves it onto his shoulder. The big woman takes my hand and we walk to the waiting horse-drawn carriage. "Hoppla," he says hoisting me up to sit next to him on the driver's seat.

His wife leans over from the backseat. "For these two weeks we are your family, hmm?" she says, smiling at me.

And so they are! They laugh a lot, and tease each other; they eat huge quantities of food and urge me to do the same, seeing how skinny I am.

At times the husband picks me up and plunks me down in his wife's ample lap, where she hugs me to her big, warm breasts and tells me how cute I am. Am I really cute? I don't know, but I really like to hear her say it.

"I've always wanted to have a little girl just like you," she says, and it doesn't sound at all like when my mother says that.

"Me too," he nods. I believe what they say, I am astounded and I like it. They let me know over and over how happy they are that I have come. They sing and laugh out loud, blow their noses with a roar into big handkerchiefs. Their heavy brown shoes clomp as they walk. It's not at all like it is at home with everyone being so quiet.

Every morning Tante Gertrude, as she wants me to call her, comes up to my room under the eaves to wake me up with a cheery

"Guten Morgen" *and pours warm water into the porcelain pitcher on the washstand. I jump out from under the plump feather cover, lift the heavy pitcher, pour the water into its matching basin, wash and dress. A big bowl of oatmeal with lots of sugar and warm, thick milk is breakfast. I wolf it down, without thinking that at home I would never touch it. They praise me when I finish it all. "We'll have to send you home all plumped out," they smile. After breakfast I strap on the green knapsack with my lunch: a sandwich consisting of two hefty slices of dark brown farm bread with butter and cheese and an apple. Now I'm ready for my walk to the clinic. The first day Onkel Karl walks with me, but after that I go alone. I am proud that they trust me to find my way. I know I can and I am not at all afraid.*

Every day, the path from the farm house to the clinic and back is a magical event. It is still very early in the morning when I leave, and the sun is not yet hot as I walk with determined steps through the meadow that belongs to the farm. The grass, sprinkled with wild flowers, sparkles with morning dew, and everything smells fresh and new. The path continues along the edge of some light woods. To my right the woods thicken and become darker, but to my left, far away along the opposite edge of a sunlit valley, a short train, like a small toy train right out of my school primer passes at the same time every morning. Its stubby little smokestack blows a plume of gray smoke, and when the engineer toots its whistle twice as it passes over a bridge, I hear the echo and can see the steam. It's a beautiful and lonely sound, but also confident and determined as if the little engine knew where it was going, just as I am, walking along my path. Sometimes I don't hear it, and then I know that I am late for my first appointment at the clinic and I start running.

In the late afternoon, on my way back, I don't dawdle to look around, for the path is now in shadow and the woods are very dark and threatening. I don't know what lurks there and I don't want to find out. As I hurry as fast as I can, I sing an old children's song quietly to myself, over and over:

Hänschen klein	Little Hans
Geht allein	Goes out all alone
In die weite Welt hinein.	Into the wide world.
Stock und Hut	He looks nice
Steht ihm gut	With hat and stick;
Er ist wohlgemut.	He is cheerful.
Aber Mutter weint so sehr	But his mother is weeping
Hat ja nun kein Hänschen mehr.	Little Hans is lost to her.
Da besinnt	So the child
Sich das Kind	Changes his mind
Und kehrt heim geschwindt.	And quickly returns home.

That helps. Quite out of breath I reach the friendly farmhouse where Tante Gertrude is waiting for me with a delicious supper.

WITH MY HEAD leaning against the window of the train, that once again will take me to an unknown destination, I find myself humming, very quietly, that little song, that long ago had helped me not to be afraid. I am older now and no longer afraid of dark woods. I think of the old couple and how cheerful they had been, and I as well; how I haven't been around carefree and cheerful people for a very long time, nor have I been carefree and cheerful myself.

I remember how on arrival at the school I couldn't believe my eyes. Had I arrived in fairy-tale land? The car that picked Ursel and me up at the station in the nearest town, drove through an ornate wrought iron gate at the entrance to the school grounds, over a stone bridge which crossed a wide moat and down a long drive bordered by taller trees than I had ever seen. They were taller than those which stood in the cemetery park in Hamburg where we had sometimes gone for a Sunday afternoon walk when I was little. I opened my eyes wider and wider to take it all in. We drove over another stone bridge across the inner moat and into the courtyard of a small baroque palace over whose heavy bronze door the year 1710 was carved in Roman numerals.

It didn't take me long to feel that I belonged at Eerde, the school whose name means earth. Most of the students and faculty were like myself dislocated or of mixed backgrounds, part German, part Jewish, part English, some Dutch Quakers, some voluntary German expatriates. I understood quickly that for the moment at least, most of the people there considered the school their home. The older students and the faculty must have been much more aware than I was that the world was on the brink of a terrible war, that the future was insecure and uncertain, everywhere but here in this place.

In my memory the physical beauty of the place is inseparable from the feeling I had that here was where I belonged. I wasn't homesick, I hardly thought of home. It now seems quite callous of me, but I never wondered how my mother was. It was the first time in my life that I was not an outsider, not on the fringes, not set apart. That feeling of belonging must have been so heady that I forgot about everything else.

I soon became a member of a group of six girls, who stuck together, told secrets, talked about boys, which ones were nice and which ones we didn't like. It was all new and wonderful to me. We mooned over the handsome young music teacher and his even handsomer buddy, the gym teacher. I liked the music teacher best; he seemed to me to know everything I yearned to know about music. Sometimes when I sat on the stone balustrade of the bridge at siesta time, I could hear him play the piano through the open window. The music sounded so beautiful that it moved me to tears.

We persuaded the director of the school to let the six of us move into one residence together. The house stood by itself about a twenty minute walk from the school. It had been a private residence and had the feeling of a real home for our little group of displaced girls. Each of us arranged our few possessions in the bedrooms we shared, two and two, and each of us put something of ours in the common living room, a book, or a picture or little statue or a favorite pillow. How I loved that room! It was airy and light and looked out on a once-taken-care-of garden. Beyond that were the fields, and in the distance one could see low hills dotted with clumps of trees. I remember how carefree I was as I hurried back and forth to classes along a path bordered first by wheat fields, where red poppies and blue cornflowers bloomed, and then through a small copse of low trees and currant bushes, whose berries, *krenten* in the local dialect, were large and purple and very sweet.

I was the "baby" in our group, the youngest by about a year. Once in a while I would notice that my friends whispered among themselves and wouldn't tell me what it was about. I was too young to understand they would say. Too young? Not understand?

Finally I insisted that indeed I was old enough to hear everything they talked about. "What about our solemn blood oath? Didn't we swear to have no secrets from each other?"

"OK, you're right. Well, we've been wondering whether those two guys are gay, you know, homosexuals."

"Huh, what does 'homosexuals' mean?" I wanted to say, but instead I pretended to understand and nodded my head in agreement. Although I tried to be more observant, I could never figure it out.

I noticed another secret activity of my friends from which I felt excluded. It had to do with their complaints to each other about not feeling well, being excused from gym and going to the bathroom often, and with certain cryptic remarks about how it was this month compared with other months. And then, one day I discovered a bright red spot in my underwear.

"Didn't your mother explain?" Mia, who was a year older than I, asked in surprise.

The group held a conclave and decided that it would be best if Susie, Edith's sixteen-year-old sister, would take me aside and clarify this event for me and explain what I must and must not do. It was an interesting story to ponder and I felt important, but of course I was also terribly embarrassed, more about being so ignorant than about hearing all the gory details. Even so, I was happy, for now I felt that I really was a full-fledged member of our group. I was no longer the baby.

Another big event: I stopped wearing glasses.

"You don't need them any longer; you're really not cross-eyed any more." Edith spoke for the group. "We've decided for you. Try it." How I hated the word cross-eyed! I walked over to the mirror and looked. Well, maybe it was a little better, I thought.

"Try not to think about it so much," Inge suggested. "It's really not so bad. Only a little bit, now and then."

"It makes you look kind of interesting," Rosemarie ventured.

All five of them were standing around me in a circle as I tried to establish whether the girl in the mirror really looked alright. I rolled my eyes to the right and to the left. Maybe they were right, maybe I looked OK. Mia picked up my glasses from the dresser and ceremoniously deposited them in the wastepaper basket. Everyone applauded.

"While we are at it," Edith said, "you need some new clothes.

Here, try this on." She handed me a shirt which I could have sworn I saw Inge wear only yesterday. The others produced a yellow sweater and a navy blue skirt, and even a jacket, which, though the elbows were a little thin, still had some life left in it. The shirt was a bit big, but everything else fit.

"But these are yours," I protested meekly. "Don't you need them? I'm really OK."

"Take them. We insist. We don't need them. Besides you can put yours in the clothes bin for others. Done!"

I was astonished and felt embarrassed but also really wonderful to be so important to my new friends. They were taking care of me; they really liked me, I belonged. I guessed that they had seen me put on weight and that my clothes no longer fit me.

In fact, I was well on my way from a skinny little kid to an adolescent girl. I hadn't noticed the changes, and even though I was not an athlete, I liked to run and bicycle and skate and play soccer and field hockey as well as the other girls. I liked to climb trees and even, after much practice, had learned to turn cartwheels on the lawn. I was unaware and not prepared for the changes to be expected at adolescence, since neither an older sister nor friends nor my mother, had warned me. I hadn't even noticed that indeed my right eye was much more centered than before. But the girls noticed and because I was one of them they cared and wanted to do something about it. They didn't want gratitude or love in exchange, the way I had always felt my mother wanted it when she did something nice for me. That was astonishing for me, something I had never experienced before.

Whenever the six of us had a disagreement we would ask Susie to be the arbitrator. To me, the give and take of talking things over together was a new and fascinating experience. In the German schools the teachers would make the decisions according to what they might consider the "German Way," and we girls would imitate them, select a leader from the group who would then rule. At home there was no one to disagree with except my mother, and that was an altogether different matter.

And then there was Eva. She was a year older than I was and in my eyes she was the most beautiful girl I had ever seen. Her short straight hair was very black, as were her large round eyes, which looked out into the world with a kind of calm confidence I admired. She was not much taller than I was, and even a little chunkier, but she moved with a kind of dignity I wished very much to be able to possess myself. The clothes she wore always seemed to be made just for her in their tasteful simplicity. It was the way she wore them that made them elegant. Whenever we took a walk together, her cheeks would become rosy and flushed. I couldn't get enough of looking at her. She liked being looked at, she liked being admired, and she considered me her best friend. We had long serious conversations about the nature of beauty and love, art and poetry as we sat in her room in the tower of the main house, the *Kasteel,* a romantic round space which customarily was only given to seniors, or during our walks through the fields. Our favorite place was a large outcropping of rock on a nearby hill from which we could see the castle and the canal leading away from the outer moat through the fields and the distant woods.

She wrote her mother in Amsterdam at least once a week, and every week her mother wrote back. I admired the array of photos of herself alone, or with her mother, that stood on her bookcase. On all of them daughter and mother looked happy and loving. It hadn't occurred to me to bring a picture of my mother with me, and letters between us were only sporadic. Eva made me think, she made me feel attractive and valuable in a different way than the other girls did. I was in love with her.

I was torn. The girls in the group didn't like her; they thought her stuck up and snobbish and egotistical. She didn't like them much either, thought them common and superficial.

"Why do you hang out with Eva so much?" Mia asked one day. They had obviously discussed the matter, and Mia had volunteered to talk to me.

"I like her," I dared to answer. I tried to explain, but from then on I felt a circling of wagons, leaving me outside in the cold. Eva couldn't understand why I wanted to belong to that group of silly girls, and there was no way I knew how to explain to her what they meant to me. She wanted me to choose, and I didn't know how.

Soon however my problem was solved. One of the older boys had noticed Eva as well and pursued her with vigor. He was handsome and self assured and Eva began to spend more and more time with him. At first she would tell me how wonderful he was and how much fun they were having together, but soon that stopped, and whereas she insisted that I was still her best friend, things had changed. It saddened me, but I was relieved too. The group opened their arms to me again and I was once more one of them. Maybe they had been right after all, I thought.

Since this was a Quaker school, there was Sunday Meeting. We wore our Sunday clothes, and before entering the great hall of the castle we took our shoes off and left them lined up against the walls in the hall to protect the beautiful old carpet. To me the removing of shoes became an important, festive ritual. We sat on cushions on the floor, and I found ample time during that endless twenty minutes of silence with which the service began, to study the scenes depicted on the tapestries that covered the walls. There was a hunting scene in which a gorgeous white horse reared up on its hind legs confronting a huge stag, from whose flank the deadly arrow protruded. Hunters in elaborate getups, sporting plumed hats, stood on the flower-strewn meadow, surrounded by trees whose strangely shaped leaves cast deep shadows in the background. On another tapestry shepherds and shepherdesses were having a picnic in a clearing in the woods, while sheep and goats were grazing contentedly near a little tumbling brook. It was all so romantic and beautiful and happy.

Finally an adult would stand up to speak. Others followed, students as well as adults, to express a thought or recite a poem or read a brief story. Sometimes we listened to a performance on the piano or the violin and we usually sang one or two songs together. At one service I played a movement from a Handel sonata on my recorder, encouraged by Hildy, the handsome music teacher, for whom in any case I would have gone through fire. I was terribly nervous, but also felt proud to stand in front of the whole school, recorder in hand. It was another sign that really and truly I belonged.

Of course there was learning as well: English and Latin, and everyone read poetry. In our isolation, books were passed from one student to the next, so that eventually almost everyone had read the same things. There would be endless discussions and I listened in wonder at how much everyone else seemed to know. I even learned to speak a little Dutch, and when at spring recess one of the Dutch girls invited me to come home with her, I was ready. For a week I was included in all their family activities, big family meals and trips and picnics and canoeing with a mother and a father and two girls who took all that for granted.

During the year on rainy weekends, some of us laid claim to a corner pavilion in the high wall that surrounded the castle where we played nonstop Monopoly games. The rain pelted on the slate roof of the little round room with its few austere furnishings, through whose dusty windowpanes we could see the branches of the old trees being blown about by the wind. The dim light shed by two antique iron wall sconces combined with the isolation away from the main buildings of the school contrasted deliciously with our games of financial strategies. When the weather was fine we went on weekend hikes, rode our bicycles into the nearby village, and in the winter skated on the canals, which crisscrossed the surrounding meadows.

THE HIGHLIGHT of that winter was the annual ice festival. On one of the coldest days of that cold winter a huge bonfire burned for hours in the center of one of the frozen canals. Burning sparks shot up into the cloudless sky, and as the sky started to darken and night fell and the first stars appeared, it looked as if sparks and stars were reaching out to each other to join in the festivities. We drank hot chocolate and mulled cider, while the kitchen staff, old-fashioned wooden skates strapped to their shoes, roasted chestnuts, apples and potatoes. Mounds of sandwiches were piled up on long tables. Families from the nearby villages had come, bundled up in their warmest and most colorful jackets, and everyone skated to waltzes and polkas blaring from loudspeakers. I remember that toward the end of the evening I skated off alone along the dark canal to where the music was barely audible and the stars shimmered in the night sky. It was then I thought of home and my mother, and wished that she could be there with me.

I have often wondered why among all my recollections of childhood, the ten months I spent at the school stand out so magically as such a happy time. True, I was in the process of growing into an adolescent with all the changes that entails, true that the anxieties of living in the Third Reich with its blaring hatreds and its anti-Semitic laws were absent there, true

169

also that I loved the countryside more than I had ever liked the city, yet there was something else, something more my own, something deeper, more significant. Here in the atmosphere of the school where students and staff were treated as equals, the deep doubts as to my worth were dispelled. Here I was accepted the way I was, here I was not criticized 'for my own good,' not made to feel guilty because I was not what my mother had expected of me. All my mother's doting on me, all her need for me, all her muted praise and spoken criticisms, all her avowals of the importance of my existence in her life, all that had never given me the feeling that I had a right to exist aside from her. Perhaps what I felt at Eerde was only a normal feeling of adolescence, but to me it seemed a unique and magical awakening. I was as happy during those ten months at Eerde as in the happiest moments of my later life.

THE WAR IN POLAND had started in September. In May the German army invaded Holland. Somehow, even though the adults must have been following the war on the radio and in the newspaper, they had shielded us students from knowing. To us kids in the safety of the school community the events of the war seemed very distant. But the threatening world finally invaded our paradise. The Germans were close, classes stopped, the Dutch children went home, and those students whose families were in Holland joined them. The director of the school and his wife disappeared. It was rumored that they were trying to find their way back home to England. Their leaving was discussed and much resented by the faculty who stayed. Wasn't the director responsible for all of us, wasn't he in charge? What had happened to this formerly caring man? Suddenly it became important who you were: Jew or Gentile, German or Dutch,

Polish or Russian, of mixed parentage or not. Suddenly each of us was forced to think where and with whom we belonged. The students grouped themselves with others according to their backgrounds. We six girls realized with shock that Ursel and Rosemarie were in more danger than the rest of us who were of mixed parentage, because both their parents were Jewish and because they had no place to go. Out of our concern for them we came up with all kinds of mostly hare-brained schemes of what they could do, but in the end it was in vain, for the rest of us had our own arrangements to make. We were no longer 'the group,' we could no longer be as close as we had been. Mia and her brother were to go to a non-Jewish relative in Amsterdam, Ilse to a family of Dutch friends, Edith and her sister were spirited away to someplace where they were going to be safe, Eva went to her mother's, and I was to go back to Germany. I took the train home to Hamburg. Our plan to embark from Holland for America had come to nothing, and my mother thought it best that we should no longer be separated.

CHAPTER FOURTEEN

O N MY RETURN HOME at first sight everything seems to
be the same. The tiny second floor apartment which we
share with Herr Mannheim, our roomer, is unchanged. The
grapevine on the trellis that surrounds the balcony off the living room is leafed out; sitting there, Mother and I seem shielded from the outside world. But that world has changed since I
left; it has become more and more threatening. Of course I have
changed also. I am taller and heavier and I have started to have
pointy little breasts. I am no longer that skinny little kid wearing large round glasses who was put on a train to Holland less
than a year ago, not knowing what would await me there.

Mother keeps looking at me with wonder; she can't believe
her eyes. I can see that she is happy we are together again, but I
can tell how terribly disappointed she is that our plans to leave
Europe on a Dutch ship have come to nothing. She doesn't say
anything to me about her worries, but I know from the way
she looks, with deep circles under her eyes and sadness that
her forced smile, put on for my benefit, can't hide. She asks me
to tell her about my experiences while I was away, how it had
been for me there at the school and what happened at the end.
But I don't want to talk about it much, especially about the last

weeks. There is a deep abyss between there and here that I can't cross, a deep divide between then and now.

During the first week Mother gives me a summary of the things that have happened while I was away. Cousin Alfred and his wife Alice managed to get away to America; fortunately both the old aunts, Lina and Emma, had died before he left; there are now many more restrictions for Jews being enforced. Tante Bertha had to move again to a different place with different people, even farther away. She wants me to know it all, she is so happy that we are together again. But something inside me closes off against knowing. I listen with half an ear only. Mother realizes how distracted I am, how little interest I show in what she tells me, and so she stops telling me more. I feel far removed; it all seems to have so little to do with me. I am still walking along the path through the fields to class in a Baroque castle; I am still having long discussions with my friends, still playing Monopoly games in a little round stone pavilion overlooking a moat.

Everything I see and hear is as if filtered through a scrim before it reaches my consciousness. Something inside me is disconnected. I don't feel anything as I walk through my days, not anger, not joy, even about being home with my mother. My year in Holland is becoming a shadow as well. I am not here and not there. I am nowhere. But little by little I am forced to pay attention, to observe, to react, to pick up the routines of a life which has become very difficult for Jews in Germany. I have to do my part back here in Hamburg in our small attic-apartment, in a house which is called a Jew House.

As I walk up the narrow dark staircase I pass the room where old Trude and her adult daughter Elsa live. They must have moved in during my absence. Elsa has cerebral palsy, St. Vitus Dance, and even though she smiles at me and stutters a greeting as I pass, I don't look at her. Her mother is at her side as always. She too smiles at me with her sad old face as if to say: see we are really ordinary folks. She tries to protect Elsa from the world, Mother tells me. Their room smells of old food and musty furniture. On the rare occasions when I see them go out, Elsa weaves and wobbles, one arm waving wildly from side to side, while Trude holds on to the other.

Mother does not like to go out. She goes only when it is unavoidable. I think she does not want to see all the anti-Semitic billboards and is afraid she might witness Jews being cursed out or spat at. Even though she feels she can "pass" as Gentile if need be, still she is worried in case there is an inspection of identity cards. There is a big J on hers, and 'Sara' as middle name. Besides, where should she go? She no longer has a job, none of her Jewish friends who have not yet emigrated live within walking distance, and Jews are no longer allowed public transportation or to visit parks or museums or movies. Beginning at sundown there is a curfew for Jews. She does not dare visit her non-Jewish friends.

I remember that later she did not want to wear the yellow star with the big black fake-Hebrew script J in the middle, although of course she had one, like all Jews. When was that? When I looked it up recently I was astonished to learn that the star law was enacted in 1941, when I had already been home for a year. In my memory the weeks and months of that last year had coalesced, perhaps because I had wanted so much to forget. She had sewn the star on the lapel of her old winter coat which hung in the wardrobe in our bedroom.

"Just in case there is an inspection," she had said.

As a *Mischling* I didn't have to wear the star, but Herr Mannheim of course did. I would see him going quietly in and out of the apartment, the yellow star on his black coat the only bright thing about him. He seemed so sad, so hopeless.

Whenever our paths cross he smiles at me in a friendly way, but I can see how tired and worn out he looks. He leaves the house very early in the morning and in the evenings I hear his footsteps dragging on the stairs as he returns to the apartment. Mother says he has to work long hours in a factory, under terrible conditions. She believes the work is slowly killing him and besides she knows he doesn't get enough to eat with the meager rations Jews can buy with their J ration cards. We don't have too much either, but since I have a normal card with which one can buy more and different things, and since Mother knows how to economize and make do, we do a little better. She sometimes offers him some of our dinner. He doesn't want to take it; "Give it to the child," he says, but when she insists, he eats with relish.

Mother's Gentile friends don't dare enter our house. They write her letters or now and then meet her briefly in the street. Once only do I see her friend Paula approach our house. I watch her from the window as she looks around furtively, hesitates a moment and then quickly enters the front door. I greet her at the door, but she barely acknowledges me. She seems preoccupied and in a hurry. She and Mother go into the living room and close the door behind them. After a while she leaves, carrying two bulging shopping bags. From my window I see her hurrying down our block. Now and then she looks over her shoulder, but there is no one there.

At supper that evening in the kitchen Mother says that it was good to have seen Paula, but she does not tell me anything else. Gradually, over the next few days I notice that some things are missing: the gold rimmed Rosenthal cups and saucers, the silver plated sugar bowl and pitcher that had belonged to my grandmother, the dessert spoons which Mother would take out on special occasions. She no longer wears the silver and coral pin she had used to tie back her scarf.

It didn't occur to me then to connect Paula's visit with the disappearance of these things. Maybe because everything kept changing and there were so many secrets that I didn't probe into the meaning of what was happening around me.

ALTHOUGH I AM HOME for a while now, somehow it is still as if I were away. It is not from a yearning to be back at the school exactly, for I know that things there have changed as well, but I am somewhere that is not here. What is occurring now is like a dream through which I have to proceed, step by step, without thinking, without feeling, without questions.

Mother hasn't worked for a long time now. She hasn't earned any money, and as far as I know, we've never had any savings. Strangely enough, even though I am thirteen years old, I don't wonder about where the rent money comes from and where she finds the money to pay for our few groceries. I don't even guess that perhaps her friend has sold some of her things.

Many years later, after the war when we were living in San Francisco, Mother received several packages containing the things Paula had saved for her. I learned then that in 1939 Jews had to register anything of value they owned; later everything was confiscated. Even though I had been entitled to own some of these things under the detailed laws that were different according to how many Jewish grandparents one had, Mother had feared that if the Gestapo came they would not accept a thirteen year-old owning silverware and Rosenthal china and there would be terrible consequences.

She sends me to do all the necessary errands. I am glad to go because the apartment feels oppressive and confining. The store where Jews have to buy groceries is open only one day a week for a few hours. On that day, after I come home from school I take my mother's ration book containing the stamps which entitle her to buy food: a small loaf of bread, half a liter of milk, an egg, a little butter and sugar, a few potatoes, but no meat, and I stand in line to wait my turn. The store is far from home and very crowded. For each item there is a different line. Usually the wait is very long. Too bad if one's turn has not come before closing time. Sometimes they run out of supplies, and I go home empty handed. I am the only child there, and the adults wonder why I am there instead of an adult. I say something about my mother being sick. The women behind the counters are business-like. There is no idle conversation with the customers the way it used to be in the neighborhood stores in the old days.

One day, at closing time, it is just about to be my turn. I start to leave. The woman behind the dairy counter calls me back, smiles at me, and asks me what I want. *"Komm schnell, ich helfe Dir noch"*—quick, I'll help you—and she hands me an extra large piece of cheese.

My own ration card looks different from Mother's. It does no have a large *J* printed on every little stamp and it entitles me to more of everything than I can buy with hers. Shopping with my ration book is a lot easier, and there are regular store hours. At the greengrocers on the next block I can buy without ration stamps: potatoes, cabbage, turnips, sometimes carrots, sometimes apples. Mother gives me money and a list, hoping that everything on it is available.

There are still a few precious cans of peas and green beans in the kitchen cupboard, also jars of strawberry and raspberry jam. They supplement what can be bought. They are left over from the years until 1936 when Mother rented the little piece of land on the outskirts of the city and grew fruits and vegetables and put them up in jars and cans. And so we have almost enough to eat, an occasional egg, snippets of meat bought with my ration card, some hard rolls. I remember the ceremonial opening of the last jar of cherries still left from our garden, and how their sweetness brought tears to my mother's eyes.

↪

I AM AGAIN ENROLLED in the same school and the same class from which I left a year before. My classmates are pretty much the same too, but there are new teachers. Only Herr Volkert the English teacher is still there. He is always late for class and he often leaves early. He tells us he has to attend many meetings because he is in charge of school discipline and conformity to Party rules. I'm afraid of him. Often classes are canceled and the day after a night air raid the schools are closed.

I can see that not much was learned there during the year I was away, and so schoolwork is too easy for me and doesn't hold my attention. The girls ask me where I have been, and I say, "At Boarding School." They quickly lose interest in my story. They are involved in their Hitler Youth activities after school, and even during school hours there are rallies to celebrate a victory on the battlefield, or the taking of another town, or to listen to a speech by the Führer. I am the only girl in the school who does not wear at least one item of a Hitler Youth uniform to school. Do I care as I did before I went away? No, I no longer care and I feel that all that has no longer anything to do with me. I am doing time, a sentence for which length and conditions are unknown and over which I have no control. There is no waiting for something to change, no looking forward to anything. It is just a day by day life in which certain things need to be done.

Mother wants me to be sure to never repeat in school anything that I hear at home or about what we do. I don't understand what it is that we say that is dangerous.

"One never knows," she says, "someone might report us."
Of course I would never tell the girls anything about my life at
home anyway.

Since we don't have a radio or a telephone we get the news
from the newspaper which Herr Mannheim brings home.
German soldiers in Paris, successful air raids on England, the
advances on the Russian front. Much of it is propaganda and
lies, yet Mother reads the paper avidly. She and he together try
to read between the lines. There is also a thin newspaper put
out by the Jewish organization under strict Nazi supervision.
When Herr Mannheim brings it home he tells her about the
new regulations for Jews or who has died or emigrated. Mother
listens but she can't get herself to read it. Sometimes I think she
doesn't want to know too much. However, she wants me to tell
her what I see and hear outside. Have I seen any bombed out
buildings? What flowers are in bloom in the little park I pass on
my way to school? Did any of our neighbors talk to me? Usually
I am so much in my thoughts, so uninvolved that I have little
to report.

There is a letter for me from Amsterdam. It is from Eva, my
friend. She says that our boarding school is closed, that everyone has scattered, she does not know where, and that the German Army has taken over the buildings. She is living with her
Dutch mother in the city, but her Jewish father has disappeared.
She has seen several of our friends from school, but not others
and she wonders what happened to them. Eric and she are still
very much in love. She is in tenth grade now, but school is no
longer very important, what with the war and all. Enclosed a
snapshot of her and her mother sitting on their balcony.

I carry that letter around with me for several weeks. It is my
link to that place and that time which now seems so distant and
so desirable. On the dresser in our bedroom I keep the little

179

porcelain fawn Eva had given me. It is very precious to me and even when later it gets chipped and loses one ear, I keep it until finally it disappears.

A few years ago through a chance encounter with a Dutch woman who had been at Eerde before me, I saw a list of my Jewish schoolmates and teachers who had been rounded up shortly after I left, and the circumstances under which they perished . Among them were Rosemarie and Ursel. It became my personal Anne Frank Story.

THE MOON is almost full again. That means air raids for several nights. The British planes that roar overhead need a clear night to be able to hit their targets. In our apartment the dark shades are down, they cover the windows tightly. If a warden sees a chink of light shining through, he will become suspicious, knock on the door, and who knows what could happen next.

The sirens wail, and since Jews are not permitted in the air raid shelters that are everywhere, Mother, Herr Mannheim and I sit in the small hallway of the apartment where there is just enough room for three chairs. When a house doesn't have a basement, one must go to an inner room, where one is at least protected from flying glass, though of course not from anything else. That's a regulation, and we follow it, although we think it is pretty useless. Sometimes the lights go out and then we sit by candlelight. If it weren't for the circumstances it would be almost romantic. Mother can't sit still; she paces from one room to the other. It seems she doesn't care about flying glass. I sit on a cushion on the floor, while Herr Mannheim sits on a straight chair and recites poems from memory, sings snatches of Mozart operas, and reads to me from his beloved books, Tolstoy and Dickens and Greek mythology. In spite of all that is happening outside, this is a precious time for me. He and I have become friends, and he shares with me the things that are important to him: music and poetry and stories.

He talks about poetic sensibility and suggests that one can be a poet even if one hardly writes any poetry, as long as one thinks and feels like a poet. I find that an interesting thought. I haven't read much poetry yet and never written any, but Mother and her friends and also Tante Lina had often quoted some of the more popular lines from Goethe and Schiller, and other long dead poets. The meanings mostly escaped me but I usually liked the rhythm of the lines and how the rhymes fit together. It's the music in the poems that appeals to me. Mother has a book of Rilke's poems and those I really like because he is deep and his words are beautiful and his lines clever. He puts strange things together to express ideas, and even though I don't understand everything, those poems do something to me that I can't really explain. Perhaps then, according to Herr Mannheim, I am a bit of a poet. Well, maybe.

He is also interested in History and he likes to talk about his ideas. Mother doesn't much care now, so he talks to me. I think he is trying to make sense of what is happening in Germany and the rest of the world. He believes that after the war is over and Germany is defeated—he is sure it will be defeated—China will become the most powerful nation in the world, not the United States, not the Soviet Union. He continues talking about other wars and colonialism and Ancient Rome, but after a while I get sleepy and lose interest. I prefer poems and stories.

Now and then he reminisces about the boy and girl in whose house he lived before he came to us and who are now in England, how they were so exceptionally intelligent, beautiful and loving. I don't like those stories very much. How can I possibly live up to such perfection and therefore, how can he love me as much as he loved them?

Sometimes Mother and I close the door to the bedroom behind us and through a chink in the blinds look at the display of the anti-aircraft tracers in the sky. They are beautiful, like fireworks at a summer festival. We have lost much of our fear of bombs; there are few hits; the anti-aircraft guns are numerous and very accurate. Our feelings are split—we wish the British would hit something important, would win quickly and put an end to the war and the Nazis. But we also hope that we won't be hit and that no innocent people will be hurt someplace else. After a while the sirens sound the all-clear, and we can go back to bed. The long hours waiting are finally over, and I am relieved because our house is still standing and we are still alive. I don't care if it is the middle of the night. We know there will be few raids until the next full moon.

Occasionally there is a postcard from Tante Bertha. I have not seen her since my grandmother died, when we moved apart. I miss her less than before I went away to school. Still, I would like to see her and wonder how she is, but Mother doesn't think it is advisable that I visit her, for her tuberculosis did not get cured in the year she was away in the sanatorium. Now she lives in a rented room far from us and is very lonely she writes. Mother writes back occasionally to tell her that we are well, but I sense that she doesn't really want to see her sister, and even though I don't quite understand why, I too try not to think of her.

The mailman has brought some letters recently addressed to Mother in a large, bold handwriting which I do not recognize. She reads them in private, and I notice that reading them upsets her. She paces up and down, but doesn't say anything. When I finally dare ask her whom they are from, she tells me they are from Egon, the husband of her old friend Martha, the father of the children with whom I used to play. He wants to come and visit her. He says he is worried about her, and wants to know whether he can help. Mother doesn't want him to come; it is very dangerous for an Gentile man to visit a Jewish woman. What if anyone sees him? What if anyone denounces them? That would be *Rassenschande,* dishonor of the race, one of the worst crimes one can perpetrate, that surely would mean arrest and death for both of them.

"I don't understand what he wants now?" she wonders. "He was never very friendly. He only tolerated me because Martha and I were long-time friends." A hardly perceptible smile crosses her face, "Martha and I used to call him 'Ego' because he was always so cold and self-preoccupied." She now seems sorry to have said that.

She is about to write him a letter, "Under no circumstances will I see you . . . ," when the doorbell rings. Mother looks out of the window and there he stands, tall and smiling.

"Go down and tell him he can't come in," she says. I can see how agitated this is making her.

I open the door a crack and give him the message, but he pushes past me and runs up the stairs. Mother bars the door, she does not want to let him in, but he insists, pleading he must see her, and reluctantly she lets him enter. She asks me to stay in the room with them, and I don't mind because I am curious to hear what he wants. At firsts he doesn't say anything, just looks at her intently, and Mother waits uncomfortably. But then, with tears in his eyes he tells her that he is worried about her. Now that everything is so uncertain, now that one does not know what will happen, he had to come and finally tell her.

"I am desperately unhappy. I love you, Lotte. I have loved you for such a long time," he sobs. "I can't help myself." Tears run down his cheeks, and he reaches out to take her in his arms. But Mother, surprised, and scared out of her wits, pulls back.

"Egon, you can't do this," she says. "You must leave and never come back. Don't you realize the danger you are in? Don't you realize the danger you put us in? You must not come to the house; it is against the law for you, a non-Jew, to be here."

"I don't care," he says. "Nazi laws be damned! I love you, that's all. No one will know."

"What about Martha? What about your children? Don't you care about them?"

He has no answer to that.

"You must leave immediately and never come back. I don't love you, Egon, I never have and I never will."

I am taken aback by the harsh tone with which she says that. There is no softness, no pity in her voice for the man who has just declared his love for her, just fear.

After a while he leaves reluctantly. "How dare he!" she says. She shakes her head in disbelief. "Doesn't he realize what he is doing by coming here to visit me? Doesn't he realize that if anyone finds out about his visits and denounces him, we could both end up '*im KZ,*' *im Konzentrazionslager*?" And more pensively, "I had no idea that this is how he felt about me. The husband of my friend! There was never any sign of all this; on the contrary, he was always distant, almost unfriendly. I don't understand!" She continues to shake her head in disbelief.

"He won't come again," I say.

But he does. He comes several times more. He brings her presents which he leaves at the door; precious coffee and chocolates, and fruit. A pair of silk stockings, a coat. She does not want to take his gifts, but can't resist the coffee for herself and the chocolates for me. As he continues to come, she decides to see him briefly once more. She asks Herr Mannheim to join them, as a kind of protection. He manages to persuade the visitor not to come again, for the sake of everyone, especially his own wife and children. Finally the visits stop, and mother heaves a sigh of relief.

"I don't understand, I don't understand," she says over and over. "I feel really sorry for him," she adds," but to me he remains my friend's husband and only that."

After the war his daughter writes that he had been arrested for war profiteering and that he had died in prison. She mentions nothing about his feelings for my mother. I don't think she knew.

ONE DAY A POSTCARD arrives from Paris. Horst, Katie's son, who is like me half-Jewish, drafted into the German army, wants to come to visit us. Can he come and spend his furlough with us? He has no one else to visit, his Jewish mother and sister and his aunts have emigrated to England, his German father is dead. It is a strange situation: a soldier wearing a German uniform to visit us, on forbidden territory. We can't tell him not to come, we don't have his address. So there he is now, a slight nineteen year old, black curly hair under his cap. He walks in with the swagger of a conqueror, but after an hour sitting in the living room with us he becomes a lonely kid, glad to be home. His army stuff is lying around everywhere and he sleeps a lot on the living room couch. He brings Mother a silk scarf from Paris and a box of chocolates. Mother tries to produce a festive meal. She feels sorry for him in a way, perhaps as much for his mother's sake as for him. He had been a surly, unruly teenager who gave his mother a lot of grief, but now there he is, looking young and vulnerable in his white undershirt, a boy who should not be a soldier in the army that is fighting for the country from which his mother and sister had to flee, fighting the enemy which gave shelter to them.

"Paris is great!" he tells us. "The girls are pretty and the food is really good." He tells us nothing about the rest of his life in the army, and I wonder whether he has killed anyone. His presence gives me a strange feeling of legitimacy, as if we were indeed a part of the fabric of life around us. I am prepared to dislike him, but he is quite handsome, and I hover near him and wonder whether he thinks of me as being pretty. After a couple of days he leaves to rejoin his regiment. Mother hugs him good-bye. But then she heaves a sigh of relief; she has not been comfortable with his being there. She wishes there were a way to tell his family in England that he is OK, at least so far. But of course there is no way. He writes to us once more, to thank us. His regiment is due to leave for the Russian front the next day, and so he doesn't think he'll see us soon again. No one heard from him again, ever.

AND SO TIME PASSES. On my birthday that January 1941 Mother produces a birthday cake for me. Naturally there are no surprise presents, since presents are not sold at the Jew Store. I blow out the fourteen little candles and Mother and Herr Mannheim wish me a happy birthday on this my formal entry into adolescence.

In school there are fewer and fewer classes and more and more assemblies and rallies. Some of my classmates have left to stay with relatives in the country where the nights are quiet, where they are safe. Those that are left talk about their brothers and fathers at the front and the things they do for the war effort in their Hitler Youth clubs. School seems less important now to everyone. It's an unsettling time.

Coal is scarce now. Mother's ration is tiny and even though mine is a little larger it isn't enough to keep the apartment warm this winter. There is no stove in the bedroom anyway, and when I get up in the morning, the water in the washbasin is frozen and my toothbrush is stiff with ice. I get dressed under the covers and then get the kettle of hot water from the gas stove in the kitchen, which Mother has left simmering for me and pour it on top of the ice in the basin to wash my face and hands. Sometimes I try to pretend that I am on an expedition in the Arctic, that I am a tough and resourceful explorer.

Every once in a while I take out my recorder and some music and play a little. One evening a few months before my birthday Mother asks me whether I would like to play duets with someone. Who? I ask. She tells me that one of her friends wrote her about a recorder player she knows who would like to play with me. I don't understand the connection, but I say, sure I'd like to. And so the following week I take the streetcar to a stranger's house, carrying my recorder and some music.

Herr Franck is a former music teacher. He lives by himself and is lonely, Mother has told me, and that he likes to play recorder, just as I do. He smiles warmly as he opens the door for me.

"Come in, come in," he says. "Meet my friend," and he introduces me to an older man, old enough to be my grandfather. The three of us play trios. They are very good players, much better than I am. I wonder why they want to play with a fourteen year old, why they are making this effort. I have a really good time, and try to play my best, and when after an hour Herr Franck serves cookies and makes tea for us, the afternoon is complete.

The two men seem to be old friends, and both of them treat me as if I too were an old friend. They say that I play very well and that it was fun, and then suggest we meet again the following week and once a week thereafter.

"Be careful on your way home," they say. "It is getting dark."

Suddenly I have two new friends. It feels wonderful, and I am proud to be accepted by them as a partner. Sometimes they give me little presents: an orange, or a couple of bananas. I can see that Herr Franck is poor. He lives in a run-down neighborhood and the few pieces of furniture he has are old and worn out. When I arrive, and also on leaving, they look at me with affection and both shake my hand quite formally, as if I were their age.

I ask Mother about them. She warns me never to repeat what she says and then tells me that Herr Franck was dismissed from his teaching job because he had once been a communist. His friend too is against Hitler. He doesn't like to be at home because his wife and son are ardent Nazis, and he can't stand that, she says. Both of them wanted to do something kind for a Jewish family, and so they found me, through one of her old friends. We play together once a week for a month or two. Sometimes it is only Herr Franck and I.

"My friend is too busy today," he says a little too casually. Mother thinks that his wife is probably keeping an eye on his activities, and he doesn't want to make her suspicious. I miss him, his friendly smile and the way he reminds me a little bit of my father.

The air raids have become more frequent and now start in the afternoon. It is not a good time to be out.

"We'll play again after the war," they say. But neither they nor I believe that. I send a card to Herr Franck to thank him. I realize that I never learned his friend's name.

CHAPTER FIFTEEN

IN MARCH we finally receive our United States visa which is good for three months. Our American cousins book passage for us on a Portuguese ship out of Lisbon. No date is set; we are told that we'll be notified when two berths become available. It seems too good to be true, and even though we don't know when the day of our departure will be, we are hopeful that we too will finally be able to leave. I sense that Mother still accepts the need to emigrate only reluctantly. I don't understand why she does not look forward to a new life in a new country where there is no war, where Jews are not persecuted, where we would be allowed to live like everyone else. Why does she still hesitate, seeing that all her Jewish friends have left, my father and her mother dead, her sister estranged, and all her non-Jewish friends don't dare see her? Maybe my fourteen year old mind can not understand how rooted she is in Germany, how fearful of the unknown, how tired it makes her to think she would have to start all over again.

The months pass and still there is no notice from the shipping line. Mother writes to them in vain. When finally her American cousins inquire, they are told that there is no reservation on record in our name.

Our visas expire at the end of June and when Mother tries to renew them she is told that all American consulates in Germany are closed as of June 16.

Our hopes of leaving are shattered. There is no longer any hope. Mother feels helpless, but she tries valiantly not to worry me.

"Herr Mannheim has heard rumors about the war that contradict the news in the newspapers boasting of German advances everywhere," she tells me. Does she really believe in what she says next? "It can't last much longer, the war will be over soon, you'll see. Germany will be defeated and all will be as before." I doubt that Herr Mannheim agrees with her. He has never had any prospects for emigration; he has never had hopes to be able to leave as we have had; he has been resigned for a long time and is pessimistic and sad.

It is hard for me to remember now what I felt or what I might have said. I think that the many disappointments and losses I had already experienced in my short life had built a shell around my heart that was not easily pierced. Just one more unfulfilled expectation, I might have thought, not wanting to think of the consequences.

After a while our ever more restricted daily life takes over, and we continue as before. There are rumors that the Jews in Stettin, a city in the East, have been sent to Poland, to be 're-settled,' but we don't know details. I keep wondering 'why Poland?' but then I remember having been told once that German Jews came originally from there. Like my grandmother, I think. To me that place seems far away, and doesn't change anything here. Herr Mannheim is worried. He says that this is only the beginning; that Hitler wants to get rid of all the Jews in Germany. Mother doesn't want to believe that, she still seems to be fighting against the idea. Maybe she too is worried, only tries to keep her true fears from me. However, there are the everyday activities to get through, and nights that are interrupted by ever more frequent air raids.

Mother has a job. It is not a job she has chosen. A few days ago she received an official letter. In the evening she tells me almost casually that she is required to appear the next morning at seven o'clock at a place on the other side of the city to work. Six days a week, ten hours a day. She doesn't know what the work will consist of or how much, if anything, she will get paid. They have given her a pass for the streetcar and permission to be out after dark. Her words are strung together in a row, even and without expression, and she looks away from me as she tells me this.

"Maybe I'll earn a little money," she says somewhat hopefully. "I'll be home late. You can start the potatoes, if you want."

The next evening, when she comes home after the first work day, I can see she is exhausted and doesn't want to talk. She goes into the bedroom, and when after a while she appears in the kitchen, I see that she has changed her clothes and combed her hair. She looks a little less tired, but still, she will only tell me that she works in a big laundry with some other Jewish women, washing sheets and gowns for a hospital. An army hospital she thinks. I look at her trying to imagine what it must be like. Whatever she is feeling, she tries to hide from me.

Every day now she leaves the apartment very early before I wake up and returns very late. Even if air raids keep us up all night, she has to go. Each evening she can't wait to go to bed after we eat, and sometimes she falls asleep at the table. Now and then she tells me about the other women at the laundry. They are all Jewish and like her are forced to work there. She feels sorry for them, because they seem to be so miserable. Most of them are old, and for some of them the work is really too hard. They can't keep up and then they are scared that they will be punished. Doesn't Mother worry too, I wonder? What kind of punishment? Does she fall behind too sometimes?

"We don't have much time to talk with each other, but anyway, I don't think I have much in common with them. They all seem to have been left behind by their relatives who were able to leave. They can't talk about anything except their calamities. Sometimes they cry. They worry all the time. Much good it does. I really feel sorry for them."

"And you?" I wonder.

One evening she comes home, looking especially worn out. "It's awful," she says, almost in a whisper. "Elsa, one of the old women . . . they took her away. She couldn't do the work any longer. I don't know what will happen to her." Her voice trails off, but she tries to pull herself together. "Let's see what there is to eat," she says. I can see the effort it takes.

The days crawl along, and often at night we are kept awake by the noise of bombings and the swish of the anti-aircraft shells. We stop going into the hall when the sirens sound; we have gotten used to them. I can see that Mother is getting more and more exhausted from the strenuous work at the laundry and also from malnutrition. She often insists that she isn't very hungry, so that I can have the bigger portion. There is also the increasing worry, as more and more bad news about the treatment of Jews reaches our ears.

School has become very intermittent, and finally after summer vacation I stop going all together. There is no longer any learning going on, and many of my classmates are working for the war effort instead of attending classes. Herr Mannheim spends longer hours in his room, and less time out. He brings Mother the stories he has heard about the maltreatment of Jews everywhere, most of which she doesn't share with me. I can see life is taking its toll on her.

I don't remember how I spent my days when I was not in school. I read, I prepared simple meals, so that Mother would not have to cook when she came home in the evenings exhausted. Time seemed suspended and every day was only that day, with no past and no future.

One day in September a man we did not know, wearing the Jewish star, came to our house. Mother led him into the living room and closed the door. After a short while he left. He seemed to be in a great hurry. What could he have wanted? I felt uneasy; what was going on?

"Well," Mother said excitedly, "they have found a way for us to leave Germany and go to America."

"How?" I asked.

"I don't know," she answered. "He couldn't tell me much." I looked at her in surprise.

"We have to be at the Berlin railroad station the day after tomorrow at seven o'clock in the evening to meet others who got the same message as we. How can we possibly manage?" She showed me a railroad ticket and a special permit that allowed us to take the train from Hamburg to Berlin.

"Can you believe it? So much to do, so much to arrange," she sighed. "I don't see how I can do it all in such a short time."

Suddenly everything was changing. Was it really true? Maybe it was all a big a mistake. Mother had thought that nothing more could have been done after our visa expired and our berths on the ship were gone, and that was undoubtedly true. It seemed a miracle that after we had given up all hope, a way had now been found for our rescue. To this day I don't know exactly how it came about or how we were chosen. We were told that it had something to do with having had a United States visa which could no longer be renewed.

My memories of those last frantic days are vague. I don't

remember how it was all managed, but I think that Herr Mannheim became our messenger and helper. He went to my mother's gentile friend Paula's apartment house with a message that he put in her mailbox to inform her of our imminent departure, asking her to take care of some details, and to dispose of our things after we had left. Apparently Mother had previously written affidavits stating that the furniture and objects in our apartment were the property of certain Germans, naming Paula and her friend Martha, as well as my godmother in Bremen, and were only lent us temporarily, meaning me, the *Mischling*. There had been many stories of homes being plundered by neighbors after people left, and Mother had not wanted this to happen to her few hard-earned things.

Only later did I understand how courageous these friends had been to even consider partaking in such a scheme. Perhaps they felt at the time that in spite of the orderliness and thoroughness of the Nazi regime, they would take a chance that such little things would be able to slip through the many anti-Jewish rules and regulations. They acted out of true loyalty and friendship.

The visitor had given my mother a list of things that we were allowed to bring with us. They had to fit into one small suitcase and included the clothes we would be wearing. Even though our possessions were limited, it was hard to decide what to take and what to leave behind. I read the list out loud:

2 blouses and skirts or two dresses
3 changes of underwear
3 pairs of socks or stockings
1 sweater or jacket
1 coat & hat or cap
1 extra pair of shoes

2 small towels or 1 larger one
1 washcloth
Toilet articles.

No photographs, no books or written materials. Only a plain wedding ring was allowed. In any case, Jews had previously been ordered to turn over to the authorities any jewelry they possessed except for their wedding rings. Mother had saved my grandmother's ring, which she now put on her finger.

I don't know why I remember so clearly the contents of that list when I remember so little else. Perhaps its concrete nature helped to fix it in my memory more firmly than the mixed feelings of excitement, anxiety and hope which I must have had.

As an official half-Jew I had been allowed to keep a few pieces of the silver jewelry Mother had owned. Friend Paula came once more to pick them up. She hugged us both warmly and Mother and she said a tearful good-bye.

"Until after the war," they promised each other hopefully. Was Mother afraid? Did she believe there was an after-the-war?

We were told to bring enough food for a few days; there would be no food on the train. How many days? They couldn't say. Into my suitcase I slipped our small leather-bound English–German dictionary which was printed on very thin paper. As a token of my faith that soon we would need it in America. Somehow I thought it was worth risking.

Was there fear? Did it occur to me that perhaps this was a hoax and our fate lay in a different direction? Did it occur to Mother? I can't recall. I remember that she was much taken up with all the details to be attended to before leaving. She seemed almost paralyzed in her attempts to decide what clothes to take. I remember that she asked me to go to the department store downtown, to buy that beige nylon duster coat she had liked and had wanted me to buy before.

"You have to look decent when we arrive in America," she said.

I felt terrible for Herr Mannheim, who now had to find somewhere else to live. I was very fond of him; he had become part of my family, a loving uncle perhaps, and I was worried about what would happen to him now. He had entertained me during all the air raid nights; he had opened the door for me to the enjoyment of poetry and world literature. He had made me feel unafraid.

"I'm very happy for you. Don't worry about me," he managed to say as we bid him farewell. He seemed deeply resigned to whatever fate would bring him. "It's not fair," I thought, "not fair that we can leave and he has to stay."

Many years later, in my first attempts to write poetry, I wrote about him and me. I wondered whether perhaps during the "Final Solution" in which he perished, he was able to shelter another child the way he had sheltered me.

Mother wrote a good-bye letter to Tante Bertha to which I added my signature. Her words were dry and matter of fact, and I realized then that the two sisters had never managed to bridge the gap between them during all these years of upheaval and uncertainties. For the first time I wondered why their American cousins hadn't sponsored her as well.

"Why didn't Joel and Frank give her an affidavit to come to America as well?" I asked.

"They tried. She would not been able to get an American visa."

"Why not?"

"Because of her illness, her tuberculosis. America doesn't allow people with TB into their country. They tried." I looked puzzled.

"Remember that we had to go to the doctor to get examined? She didn't pass."

"How awful! How unfair, how mean of America!"

I HAVE NO recollection of how I felt leaving our little apartment under the roof for the last time, nor do I remember boarding the train to Berlin. But I remember that once we arrived there we gathered in a large dimly lit basement room in the station. There were already about two hundred people sitting on the concrete floor with their suitcases gathered around them, waiting. We were almost the last ones to arrive. A few men were nervously milling about. It was very quiet. Most people sat in silence, and when they spoke it was in whispers. Even the small children were quiet. Their mothers held them close as they sat leaning against the cold concrete walls of the large somber room. I was very tired, but I couldn't sleep sitting on the hard floor waiting. Only in recurring nightmares about railway stations and train rides that have haunted my nights for many years did the memory of that room stay alive within me. Those dreams are gone now, but with it is the memory of what I felt then.

Someone came to tell us that the train would take us to the Spanish border and that arrangements had been made for our voyage to America on a Spanish ship, which was to leave in a few days from the port in Barcelona. I remember vaguely that everyone was given a ticket with the name of the ship and the date of departure. The spirit in that basement room rose considerably at the news, and in spite of everyone's exhaustion there

197

were now excited discussions, albeit in low voices. We Jews were after all still in Germany.

I now wonder whether Mother was afraid as we were waiting in that cold damp basement for the train that promised to take us west to safety, that maybe it would take us instead east to annihilation in a camp. She knew that deportations were already taking place from several German cities; even I had heard of the emptying out of all Jews from the eastern city Stettin. That place had seemed far away and I had put it out of my mind. But Mother? Did she know of the extermination of Jews in Poland and other countries to the east overrun by the German army? What had the messenger said to her? Had she believed him? Did she have doubts? What did she think now in that dark basement room? I never asked her.

Only very gradually, and only after many years, was I willing to think about the miraculous nature of our eleventh-hour rescue. Whenever someone would ask me how we managed to leave Germany so late, in the fall of 1941 in the middle of the war, I would hide behind my answer, "Well, it's a long story." For me there is no answer to the other question which haunts me to this day, "Why me?

PACKED TEN PEOPLE into each compartment meant for eight of an ancient passenger train, with luggage stacked up everywhere, people eating, sleeping, snoring, complaining, crying, even laughing nervously sometimes, it was quite a scene. The windows were locked shut and covered by dark shades. Not only during the night, as a precaution against air raids, but also during the day. The few overhead lamps flickered and shed a dim light everywhere. The doors were locked as well; we were not allowed to get down from the train, even at the frequent, interminably long stops the train made. The odor of salami sandwiches and people's sweat, the overflowing bathrooms and accumulating dirt soon became unbearable. Once, much later, my mother asked me whether I remembered a woman in our compartment who went berserk, screamed and raved hysterically because she was afraid that she would be found out and shot for wearing an extra blouse under her dress. I did not remember that incident, for I had decided that it was better to be standing out in the corridor where it was a little less crammed than in the stuffy compartment.

No one knew where we were; there was much conjecturing, until on the second day a man standing in the corridor near me said that he had a feeling we were near Paris. That was an exciting thought to me, and so I dared push the window shade slightly to the side to peek out. Railroad tracks nearby, then houses and in the distance, on a hill a huge white church, whose cupola shimmered in the sunlight.

"That is Sacre Coeur," the man said. To me, from this noman's land of the sealed train going to who knew where, to see a famous landmark, even if only for a moment, to know that there were people living in a real world out there, was such a hopeful sign, that I began to think that we too would arrive in a real place at a real time soon.

Many years later, on my first visit to Paris, I lit a candle at one of the altars in Sacre Coeur in remembrance of that glimpse I had from the refugee train which had been slowly making its way to its destination.

I had squeezed a tiny, folding chess set into my suitcase. I had just learned to play a little, and so I was able to pass the long hours playing game after game with one of the adults from the next compartment. We stood in the corridor, and when we got tired of chess, we talked. He told me he was glad that there was someone like me, who liked to listen to his ideas instead of sitting there complaining about everything. He told me about books he had read and the kind of music he liked. I remember his name: Herr Fleischmann. The people in my compartment were glad that I spent so much time in the corridor; it gave them a little more room. Mother urged me to sit down and get some sleep, and she tried to guard my place against the encroachment of the strangers with whom we were thrown together in such close proximity. I chose to sleep on and off leaning against the corridor wall rather than go back into our compartment which was becoming more and more intolerable to me.

In semi-darkness day and night, with only the slight sway-ing of the train as it moved along, sometimes fast and often slowly, there was little that could make one know that we were connected to some sort of regular existence. Now and then the train stopped and then after some minutes would start again. For a while, to amuse myself I counted the stops and starts and listened to the chugging of the engine, but I soon tired of that game. The first day I had wanted to do a little exploring by walking along the corridors to see what went on in the other compartments, but I soon gave up wanting to adventure. It was hard enough to squeeze by all the people and all the baggage in the corridor when I had to go to the filthy, stinking toilet at the end of the car, and I avoided going even there. Everywhere people were crowded together, restless or trying to sleep or talk a little with their neighbors. Everywhere people were trying to eke out a little extra room for their legs and arms. After a while an overwhelming sense of timelessness overcame everyone. We were in a kind of limbo which moved us steadily along to an unknown destination. Sometimes I would hear people ask, "What day is it?" or "How long have we been in the train?" "Where are we?" or "How much longer?" Again and again, "How much longer?"

By now the train moved even more slowly than before, and we could tell by the way it seemed to be snaking around curves that we must be in the mountains. Finally it came to a stop. The doors were opened and we were allowed to get out. We had arrived at the French–Spanish border.

It had taken us four days to make the trip.

Blinking, almost blinded by the unaccustomed midday brightness, I stretched my legs which were cramped from being in one place for so long and took a deep breath. I looked around. It was a beautiful sight. High mountain peaks covered with tall pines and a meadow with blue flowers. People were gathered in small groups, still whispering, still unsure and apprehensive. There should have been some demonstrations of joy among us for we were almost safe, finally out of Germany and the Nazi laws. But everyone was too exhausted, too uncertain still as to what would happen next. We were all used to waiting for others to make decisions about our fate. People walked around a little, tentatively and hesitating, as if they were not sure that it was really all right to be released from the train. Mother seemed dazed; she stood as if rooted to the spot, not sure her legs would hold her up. Finally I saw her move to join other refugees who were talking anxiously in lowered voices. Someone had noticed that the two men who seemed to be in charge of our transport were arguing with the border guards in Spanish about something. People stiffened full of apprehension. What was going on? What was the problem? We could see the Spanish train waiting on the other side of the border. Why weren't we allowed on? Again, fear and hopelessness among the refugees. I too started to feel tense, but then as I looked around me at the cloudless sky and the steep mountains I began to feel happier. I saw a narrow path nearby that led into a copse of small trees. As I started towards it I heard my mother's anxious voice calling me.

"I'm not going far," I called back, hoping she'd think I was looking for bushes to pee, when really I just wanted to get away a bit from everyone. I wanted so much to be alone, even for just a little while, but she insisted I stay with her. I sat down on a nearby rock, waiting. I did not want to listen to her conjectures as to what the problem might be. After a while she gave up talking to me and rejoined the group of anxious adults. I remember that it took a couple of very tense hours before the problem, whatever it was, was resolved. Much later I learned that the Spanish border authorities had changed their minds about letting us enter. I suspect a good sum of money had to change hands in order to convince them.

Finally we were able to board the waiting train on the other side of the border. It was ancient and rickety and the wooden seats were not too comfortable, but there was enough room for us to spread out. There were no blinds on the windows this time, and though I was very tired and the windows were very dirty, the mountain scenery I saw during the few hours it took to travel to Barcelona was one of the most glorious sights of my life. Little by little I began to have a sense of anticipation of what might lie ahead, of better times to come. We expected that in a couple of days we would board the Spanish ship that we had been told would take us to Cuba, and from there we would go to the United States. We were safe and the future looked bright.

MANY YEARS LATER I found out that Germany closed its borders to Jews on October 1, 1941. Those Jews who were still there could no longer leave. We had arrived in Spain in September, thus confirming what I had always suspected: We were among the last few hundred Jews able to escape from Nazi Germany.

PART FOUR

CHAPTER SIXTEEN

IT WAS LATE in the afternoon when some of us were brought to a small hotel, the Hotel Navarra, on the Rambla de Cataluña, one of the wide avenues which branch out from a central plaza. We didn't mind the tiny room; after all, it was only for a few days before our sea voyage across the Atlantic. The future looked bright and I was happy.

And then a bombshell fell: there was no passage booked for us on a Spanish ship; there was not even a ship by that name. It had all been a hoax, it had all been fake, a trick.

Questions, confusion, doubts, anger rose up among our small group of exhausted refugees. Rumors flew: a mistake, a misunderstanding; hadn't it been in black and white on our exit visas? Someone was cheating. No, it can't be true! What's going on? Now what would happen to us? Despair everywhere. It was as if here in this real place, in this beautiful sunny city with its soft Mediterranean air my mother and I were again suspended in a vacuum. For the next days we lived in a daze as if time and place did not exist. Mother tried to find someone who knew something concrete; but no one seemed to know anything; and so she decided that she would no longer listen to any of the rumors going around.

One day followed the next with no change and no news as to our fate. Tensions rose among our small group of refugees. People kept asking each other for news, but no one knew anything. Our lives were still in the hands of others, a committee somewhere in Madrid, some organization somewhere in America, perhaps a sympathetic Spanish government official or a greedy one—we didn't know. What our future would be no one would tell us and maybe no one knew.

Many years later I found out that somehow the Churchill government had put pressure on Spain, under the threat of trade sanctions, to provide permission for a temporary stay in Spain for this small group of Jews, who had been able to leave Germany at the last minute with entry documents to Spain and passages on what later turned out to be a non existing ship. But in 1941, on those sunny September days in Barcelona, we knew none of that.

There is a big to-do in the hotel. One of the families, an Orthodox cantor and his wife, want to have a public ceremony for the Jewish New Year. The husband always wears a small black cap and his wife wears a wig. They were told that in Spain it is against the law to celebrate anything religious that isn't Catholic, and that we refugees are in no position to break the law. It seems to be very important to them to stand on their principles; they insist that it is our right to get together for a holiday service. There are heated debates going on among the refugees, but all in whispered tones or behind closed doors. Finally, that family decides to hold the ceremony in their own room.

Mother and I aren't going. She isn't religious the way they are, and she doesn't like it that the couple is very inconsiderate and stubborn by putting us all in danger with the authorities. She thinks that being orthodox is very old fashioned. I would like to think better of them because I have fallen in love with their two-year-old son, Jethro. He is chubby and cuddly and charming and very smart. His mother combs his fine brown hair into a droll little curl on top of his head, which I find absolutely adorable. To me he seems wonderful and more interesting than any of the adults around.

We haven't given up hope that soon a solution can be found and that we'll be able to leave. Perhaps another ship can be found? But the weeks drag on and there is nothing new, except that some of us are being moved to another, cheaper location.

The little boarding house, the Pension Vidella, our new home, is in a different part of the city. Mother and I share a very tiny room, with one single bed which is lumpy and very narrow for the two of us, a wash basin and a tiny chest of drawers. Since we have so little stuff, only one small suitcase each, it doesn't really matter.

Now Mother and I are living together more closely than ever before. We sleep in the same small bed in our tiny room, we wander the city together, we sit day after day at the same table in the dining room eating the same food and talking to the same people. We have no money that might enable us to afford separate activities. We live not knowing what the next day might have in store for us. Taking care of me, watching me and worrying about me seems to be Mother's main concern, but in return she wants me to be there for her in ways which I find oppressive. Since there is nothing for her to do which might give her some personal sustenance, no housekeeping, no job to go to, no money to manage, and no schedule to keep, I have become her focus as never before. I try resisting her efforts to keep me close. I am irritated by her demands that I should always tell her what I am feeling, that I affirm that I love her the way she wants it. I don't want to be thrown back into that tight mother-daughter orbit from which I had struggled so hard to extricate myself. My hard-won feeling of separateness from her, which had grown during my year at boarding school and which despite our physically reduced circumstances in Germany had not diminished, is being sorely put to the test. I guard my feelings even more tightly than before, not realizing that I deprive myself of feeling much myself. Being fourteen years old and thus more resilient than most adults, I don't burden myself with the same worries she does. I want to look at life day by day, as promising something new and interesting, even though in reality nothing changes.

"I don't feel anything," I say and "yes, you know I love you." But that does not satisfy her. She can tell that I am annoyed to be put on the spot by her questions about my feelings, just as I know how disappointed she is in me. After a while she gives up asking, and we reach a kind of detente in what we expect and say to each other.

I didn't realize then, as I do today, what it must have cost her to live a life of such uncertainty even if safe from Nazi persecution. We were unwelcome refugees in a foreign country in which there was no place for her, where she didn't know the language, where we were dependent for everything on the decisions of a committee of strangers and where there was no work for her to support us. Though we were now probably safe, maybe she felt even more powerless than in Germany, where so much of life, in spite of its ever-increasing restrictions, was nevertheless still familiar to her.

With time on our hands, we have nothing to do except to wait and worry. We are not supposed to tell anyone that we are Jews, because Spain is a friend of Hitler and Jews are not welcome.

One morning Mother says, "We can't sit around doing nothing. Let's go out and see what Barcelona is like. It's warm, the sun is shining and we have lots of time. Let's take advantage of it. Even if we don't know what will happen next," she can't help but add.

In spite of our precarious situation she seems to have recovered some of her old spirit. Why not, I think. For me being here has become a bit of an adventure. I haven't been anywhere for a long time. And so we start walking, down the Ramblas, into side streets and across small plazas in which fountains play and plane trees throw mottled shade on the little metal tables and chairs of outdoor cafes. It's all so interesting that sometimes I forget our difficult life.

We walk everywhere and look at everything and have gained quite a reputation among the others in our group as the adventurous ones. Most of the others just hang around the pension, waiting for something to happen, some change, something to give them hope. They seem tired and depressed, complain constantly and bicker with each other about every little thing. I'm glad to be away from the pension.

Mother keeps insisting that we have to continue our walks around the city. We don't want to go crazy doing nothing, she says. We walk and walk and walk: To the harbor to see the ships (one of them was supposed to have carried us to the United States); we visit all the parks and climb the hills to the affluent neighborhoods with their villas and their views over the city. Day in and day out we sally forth into the sunny streets in order to keep our spirits up.

I don't know where Mother gets her energy. She is adamant, and I admit now I enjoy it too, for the city is really beautiful with wide avenues and little narrow streets in the old quarter near the cathedral. There are very few cars and the old black taxis burn charcoal in a contraption attached to the rear. The war all over Europe has its effects here too, even though Spain is supposed to be neutral.

On one of our daily walks, we visit La Sagrada Familia, a colorful church built by the architect Gaudí before the Spanish Civil War. It had become neglected, the inside gutted by fires and vandalism, stinking of excrement.

We are now given a few pesetas every week for toothpaste and soap and stuff like that. It's not enough for streetcar rides, not enough for some cheese to go with our morning roll. That roll is small and round, hard and grainy and pretty tasteless, so some cheese or jam would really dress it up.

As we are passing the big outdoor market in the old section of town in front of the cathedral, we discover pomegranates. Mother knows what they are from her old horticulture books, but I have never seen them. We notice a woman who has one in her hand. She is picking out the sections and sucking out the juice. Mother thinks we should try them; they can't cost too much. We buy one to share and the old lady, who sells it to us, cuts it in half. I slowly pick out one tiny red grain at a time, suck out the juice and spit the seed out. It turns out to be delicious, sweet and juicy. Eating that way has its advantages; it's a slow process, and it feels as if I were really eating something. Besides, it's something to do while walking.

We are picking up a few words of Spanish: *gracias, buenas días, donde está* from overheard conversations, but not much else. On a long walk to the harbor Mother wants to ask a passer-by for directions to a public bathroom. Since neither one of us knows the correct word, and our pronunciation of 'toilet' brings no response, she is not at all shy about using graphic gestures. How embarrassing! We learn the word to use next time: *retrato*—some place to retreat to. I wish I could have a retreat of my own, some place where I can do what I want when I want it, a place where I have at least my own bed. Oh, well . . . Now and then I get mad at Mother for dragging me around the city all the time. But she insists we go. It makes the days pass.

We are served three meals a day, if one can call them meals. It's always the same, day in and day out. Breakfast is coffee or watery hot chocolate and a hard roll made of corn flour. For lunch there is a small plate of rice and beans mixed together with tomato sauce. Dinner is a small round fish with large bulging eyes, about ten inches long, curved around on the plate so that the end of its tail is in its mouth. The first time I saw it I felt sick to my stomach, but I slowly got used to it. It sits there on its lettuce leaf and looks at me with its fish eyes and dares to have me cut into it and eat it. There are many small bones and by the time the meat is clear of them there is really very little left to eat. Once in a while there is flan for dessert; now and then there is an orange or an apricot. It's enough to keep us alive. Still, I'm always hungry. I sometimes fantasize the huge wheels of cheese that were kept in the pantry behind the kitchen at Eerde, from which we kids would cut big chunks to slap on thick slices of farm bread and devour to assuage our adolescent appetites. I see large plates of buttered noodles and bowls of thick pea soup with slices of sausage floating on top, and I wonder why I was never this hungry before, even during the worst times in Germany. Over time I feel less hungry and sometimes Mother and I don't even bother to return to the pension from our walks at lunch time. It's not worth it.

Mother says we must keep our hope up that something will happen to get us out of our precarious existence here and on the way to America; but nothing changes. At least we escaped Germany and for that we are grateful. We now know that the Germans are rounding up Jews from all over and sending them to the East to places no one has ever heard of.

There is a brief postcard from Tante Bertha. She says good-bye to us and wishes us luck in our new life in America. She doesn't know whether she can write again soon, for tomorrow she has to be ready to leave. She'll write when she can. "Don't forget your Tante Bertha, Elisabeth," she writes. After we read it Mother doesn't say anything, and neither do I. It's been such a long time since I last saw Tante Bertha that it's hard to think about her. Does Mother? After all, they are sisters. I ask Mother why she didn't try to leave Germany for America like us.

"Remember, I told you that America wouldn't let her in because of her sickness and there was no other place for her to go." I can tell that this time it is Mother who doesn't want to think about something.

"That's not right, the Americans are not fair; it's an inhuman thing to do," I say. "After all she can't help it that she is sick."

It strikes me that Bertha hadn't fit America's' laws the same way that I hadn't fit the laws in my German school. It hadn't been so bad for me, but for her it meant suffering and perhaps being killed. Did America think of that when they made those rules? I am angry and very sad.

The next day there is a short letter from Mother's friend, Paula in Germany. Mother is surprised; she thought Paula would be afraid to write to us. Bad news too: old Onkel Leopold and Tante Lina were rounded up and sent to Theresienstadt. "It's not supposed to be so bad there," she adds.

"Let's hope so," Mother says softly, but without conviction.

I don't know how she deals with all the bad news from Germany. She seems to manage without breaking down. I guess she too tries not to look back. She knows, without really knowing why, that we were saved in the nick of time through sheer luck.

I tell Mother, that I miss Jethro. "Can I visit him?"

She isn't too thrilled. "How will you get there?" None of us has a phone.

"I'll walk. It's not too far." Actually I'm not sure how far it is.

His parents are glad to see me. He remembers me and gives me a little kiss. Since there is nothing I have to do all day long, I have offered to take care of him whenever his parents want it. They agree and I love it. I play songs on my recorder for him and teach him the words to some of them. It's a lot of fun when he sings them with me. It makes us laugh and hug each other. I call him my sweetheart and my treasure. In the morning I take him to the big central square, the Plaza Cataluña, where we feed the pigeons with the roll I saved from breakfast. Sometimes he sits on my lap and I tell him stories. I enjoy listening to him say his Hebrew prayers. He wants me to know them and repeats them for me until I can say them with him, baby accent and all. When he puts his little arms around my neck and puckers up his lips to give me a good night kiss, I am in seventh heaven. I'm always sorry when I have to leave and then the evening drags on with nothing to do. Mother feels that his parents are taking advantage of me, their volunteer babysitter. She feels neglected when I don't go with her on our daily walks.

My monthly periods have stopped. It's a good thing, for before that I had to use cut up pieces of one of the two terry-cloth towels which we were allowed to bring along. No money for pads. They were rough and scratchy and I had to wash them out in the sink. Disgusting! I refused and made a scene! Finally Mother did the job for me. Now we are both free of that chore.

I seem to be able to sleep OK, but Mother is restless. Maybe it's because of another letter she got from Paula. It said that she had been informed that Lina and Leopold were dead, had killed themselves in Theresienstadt, she thinks.

"Rather than live out their lives in that place," Mother whispered to herself. *"Schrecklich, schrecklich"*—terrible, terrible—she said and cried.

⭏

THERE IS ANOTHER mother and daughter pair in our group. Ilse and I have started to become friendly. And so have the mothers. Ilse is seventeen, from Frankfurt and talks with a funny accent; *Frankfurterisch* Mother calls it. Even though she is three years older than I am, we get along well.

Mother has asked them to go with us to explore the city. Ilse sometimes does, but her mother doesn't feel up to it. Too tired, she says. I don't know what she is tired from. There is nothing to do except wash out one's underwear and try to look halfway decent. I guess she is discouraged because of all that uncertainty. Ilse is very attached to her mom and I think she wants to stay close.

Gradually we get to know all the other refugees in our pension. There are only two other girls here, sisters. Their parents won't allow them to leave the building for fear that something terrible will happen to them. I feel sorry for them; they must be bored out of their minds.

Mother likes Herr Peisach who used to be a lawyer in Germany. Over dinner they talk about things other than our situation, like books and philosophy. His pretty young wife seldom eats in the dining hall with us. He says she prefers to eat in their room because she is shy. People are curious about her and think she is a snob. Besides she is not Jewish, and that makes some of them suspicious. When she does appear she is always very well dressed, with makeup and costume jewelry, and her hair is always in place. Not like some of the other refugees, who are really letting themselves go. I am learning a lot about different kinds of people, how they behave in a situation like ours.

As time goes on, everyone's nerves are getting more and more on edge and there are many arguments about unimportant things. Somehow people think that others have an 'in' with the committee and are getting privileges and are better off than they are.

Once a week we have to go to the police station to have our document stamped. It's a routine, and yet one is always a little scared.

The meals continue to be the same: rice and beans, those little fish and hard rolls made of corn flour. There is less fruit than before; maybe it has become too expensive. The patron's wife does all the cooking and serving. She looks much older than her husband and is very sad looking. He sits at a table covered with a white tablecloth with a young woman who wears her long black hair held up with big combs, really bright clothes and lots of makeup. They drink wine and eat all sorts of wonderful food, not the kind we get, and they laugh a lot really loud. Everyone assumes she is his mistress, and Mother feels sorry for his wife. I remember how when I was little I didn't know what a mistress was! Once in a while he comes over to us and talks in Spanish to someone. I'm beginning to understand some of what he says. Having studied a little French once helps.

On our walks we often pass a large somber stone building whose tiny windows have iron bars over them. It must be a jail. There are always long lines of women waiting in front of the gate carrying bundles wrapped up in colorful scarves. We think it must be food they bring to their relatives in the prison. Mother says that the prisoners inside are probably from the Spanish Civil War that ended not so long ago.

There are many bombed-out buildings, where children play among the stones. Even little children stay up really late here, way past midnight, not like in Germany. Of course Mother thinks that's no way to bring up children, but then everything is so different from what we are used to. I guess that is what keeps us interested.

The *Guardia Civil*, the police, are everywhere in their uniforms and shiny black helmets. One of them sometimes eats in the dining room with the patron, and all of us feel very uncomfortable when he is there. It is strange to be both hidden and not hidden, and to depend on the goodwill, or whatever it is, of others.

Sometimes when we walk along the streets in the nicer neighborhoods we find ripe figs on the sidewalk that have fallen off the trees in someone's front yard. We take them to our room to wash them before we eat them. They are delicious, sweet and juicy. We also pick the brown pods from breadfruit trees and chew on them. They are sweet too, but they can't be eaten. I never before tasted any of these things. Being hungry makes one try new things!

One day followed the next without change, without variation, without hope or despair. This was now our life, and as I gradually got used to it and settled into it, I began to take stock of myself, more than I had done before. I don't think I was ever really sad or happy; I focused only on what I experienced at the moment. If I was suddenly angry, it was about some disagreement with my mother; if I was pleased, it was because the sun was shining and the city looked beautiful, or because Ilse had told me an amusing story.

There was the matter of the single bed we shared. I remember that Mother and I had certain routines: I got into my pajamas and crawled into bed and was usually asleep before she herself was ready for bed. When during the night she seemed to take up more than her share of space, I would crunch over to the edge of the bed in order not to wake her, not to smell her

215

breath, not to have our bodies touch accidentally. In the morning, Mother would usually wake up first and get out of bed, and then I would stretch out and luxuriate in the privacy of the unshared sheets.

↣

MANY YEARS LATER when I was in my twenties I accidentally saw her partly unclothed as she was getting dressed. I was struck by the whiteness of her skin, and how the nipples on her small breasts were of such an unobtrusive pink color. They looked to me as if no one had ever touched them. It occurred to me that I had never seen my mother naked. We had shared the same room throughout my childhood, and even when I was little she managed never to let me see her unclothed. Even later in America, when we still shared the same room, I never saw her undressed. Was it shyness? Modesty? Or a kind of old-fashioned reserve, learned early from her very Victorian mother? Or was it I who didn't want to see? I think I never imagined what she might look like naked, never visualized the way her skin covered muscles and bones, the way pain or pleasure might manifest itself. Her body was a guarded, hands-off place for me. I don't remember many embraces, and even the compulsory kisses we exchanged on arrival or parting in later years were disembodied, neutral events.

When my mother was in her late seventies, sick for quite a while with advanced angina, she asked me to help her change her nightgown. That was the first time ever that I touched her naked body. She had turned away from me, perhaps still shy about being seen. I reached out to stroke her back. My hand brushed against the wrinkled folds at her waist as I pulled the fresh nightgown down over her upper body, while she made sure that her lower body remained covered by the sheet. Her skin felt so fragile and vulnerable that shivers ran down my back and tears collected in the corners of my eyes.

⤙

THE PENSION had no bathtubs or showers for us to use; a sponge bath at the white enameled sink in our room was the way to get clean. I recall that I would try to finish washing my body as quickly as possible while my mother was using the toilet down the hall. I dreaded the scrutiny she gave me every day; her eyes roving over my body told me that she was worried about me. I tried to hide from her how uncomfortable her inspections made me.

"I'm OK," I might answer her, scowling, when she asked me how I was. "Let me figure things out for myself. Just leave me alone and don't think so much about me."

"But I only want the best for you, don't you see?" There was that old jousting stance between her and me again, more acute even, now that I was older. I should have realized that her worry about me was a normal response considering our circumstances, but my teen-age ego resented her devotion to my welfare, even if the origin was a mother's love. It occurs to me now, that I probably would have missed it if she had stopped worrying, but at the time it seemed only an intrusion.

My mother made sure my clothes were clean and mended; she washed my hair with soap in the sink in our room at least twice a week; and often when she saw me picking at the fish on my dinner plate she gave me her roll, insisting she didn't want it. Since I was always hungry, I took whatever she offered, while at the same time I squirmed under her solicitude.

Years later as I looked at snapshots of my mother and me taken in Barcelona by another refugee, I wondered what some-one who wouldn't know the circumstances under which they

217

were taken might think. Are we carefree inhabitants of this city, out for the customary Sunday stroll after church and lunch and siesta? Are we tourists seeing the sights? The palm-lined avenue on which we are standing, the long jetty in the harbor, the ruins of an old fort, the Gothic cathedral in the old square, all as settings for the two of us, mother in a simple dark hat, her handbag tucked under her arm, daughter in white blouse and pleated skirt and stockings. We are standing together or sitting close together, smiling at the camera. On several pictures I carry white gloves and my hair is done up to resemble that of a current movie star whose name I have forgotten. For me these photos are what I like to remember about our sojourn in Barcelona, even though I know they are anything but the whole truth.

Ilse, who had started to learn hairdressing in Germany and who spent what to me seemed an inordinate amount of time on her own hair, insisted that something had to be done with mine, to make me look more attractive. I felt myself above such vanity and thought of coiffed hair as being a sign of a superficial nature. But then, everything was different now, and Ilse was very persuasive. Besides, she was my friend. She combed and fluffed my straight brown hair into artificial waves with her curling iron, snipped here and there to make it more stylish and told me to let it grow, so that I would look more glamorous.

TO OUR SURPRISE, a new person joined our little group at the Pension Vidella. Frau Burg was Swiss, and we wondered what had brought her to Spain in the middle of the war. She was not a refugee as we were but I remember that it had something to do with her Jewish husband in the United States. I also remember that when I met her for the first time I was struck by her beautiful expressive face. There was no fear in her eyes, no hesitancy in her behavior. Almost immediately she and Mother took to each other. Mother said that she liked her because she was good to talk with and very thoughtful.

When Mother told her a little about our circumstances she was appalled.

"Aren't the children going to school?" she asked.

"No, there doesn't seem to be a way," Mother answered.

"Something has to be done about that. Let's see what I can do."

And so to our great astonishment she arranged with someone she knew in Switzerland to provide a scholarship for me to be able to attend the Swiss school in Barcelona.

"I could only get them to provide for one student, though. I told them about all the children. They were adamant. 'Only one,' they insisted. Well, that's still better than none."

What a chance for me! I waited with great anticipation and considerable anxiety for my first view of the school. In the middle of spring, on a typically bright sunny day, I went with Mother for an interview. The school was about a half hour walk from our pension in a pleasant residential neighborhood on one of the hills where we used to walk now and then. The building did not look like a regular school; it was more like the rest of the private houses in that neighborhood, only larger and less well kept. I wondered what it contained.

I don't remember much about what was said during the interview, but I do remember the man who spoke with us. Señor Gutierrez was a dark man: black wavy hair topped his swarthy face. He had a small black mustache and very dark serious eyes under bushy black eyebrows that looked at me unsmilingly. His clothes were dark as well. He spoke to us in perfect German with a slight Spanish accent. He seemed stern and not particularly friendly and I started to have second thoughts about wanting to go to his school. Later on I became aware that he was a most unusual person: Protestant minister in Catholic Spain, biblical scholar who knew Hebrew and Greek as well as many other languages; a teacher who expected extraordinary things from his students and got them; a poet and translator of poetry from German into Spanish. Above all he was a courageous and kind man, who perhaps through his steadfast faith, was able to endure living a narrowly circumscribed life because he would not renounce his faith and would not leave his beloved Spain.

On the top shelf of my bookcase I keep the Spanish books I used then, cheap paperback editions of Cervantes' *Don Quixote,* Lope de Vegas' *La Vida es Sueño,* and others whose pages had to be cut before they could be read. Among them a book of poems, whose light blue cover with its edges browning and brittle with age carries the author's name: M. Gutierrez. It is an anthology of German poetry translated into Spanish. On the flyleaf, in his bold handwriting the author thanks me for being his faithful helper. His faithful helper? I remember that after my first few months at the school he asked my mother whether it would be all right if I helped him with his book. And so, once a week I would go to his house and he would ask me to look at his translation to make sure he had understood the German correctly. His wife would bring us cookies and hot tea served in delicate porcelain cups. How luxurious it felt to be in a real house, with people who lived a real life! I wonder how he could have had enough confidence in me, a fifteen-year-old, who had just learned a little Spanish to ask me to help in the translation? Did he want to give me a boost and lift my spirits? I don't think he really needed my help, especially since his wife was German born.

Going to school seemed like a glorious adventure. Señor Gutierrez taught Spanish history and literature. He had his students read Cervantes and Lope de Vega, because he wanted them to get an idea of the richness of his beloved Spanish. I struggled mightily with the language and I did my best to write the short essays he assigned, making copious use of dictionary and grammar book. He gave me no quarter, and so my papers were full of his corrections written in green or purple ink. Now and then I got angry with him for making no allowances for me. But in the end he gave me good marks and I was proud of myself. To this day, although I have forgotten most of the Spanish I eventually learned, I retain a special fondness for its cadences and sounds. Sometimes at an airport when I hear people speaking Castilian Spanish, I want to say to them "I love to hear your language. I was in your country a long time ago and I have never forgotten how beautiful it is."

❧

MY LIFE HAD CHANGED. Once again I started living in two worlds, not completely belonging to either. In the morning I would hurry from the pension to be on time for the first bell, while the other people in the pension were moping around trying to make time pass until lunch. Going off to school felt almost normal, except that I was acutely aware that the books and writing materials I carried had been provided by the school, because I did not have the money to buy them.

I don't remember much about those first days there. On the playground the boys and girls, who ranged in age from perhaps twelve to eighteen, talked to each other in many different languages: Catalan, French, German and Switzer Deutsch, a dialect nearly impossible to understand. Spanish, which everyone could speak more or less well, was the lingua franca.

The Escuela Suiza was a small school in which everyone

knew everyone else. It reminded me of my old boarding school, familiar in its size and diversity. But here everyone went home to their families at the end of the day, to their regular lives in houses or apartments, while home for me was still our small room in the pension. For the first week or so I stood alone on the playground watching.

The second week, a boy who was in some of my classes approached me at recess. He suggested, speaking in German, that we walk home together after school, since we lived not far from each other. He smiled shyly as he spoke, almost embarrassed, and I wondered how he knew where I lived. The bell rang and there was no further talk, but at the end of the day there he was, waiting for me at the school door. Again he smiled shyly and we started walking without saying anything. He was about my age, not very tall, with dark eyes and hair. Was he Spanish? I didn't think so, for he spoke German without an accent. He told me, with some embarrassment that Señor Gutierrez had asked him to help me get settled at the school. He had found out where I lived from his father, who worked for the refugee committee in charge of our group. I remember that I felt funny that a boy had been charged with my care; I did not think I needed anyone to take care of me. But I was flattered too, and strangely excited.

Every day from that first day on we walked to and from school together. Gradually he told me about the teachers and our classmates. He had few questions for me, and I did not volunteer much information about myself, since he seemed to know in general about my situation. I soon noticed that, after some initial shyness, he started to like talking to me, that he seemed to like being with me. I liked him too, and so gradually our relationship turned into a teen romance, my first and his as well. When our classmates noticed that we tried to sit near each other in class, talked with each other during recess, and walked together back and forth to school every day, they teased us mercilessly. Especially when they saw that Gert sometimes carried my books! But we didn't care. We started to take walks in the parks on weekends, we went on hikes in the hills above the city, and there one evening, as we sat on a rock and looked down at the lights of the city below us, we exchanged the first crooked little kiss. From then on we were inseparable and spent all our free time together.

Even though he had spoken about his family, I had never met them. Finally, he invited me to have dinner with them.

"Will you come? I would really like you to come," he emphasized. "My mom is a really good cook." I was thrilled. A real family dinner! In a real dining room, in an apartment! Especially with Gert!

To this day I remember the sweet noodle dish with raisins his mother served; the big slice of pot roast she put on my plate with gravy and mashed potatoes; things I had not eaten for a very long time. The next day Gert confided in me that his mother did not like the idea at first, but that he persuaded her and that she finally relented. I think she was probably relieved when she saw that I had good manners and seemed generally acceptable, in spite of being a poor refugee.

Often we would sit in his room to do our homework together. We had to keep the door wide open, to pacify his mother who was firm in her belief that a young girl should not be in her son's room.

We liked to go up to the roof of his house where we could look down on the city below us. There we played duets together, he on violin and I on my recorder, and even though neither one of us was terribly proficient on our instruments, I thought we sounded wonderful. He taught me the words and tunes of Spanish popular songs, which with many giggles, we belted out together. We talked about our beliefs, about our families, and always about music. He shared his lunch with me at school and I helped him with his math homework. We became inseparable.

Was I falling in love? It felt so good to be together and thrilling feelings rose up in me, unfamiliar and new. He told me he loved me and that it was the first time he had ever felt that way with any girl, and that it was a wonderful feeling and also a bit confusing. I nodded my head, yes, yes, wonderful and confusing.

I became part of his group of friends, boys from school and from the conservatory where he took violin lessons. Now and then we all went to the movies together where we sat in the last row, and where during the romantic scenes Gert and I secretly held hands, and where during horror movies we hollered and whistled and yahooed. It was all so amazing!

I thought that perhaps Gert, being from a German-Jewish family, whose parents had come to Spain in the twenties, considered himself as not quite belonging either. He was not Spanish, not Catalan, nor German. There was something about him that was different, something hidden, a promise of an unfulfilled yearning which attracted me. His friends were usually the oddballs, the kids that were different, often kids from Catalan families who were not in sympathy with the Franco government and who spoke their own forbidden language secretly at home.

I was going to school; I was in love. I had a life. Events at the pension, the tensions, the boredom and the worries no longer mattered to me .

Mother, through the efforts of Señor Gutierrez, had in the meantime started a job as a nanny, a *Fräulein* as they called her, for three little spoiled children, whose wealthy parents wanted them to learn German. They paid her almost nothing, but she received a good lunch and sometimes brought back with her all sorts of luscious things for me to eat. She would come back in the evening and tell me stories about the children and the other servants and about the *Señora,* who was beautiful and bored and sad. She was always nice to Mother and seemed glad that she did not have to deal with her three unruly little children. They took advantage of Mother's very limited Spanish to engage in all sorts of capers which my mother was certain, were not allowed by their parents. They told their mother that *Fräulein* had given them permission. This led to some difficulties for her, but the cook and the maid took time to explain to the mistress that it was only a misunderstanding due to language. Mother learned how to say no to the children and gradually her Spanish and her relations with the *Señora* improved.

Thus, both of us managed to lead a less limited and restricted life. Even though I often felt guilty for having achieved such a special status and wished that some of the other children could also go to school, most days I felt on top of the world and our precarious, uncertain situation became less important to me.

Sometimes my friend Ilse and a young Spanish man whom she had met joined Gert and me on our hikes in the nearby mountains, and sometimes we would take the bus to the beach just outside the city limits.

On our return from these outings Ilse and I would talk about having a boyfriend, whether or not we were really in love and how it felt to be kissed, all the usual kinds of teenage-girl topics. I knew with great certainty that Gert and I were meant for each other. We agreed that once I was settled in the United States, he would join me, and later, after we finished High school, we would go to college together and get married. I felt bad that Ilse's "young man" could not also follow her to America.

"He has to take care of his mother and his younger sisters. I think they don't have much money and his mother isn't very strong. Otherwise we too would get married once I get to America, she explained a little plaintively.

Paolo was a tall, quiet boy with blond hair and the beginnings of a small mustache. I noticed that there was something different between them from what Gert and I felt for each other in our chaste romantic puppy love. When she confided in me that she felt that somehow kissing wasn't quite enough for them, and that she really didn't know whether or not it was all right for them to "go all the way," I must have looked at her blankly, for she asked me, "Don't you understand? Didn't your mom ever talk to you about all that?"

I was still incredibly innocent; other than that vague romantic admiration of the two attractive young teachers at the boarding school I had felt when I was thirteen, boys and young men were an unknown quantity for me. Ilse decided to instruct me in the facts of life. I listened with great interest and awe to the details of man–woman sexual relationships.

"Of course only when you are in love and plan to get married soon," she had added, trying to guide me, or perhaps herself too. Since she assured me that she did not want to stay in Spain, and Paolo couldn't leave, I could see her problem. Gert and I were both feeling the first tentative longings to reach out to a member of the opposite sex, and meaningful looks, gentle kisses and a lot of holding hands seemed to be quite sufficient, so that this new knowledge didn't seem to apply to that romantic feeling we had for each other. Even though Gert and I talked about everything, and assured each other that we were both very mature and no longer children, we never spoke about what was actually going on in the world, or what had brought me and my mother to Barcelona.

Paolo asked us whether we would like to meet some of his friends. I was delighted—another new experience. Ilse told me later that he had decided that we could be trusted not to talk about what we might see and hear.

He took us to a house on a narrow street in a different part of the city, and knocked on a low door. Someone opened a little peephole and then let us in. We entered a large dimly lit basement room full of young people sitting at long wooden tables or standing about, who were all talking Catalan, laughing, drinking a bubbly cider and having a good time. Someone started to play guitar, and everyone began to sing Catalan songs. They all knew many verses by heart, and the singing became more and more lively. I only understood a few of the words, but that didn't matter. Paolo translated some of it for us, and the spirit in the room was so open and joyous and friendly, that we felt really welcome and had a wonderful time.

After a while the tables and chairs were pushed aside and the dancing began. Everyone joined in to dance the regional Catalan folk dances and we were invited to join as best we could. There was a special camaraderie among these young people, a special closeness, that I understood came from their common goals, and the risks they were taking together.

Later that night, on our way home, Paolo explained. "It's against the law to sing Catalan songs and dance Catalan dances, even to speak Catalan. The government says that's radicalism and communism and Catalan separatism. But we don't agree. We want to keep our traditions alive, because one of these days Spain will get rid of Franco and his crew and we'll be free again. That's why we have our secret clubs." It made me feel really proud that he trusted us. Maybe Ilse had told him about Hitler's Germany?

She told me the next day that Paolo's father, who had been on the wrong side in the Civil War, was still in jail, and that his mother and sister went every day to bring him his meals. I now avoided passing the street where I had seen the long lines of women waiting in front of the prison. Perhaps I didn't want to let the ugly world enter my present happy state.

Gradually, as I walked to school, sat in a classroom with other kids my age, as I went about with Gert, took part in conversations that had nothing to do with being a refugee with no home of my own, it felt that I belonged at least in part to a different world than the refugee world; a more normal, more stable world, a world in which even oppressed people had hope.

CHAPTER SEVENTEEN

I N THE LATE SUMMER of 1942 the free zone of France was invaded by the Germans. Many people, Jews as well as others who feared for their lives, fled into Spain. They came on foot across the rugged Pyrenees. We saw them arrive, dirty, hungry and worn out from their long trek across impossible terrain. We listened to the stories they had to tell about what was happening across the border in France, how now the French Jews were rounded up as well and sent away. We were happy for the newcomers who managed to escape, but perhaps because of the influx of so many new escapees, the Spanish government changed its policy. It decided to send all illegal refugees back to the countries from which they had come; at least that was the way the story came down to us. We refugees knew very well what that meant. We waited in helpless fear and trepidation for the day the call would come to board the train back to Germany.

The next week passed without anything happening. This only increased our anxiety. Our little group of frightened refugees was at dinner, when a man from another refugee group arrived to tell us that we could stay after all. The Spanish government had changed its mind again, he said.

"I can't tell you anything more," he said, moving towards the door as if to leave. He was very nervous.

"Wait," someone shouted. But he was gone. What did this mean? Could we believe him?

"We must believe him, we have no choice."

"Let's hope it's not some sort of a trick."

"Just another rumor."

Everyone had an opinion, speculations flew. Was it true? Were we being lied to? We didn't know what to think. Agitation, hope, resignation, skepticism were all there in that dining room. I fled into our room while the adults continued their anxious speculations.

Once again, as I found out recently, the Allies had been able to put economic pressure on the Spanish government, this time to dissuade them from going through with a policy that meant certain death for hundreds of people. Again we were saved in the nick of time!

We now had to check in at the police station every day instead of only once a week as before. No reasons were given. What were they planning to do with us? Again different opinions, worried arguments, barely suppressed fears. A few days later there was an empty place at dinner. Herr Schreiber had been kept back at the station house. Arrested. What had been his crime? No one could imagine what he might have done. The next day all the other single men were arrested, and after a few days it was the single women's turn. No one knew who would be next; no one knew what had happened to those who were missing. Only whole families were now left in our pension. Rumors flew. What was going on? Apparently the government was reneging on its promise not to send us back after all. Those of us who were still there started to prepare for the worst. Mother packed her few belongings and told me to do the same. She insisted that I continue to go to school. She would register for me at the police station. I argued that whatever happened we should be together, no way would I leave her. But in the end she won, and reluctantly I continued going to school.

Suddenly the arrests stopped. Single people had been arrested and only families were left. How long until it would be our turn?

Mother had slowly been feeling more positive about our situation, even a bit optimistic that all this would end some day and we would finally settle somewhere. She enjoyed being a nanny; she had become fond of the children in her care, and had come back every evening with stories and new Spanish expressions which she had learned from the other household employees. We were both eating better, and even had a little money to spend. Now, with the news of the arrests, not surprisingly, she fell apart. She was convinced that this was the end for us; that now there was no longer any escaping our fate. I tried to persuade her, and myself, that maybe the arrests had really stopped and that so far no one had been deported back to Germany, but to no avail, her fortitude and optimism had finally given way.

I was in class when the school secretary came into my room to tell me that Señor Gutierrez wanted to see me in his office. Slowly I got up and followed her. What was this about? What had I done? Suddenly a terrible foreboding: Something happened to Mutti! Had she been arrested after all? It even flashed through my mind as I ran up the stairs to Señor Gutierrez's office that she might have died of a heart attack, like my father had when he had given up all hope of ever seeing us again. I knocked at his office door, trembling, hardly able to breathe.

"Come in, Elisabeth," he opened the door for me. "Your mother is all right," as if he had guessed my thoughts. He paused and sat down at his desk again and gave me a sidelong glance as I stood there twisting the fingers of one hand into the other. "She is in a small private clinic where she can get good care."

"What is wrong with her?"

I was barely able to finish asking before Señor Gutierrez broke in. "She will be safe there until the danger has passed." He now looked at me fully. "Don't worry," he said, "Don't worry. My wife and I will take care of you in case something should happen to her."

His words were undoubtedly meant to be reassuring, but what did he mean? Was she safe or not? Why did he say that? I was so fixed on the thought that my mother would be safe that I was unable to think past that. I noticed however that his voice had become uncharacteristically soft. He looked at me with such concern and sympathy that I felt extremely uncomfortable. I stood there not knowing what to say or do.

There was a long silence during which the expression on his face gradually returned to its usual stern and distant state. The tone of his voice became matter of fact.

"You have to be very grown up now. You are alone in the pension. You must continue to go to school and do your homework."

But then his voice changed again to something softer. "If you need anything, come to me. In a few days, as soon as your mother feels better, you will be able to visit her."

I sat in the classroom for the rest of the day, dazed. On my way home I told Gert what had happened. "I know," he said and took hold of my hand and held it firmly all the way to his house.

"I'll take care of you, don't worry," he said when I confessed that I didn't think I could ever ask Señor Gutierrez for help.

"He's so awe inspiring, so stern. I'm a little afraid of him,"

I confessed. Gert tried to reassure me that he would always be there for me, and that besides, everything would turn out alright in the end. Yet I couldn't forget Señor Gutierrez's words. Was there something he knew which I didn't and that he wouldn't tell me? His words had made me no less worried about my mother; on the contrary, I was suddenly convinced that my mother would indeed die soon and that Señor and Señora Gutierrez would then adopt me. It even included, in my more disjointed moments of fantasizing, the scenario of my finishing school and then marrying Gert. Those thoughts became so firmly planted in my mind that for a few days I could think of nothing else.

The next week or so I was as if paralyzed. I couldn't think, I couldn't sleep, and when I was in school, I couldn't pay attention. Suddenly I was alone in our room in the pension. I sat alone at our table in the dining room during the few meals I ate there. When the others asked me about my mother, I told them that she had become ill and had to be hospitalized.

"Can she have visitors?"

"I'm sorry, she is still too sick. Maybe later," I would answer. I was not supposed to tell where she was. No one knew what was going to happen next, and if and when the arrests would continue. There did not seem to be any particular plan, everything was haphazard and uncertain. The refugees in the pension were scared, jittery and on edge, and many of them seemed close to losing the little composure they had left. There were many quarrels about unimportant matters, and I felt a lot of antagonism towards me, for again Mother and I seemed to have received special treatment the others did not share.

As it turned out, for some to us unknown reason the arrests really stopped. We assumed that those who had been detained were somewhere in prison, perhaps even in the one so close to our pension. We were not told.

Only much later, when my mother and I were by then safely in America, did we find out that they were not released until a year later. They had been sent to the notorious Spanish detention camp Miranda del Ebro where they suffered great hardships.

Two weeks passed before I was allowed to visit Mother in the clinic. There had been no news or phone calls from her during that time, except for a couple of postcards from her assuring me that she was beginning to feel better. My fantasy of her death had faded, but beyond that I couldn't imagine what was wrong with her,

She was lying in bed in a pleasant, sunny room. She looked pale and tried to smile. I could see that she could hardly raise her head from the pillow.

"I'm so happy to see you," she whispered. How are you managing? Did I eat enough? I assured her that everything was all right. When I asked her whether she was in pain, she said no. Did the doctor tell her what was wrong with her? He wasn't sure, she said. I put my hand on hers lying on the coverlet and bent down to kiss her cheek. The nurse was standing in the door, motioning to me that the visit was over. My mother had closed her eyes.

Now that I had seen her, my spirit settled a little. She wasn't going to die; eventually she would be all right.

I never found out who had made the arrangements for my mother's admittance to the clinic, or who paid for her stay there. She was told she could remain until she was completely recovered; by which I guessed they meant until the danger was past. Later, when she started to feel better, she complained that the doctor would not let her get out of bed for more than half an hour a day. Maybe if she were declared better, they would have to dismiss her. No one knew whether the danger had passed.

I visited her often after school. It was strange to see her in a hospital room when I couldn't even remember her ever being sick enough to take to her bed. Usually I would sit on a chair at the side of her bed, its white sheets reflecting the sunlight shining through the large window, while she seemed remote and hardly spoke. Or I would go to the window and look out into the garden below. Everything there seemed remote as well, beautiful and peaceful and somehow not connected with the danger which had brought my mother to this room.

Even though I missed her and felt lonely without her at the pension, school and the time I spent with Gert kept me from becoming too despondent. Somehow I could not believe that she was really sick; somehow I thought that after a while all this would pass.

As time passed, when I visited her she seemed quite cheerful. Maybe it was only for my benefit she put on this display, for the doctor still did not let her get out of bed, did not declare her well enough to leave. There did not seem to be anything particularly wrong with her any longer that I could detect. She did not complain about pain, only weakness. I was puzzled, but I could see that she was not her usual self. I told her a little about school and we talked about the inhabitants of the pension, but never about what had happened and why she was here. I did not want to tell her about Señor Gutierrez's offer. Better wait until later.

She saved some of her lunches or dinners for me, insisting that it had been too much for her. I knew better, but I also welcomed the cheese, the fruit, and the occasional piece of cake she gave me. The pension still served the same monotonous menu of rice and beans and little fish, only even smaller portions than before. I was sick and tired of it all.

Another time on my usual visit I saw a young woman from

our refugee group occupying a second bed in the room. She too seemed only slightly ill; perhaps she too was there to avoid being sent away. I also noticed how she and Mother gradually became friends; perhaps from a sense of their shared adversity. Now and then I heard them laugh together about something I didn't understand. I felt that perhaps my mother had told her things I didn't know; that they had shared secrets with each other of which I knew nothing. To my surprise I found that I was jealous.

Sometimes as I sat in our room alone after visiting her, I would wonder what had happened that morning while I was in school that sent her to the hospital. Had she suddenly become really ill or had it been something else? Had her courage finally given out so that she had collapsed? Had Señor Gutierrez decided to arrange a hiding place for her because he had taken a special interest in us? I didn't ask, for I saw that she was comfortable, that she was slowly getting better and that for the moment she seemed content to be taken care of. When I asked her many years later, she did not want to talk about it.

The days and weeks passed, and summer turned to fall and into the balmy Mediterranean winter. I don't remember how long Mother was in the hospital, but it seemed to me a very long time before she was released.

Even though she regained her balance, it took her a while before she was her old self again. I noticed that she was less energetic and often very tired. She seemed sadder than before, which made me think that she had probably given up hope that we would ever be able to get to America. The war was raging on all fronts, and even though Spain was not directly involved, we couldn't imagine how the fate of a few German-Jewish refugees stranded there was of any importance.

In her absence I had changed as well. I had been on my own

and had managed without her, with the result that I became less concerned with making a point of being different from her as well as less sensitive to her criticisms. I had not fallen apart during the time she was in the hospital. I had learned a good deal of Spanish in the meantime and I felt comfortable speaking it. I was relieved and happy that my mother was back, and with the resiliency of the young, I didn't think much about the future. I had become much easier to live with, less defensive, less bristly towards her.

When she decided that we should go to the little Protestant church the Swiss community maintained where Señor Gutierrez was the minister, I at first demurred. I did not want to go, for I was suspicious of churches. I had had a taste of it in Germany, when after having been baptized at the age of twelve, I had to go to Lutheran catechism class and attend services in order to be confirmed. That had been a maneuver which Mother had thought might establish my non-Jewishness, just in case. She herself had no qualms about going to church on Sunday morning and finally persuaded me to go with her. She said that It would give us a place to spend Sunday mornings and a feeling of belonging. Besides we owed it to Señor Gutierrez. Once a week therefore we took the very long walk to the church and back after the service.

To my great surprise I began to enjoy those Sundays in church. I would see some of the families of my schoolmates there, and even though at the beginning some of the adults looked at us askance, not quite knowing how this mother and daughter pair fit into their community, the children who knew me were friendly. I loved the singing of hymns; I listened closely to Pastor Gutierrez's sermons, which were always scholarly and thought provoking.

Once after we had been coming for a few weeks, he made

indirect reference to the life of people who had to leave their native country, obviously with us in mind. I remember that at first I was disappointed that he had been so circumspect and didn't tell it as it really was, but later I understood that he had to be extremely careful in what he said. I don't remember who had told me this, but the way the Franco government dealt with Protestants who in their opinion were too outspoken, was to banish them to a provincial town, where they would be totally ostracized to the point where no one would even sell them food. I sensed that maybe he too was someone who didn't belong, who made his life among strangers, preaching to this small community of Swiss business people.

On Christmas Eve the church was aglow with candlelight, redolent with the smell of pine boughs that decorated the walls. Baroque angels perched on the Christmas tree in the corner near the altar. When the congregation sang the Christmas songs I knew, I could not hold back my tears. I remember that I felt embarrassed to be overcome with emotion at the sound of the familiar melodies. I turned my head away from my mother so that she would not see me. I had not cried in a very long time and I was ashamed of my tears. At the same time I felt a curious sense of relief. The music had freed me to feel the sadness, the loss and the loneliness which for too long I had not allowed myself to express. I felt exposed and vulnerable. I worried that later my mother would ask me to explain my feelings and would want to comfort me. I decided not ever to cry again where my mother could see me and to always act tough as if nothing could touch me.

We walked back through the dark streets to the pension, side by side in silence. I don't know what Mother was feeling, but to me the fact that we had no home to return to, that we were not going to celebrate with presents and laughter and feasting, was overwhelming. We could not even talk about where we had been; the others refugees would have considered it unforgivable for Jews to have attended a Christmas service.

In early spring a German opera company came to Barcelona. Gert and I waited in a long line in front of the opera house to get standing room tickets for *Tristan und Isolde*. As dusk settled in around us and soft rain started to fall, we huddled close together under his jacket to keep dry and warm. It was a long wait, several hours, but we didn't mind. We were both excited in anticipation of the performance we were about to see, and as we stood there close together, surrounded by other young people, Gert put his arm around my shoulder, and I forgot about everything else and only wished that this happiness would never end. The streetlights had been turned on, and as our line snaked slowly towards the box office, we watched as the ticket-holding audience arrived, dressed in all their finery. We made comments to each other about some of the spectacular outfits we saw, and speculated about who these people might be. We stood behind the seats of the fifth tier, 'the heavens.' I hardly felt that my feet were getting tired during the long hours the opera took to unreel. During the intermissions we sat on the floor and hardly talked. Wagner's music of love and passion seemed to speak to our own feelings. I forgot that the singers, in true Wagnerian fashion, had large adult bodies and that they hardly moved as they sang those endless phrases. When the final curtain dropped it seemed to me that the performance had been for Gert and me alone; that the music of love and loss was ours. I would have preferred it if the lovers had been able to live happily ever after; even so, the sad ending of the story added a sense of sweet melancholy to the evening. As we walked back to the pension through the dark deserted streets of the city with our arms around each other, we were silent. Perhaps we were too tired to talk; perhaps it was that we didn't want the magic of that night to end.

In the spring of 1943 the unexpected happened. We were told that it might become possible to leave Spain. Rumors had been floating around in our community for a while that a solution to our plight was being explored. I did not know who was doing the exploring, and I suspect that neither did many of the others. Some thought that perhaps the "Joint," as we called the Joint Distribution Committee which had been supporting us, had found a way. We did not know how it was decided who could leave and who would have to wait. We refugees now became very secretive about our comings and goings and very suspicious of others. The atmosphere among us became tense and unfriendly. Some suspected that others had special status with the committee and would be chosen first. There were whispers and secret glances when those who had received good news entered the dining room. People who had been friends for a year stopped talking to each other. Mother and I hated all that and tried to keep out of it. Why, I thought, when there was finally hope, did people become so mean?

We waited impatiently to be told that it would be our turn. I don't remember the details, how we heard, or from whom, nor how I felt the moment we knew. Perhaps I didn't really believe it. Perhaps I really feared it. After all, again I would be leaving the known for the unknown. I had gotten used to my life in Spain; I was going to school, had a boyfriend, and had learned to speak Spanish. Even sharing one room with my mother, was something I had done almost my whole life anyway.

What did I do during that month between April 14, 1943, and May 14 when we crossed into Portugal? I don't remember much, except that I could only think of one thing: How could I possibly part from Gert; how could I live without seeing him every day, without being able to share with him all my thoughts and feelings, without our closeness, our holding hands and our sweet kisses. We promised that we would write often—once a day, once a week? He promised that when he finished high school and the war ended, he would persuade his parents to let him continue his studies in America and we would be together again. I hung tightly onto that promise. It helped a little, for I couldn't imagine life without him.

During the last week before we were to leave, he told me that he could no longer spend a lot of time with me; that his father had asked him to help in the office; that soccer practice was taking more time. I couldn't understand it. Didn't we love each other? Didn't he want to spend the last week together with me? Finally I asked him. Could I understand, he replied, that this was the best way for him to deal with the inevitable?

CHAPTER EIGHTEEN

I HAVE IN MY POSSESSION a large piece of paper, an affidavit of sorts, in lieu of a passport, signed by the American vice consul in Barcelona. Pasted on it are pictures of my mother and me; there are many official stamps and signatures in Spanish, English and Portuguese. Our immigration quota numbers, #817 and #818, are dated April 14, 1943. One stamp tells me that we crossed into Portugal on May 14, and another one that we embarked on the Portuguese merchant ship, the Serpa Pinto on June 8, 1943.

Finally everything was ready. We said goodbye to the members of our group who were still left behind, and tried to assure them that their turn would come soon as well. Gert took us to the station for the train to Madrid. I remember how desolate I felt, how I could not control my tears as we said good bye. As his figure on the platform grew smaller and smaller until he disappeared from my sight, it seemed to me that once again events unrolled automatically without my consent and that once again, as when my father had waved to us from the station platform so long ago, I felt that something important was being torn out of my life.

Mother and I spent a day and a half in Madrid, impatiently waiting for the train ride to Lisbon. She wanted to pay a brief visit to the Prado, and even though I was too impatient to go and was in no mood to look at pictures, I trotted bravely through the halls, impressed by the sheer size of the museum and the quantities of paintings that hung there. I remember especially the large hall covered with enormous paintings of battle scenes by Velasquez and by the elongated figures in El Greco's paintings which Mother pointed out to me.

As we crossed the border into Portugal I finally realized that now we were really on our way to the Promised Land, that we would be leaving Europe for good. There were so many new impressions, so much to think about, that I grew more and more excited at the prospect of the new life ahead. I held on to the promise Gert and I had made to each other that in a few years we would be united, and though I wrote to him every day, my letters became shorter as time went on.

In Lisbon we were put up in a pension on one of the major boulevards of the city. Our room was large and sunny, with big windows that looked out on the tree-lined street. What a change from the tiny dark room we had shared for so long! It felt like heaven to us. And miracle upon miracle, there were two beds! The shiny parquet flooring seemed the acme of luxury; but even more amazing was the bathroom down the hall, where we could soak in an oversized tub filled with hot water.

Even though we were not told how long we would have to wait for a passage on a ship, it felt good to be out of Spain. Mother, especially, was much more relaxed, and again urged me on to see as much of the city as possible. I remember Lisbon as a city of many hills, with pastel painted houses that seemed to be marching up those hills, with wide tree-lined boulevards and many Baroque churches.

When on our first day in Lisbon we returned to our beautiful room from a short evening walk and turned on the light, a swarm of brown inch long creatures scooted away into the crevices between the walls and the floor: cockroaches! I remember them as being larger and more numerous than any I have encountered since, and even though we were at first aghast, we got used to them and learned to give them enough time to vanish after we turned on the light before entering the room. We made sure however to shake out our shoes in the morning before putting them on.

I don't know why that particular trivial image has remained so vividly in my memory when perhaps other more significant ones have disappeared. Maybe those dark creatures that scooted away in the light were a sign of the dark things we were now about to leave behind.

Every lunch and every dinner at the pension was an absolute feast for us. So much to eat! We stuffed ourselves at those meals; we could not help it, for we had been hungry too long. The most astonishing part was that in the center of our table stood a basket that overflowed with white bread and rolls, the likes of which we had not eaten for many years. All that for us? After we had finished our first dinner in the dining room and there was still a lot of bread left in the basket, Mother and I gave each other a kind of conspiratorial look, laughed, and without saying anything, secreted the remaining bread into handbag and pockets, making sure no one saw us. "For later," Mother said as we left the dining room, our pockets bulging.

We didn't eat the bread that evening and hid it in a dresser drawer. The next day at lunch, the breadbasket was full again, and again we took bread up to our room, and again at dinner, and at the next lunch and dinner. We couldn't believe that there would indeed be more and that this abundance wouldn't have to stop soon, and that we would really not be hungry again.

The bread accumulated uneaten in the drawer, and we finally understood that there would be more at every meal. There was no way we could throw the bread away. What to do about it? Mother suggested that we feed it to the carriage horses in the park. The horses enjoyed the feast, the carriage drivers didn't mind, and we were able to laugh in retrospect at our strange behavior.

I remember how pleasant it was to be visiting a family in their attractive house on top of a hill. As we sat on their balcony and looked down at the clay-tiled rooftops of the city below us, rosy in the light of the setting sun, I suddenly felt very sad and found to my surprise that tears were gathering in the corners of my eyes.

I remember the young man, who stood every evening for many hours in front of an apartment house across the street from our pension. He looked up at a second floor window, where a girl was leaning out as far as she dared, while he craned his neck up to talk to her. Even though I could not understand what they were saying to each other, I imagined their conversation, and wondered whether they would ever be allowed to be together, the way Gert and I had been. One evening he brought some of his friends and they serenaded his girl with romantic songs accompanied by guitar and mandolin. It made me feel romantic too, tinged with an undefined wistful longing.

WE REMAINED in Lisbon for almost one month. On June 8, 1943 we finally boarded the *Serpa Pinto,* a Portuguese freighter bound for America. Walking up the gangplank I didn't notice that the ship was old and not too clean and quite small. Even though I tried not to show it, I was very excited at the prospect of the coming voyage. My imagination did not extend to our approaching arrival in America; that was too far in the future, too vague and indistinct a concept, but an ocean voyage, that was something else!

The officers who stood on deck were dressed in white with shiny brass buttons, and as the ship's whistle gave a long blast and we started to move very slowly away from the pier, all seemed glorious.

Our small stuffy cabin was below decks, and since we shared it with several other women refugees like us, it became extremely cramped and hot and smelly. Mother arranged our two suitcases in the best way possible, but I couldn't wait to get back on deck to watch the ship pull out of the harbor. As I stood at the railing, I watched the hills of Lisbon, golden in the late afternoon sun, recede gradually into the distance.

It flashed through my mind then, that this was the last view I would have of Europe. I was not sorry to leave; I did not yet want to look back at the past. After a while Mother found me, and we stood together looking out to sea. Neither one of us spoke. Once I looked furtively at her and I saw tears in her eyes. Whether from sadness or relief, I didn't know.

We knew none of the thirty refugees on the ship, none of them my age. Mother soon found people to talk to, but I remained quite alone. I discovered that I could sneak up to the afterdeck, which was off limits to us. There I spent my days lying in the shade of a lifeboat or propped up against a large stanchion.

I wrote long letters to Gert, in which I told him my impressions of our voyage and in which I vowed that I loved him and how desperately I missed him already. I read the book of Lorca poems, which he had given me as a farewell gift, from cover to cover, over and over. He had inscribed it in purple ink with: "These ordinary prosaic words cannot express the deep feelings

I hold for you in my heart. Gert. He didn't say 'love' or 'dearest,' words I would have loved to have seen on the flyleaf, but I knew how shy he was. So I imbued those 'deep feelings' with the loving words I could think of as I looked at the photographs I had of him.

I imagined us together on the last day on which we hiked to our favorite place above the city. We had spoken little then, deep in our own thoughts as we climbed hand in hand over the rocks and dry grasses to that special stone where ages ago we had kissed for the first time. As I sat on the gently rolling ship, the warmth of the sun on my back, looking at the ever changing waves all around me, yet whose rhythm seemed always the same in that vast expanse of ocean, as I lifted my eyes to a clear blue sky, whose scattered cotton clouds drifted lazily along, the beauty of it all only enhanced my longing.

Hour after hour I leaned against the rail and watched the waves. As the ship turned southward into warmer waters, I saw flying fish jump out of the water and sometimes land on deck At night I snuck up to an upper deck where I found a comfortable spot to lie, my back against a bulkhead. The soft warm air, the gentle movement of the ship and the swish of the waves below added to my mood of loneliness and longing. I spent hours looking at the stars and watched the moon gradually move across the sky. My mother had persuaded me to bring a blanket on deck, after I insisted that I couldn't sleep below in that stuffy cabin, that it made me seasick. I think she understood. The young officers, after trying to talk with me a little, soon gave up, for I was not in the mood for talk. They left me pretty much alone, except that once in a while they tried to tell me that I really must go below to my cabin. Mother and I didn't talk much either, not even about our prospects when we would land in the United States. I was too deeply immersed in my sweet sadness to be able to look ahead; I did not think about the new life that we were about to begin. I could only look back, contemplating yet another loss in my short life. My mother accepted my bizarre behavior and left me to myself. I was too immersed in my own melancholy mood to wonder what she might have been feeling.

Once however she insisted I stay with her. It became known that a German U-boat was near, and that they were suspicious of the cargo our ship was carrying. We had no idea what really went on since the Portuguese crew did not inform us. Someone spread the rumor that they were going to torpedo us, someone else that they were going to board and take us all off. In any case, the old fear of being found and sent back to Germany surfaced once more. Would it never end? Luckily, after a few very long hours of worrying, the danger passed.

The ship anchored briefly just offshore one of the Azores islands, where the Portuguese family who had traveled first class and who had been the only other passengers besides us, got off. Someone told me that they owned one of the islands and were very rich and influential. Perhaps they were the ones who had saved us from the German U-boat? As I looked down at the motor launch that ferried the family to land, I watched the young daughter who seemed to be about my age, and I tried to imagine how it must feel to come to an island which my family owned, to be rich and privileged instead of being a penniless escapee. It wasn't envy I felt exactly, but the kind of curiosity one might have about a character in a story with whom one identifies.

Next stop was Madeira, where our ship anchored in the harbor and where some of the inhabitants came out to us in small boats to sell their beautifully embroidered cloths and luscious ripe fruit. We bought a couple of pineapples, cheap and delicious. As we ate them, their sweet juice running down our fingers, Mother and I looked at each other, smiled happily and exclaimed over and over, "Delicious, yum,yum!" I had never eaten pineapple before, and this new delicacy seemed to me like a sweet omen of the new things that lay ahead. I started to look forward to our arrival in America; it seemed now truly to be the beginning of a new life.

PART FIVE

CHAPTER NINETEEN

O N THURSDAY June 21, 1943 the *Serpa Pinto* dropped anchor in the Delaware River near Philadelphia, and remained there for three days. These were the longest three days I would ever experience; they seemed almost impossible to bear. I looked longingly at the shore, at our promised land. Weren't we ever going to get there? The crew was off duty, and since it was unbearably hot and humid, those gorgeous dark-haired young officers, who had throughout the voyage never been seen by us other than dressed in immaculate white, turned into unshaven young fellows in dirty tee-shirts and shorts who lounged around on the decks, smoking and drinking beer. The cooks did the minimum of cooking, and we had to help ourselves to the little they prepared. Again that unexplained waiting, again that rising anxiety, even though we were an ocean away from Europe. We learned later that because of the war no merchant ships were allowed into New York Harbor, and since the Philadelphia docks had been crowded with war ships, our merchant ship had to wait.

Finally, on June 24 the ship docked. Mother made sure that we wore our most decent-looking clothes, my hair combed, and my shoes polished.

"We must make a good first impression," she said.

We went through the necessary formalities, got our suitcases and waited on the lower deck to be allowed down the gangplank. It was a very hot morning and as our co-passengers were pushing and jostling one another, each trying to be first off the ship and into the arms of their relatives who were waiting impatiently on the pier, who were calling them excitedly and waving their flower-laden arms into the air, Mother and I hung back and leaned over the railing to try to spot Cousin Joel. She was sure she would recognize him from the photos he had sent a number of years ago; she was sure he would be there to greet us. He was however nowhere to be seen. The crowd on the pier was dispersing and finally we were the last ones still on the ship. Slowly we walked down the gangplank.

"He must have been delayed," Mother said trying not to sound disappointed, "after all, he has to come all the way from New York."

As we waited a man, wearing a big button with "HIAS" on his shirt, came towards us, and asked whether we were the Heyn family. Cousin Joel had left a message. He was sorry, but business affairs prevented him from coming; he would meet us at Pennsylvania Station in New York. Mother's face fell with disappointment. We both felt abandoned in this strange new place. It seemed as if all the travails of the last few years had come to nothing. We had seen others being greeted with hugs and kisses, flowers and tears of joy by their relatives and friends, but there was no one here for us, except this stranger. It was a bitter moment.

Mr. HIAS put us on the train to New York and during that two hour ride we had time to compose ourselves. I remember little of that ride, but when we arrived, Cousin Joel was there to greet us.

253

"Welcome to America," he said, gave us both a little hug, smiled and handed Mother a bunch of flowers. She seemed excited and happy to see him, but I hung back, not knowing what to think.

"Let's see whether we can get a porter," he said. "What with the war on it's so hard to get help."

I reached for the handles of our suitcases. "I can do it," I said.

"OK, we each take one. I'm sure Mother must be tired." He led us through the cavernous halls of the station; he and Mother walked ahead talking, while I hung back as I shifted the heavy suitcase from one hand to the other. Wherever we were going, I wanted to get there as quickly as possible. This was New York, we had finally arrived.

Joel hailed a taxi, and during the ride he told Mother in halting German a little about his wife and children and his business, and how the war made everything so difficult. I looked out of the window at the buildings that were so much taller than any I had ever seen before, even taller than I had imagined them. As I watched the long lines of cars and buses inching along the streets, honking, revving up, and as I watched the crowds of people all hurrying somewhere, I started to feel excited. Even the hot humid air that entered the open taxi window was different. A mixture of hot asphalt, automobile exhaust and fried foods made me feel nauseous, so that I was glad when our taxi stopped.

We arrived in front of a large downtown building. Did Joel tell us that he was taking us to the Hebrew Iimmigrant Aid Society building on Lafayette Street? I must not have listened when he told Mother, for I was surprised to have arrived so quickly at a building that did not look the slightest like a private home or even an office building.

Here we were now in front of the building that is today

The Public Theatre in Lower Manhattan. It is an imposing, dark brown building, which sits among its neighbors, dingy manufacturing and tenement buildings, like an aging aristocrat among the plebeians. When the Astor Family had it built at the end of the nineteenth century it served as their private library for their collection of valuable books. Instead of a collection of books, it now housed and fed some of New York's most recent and poorest immigrants. I don't know when it had been converted, but when we arrived it was the headquarters of the HIAS our first home in America.

Joel carried Mother's suitcase to the front door, set it down on the hot pavement, reached into his wallet and gave her two ten dollar bills.

"To tide you over," he said with a smile. "I'm sorry but I have to go back to the office now." I noticed the taxi waiting.

"You can stay here for a while to settle in and make plans. On Friday afternoon I'll pick you up to spend the weekend at our house on Long Island to meet the family and relax." A quick hug. He jumped into the back of the idling cab which roared off into the traffic.

With our two suitcases and a bunch of flowers Mother and I stood in silence as if rooted to the pavement. Suddenly I felt exhausted. My clothes were sticking uncomfortably to my hot sweaty skin, and I wished that I could take a cool bath, that I could push away my feeling of disappointment. It had all been so matter of fact, our arrival, so terribly ordinary! The exhilaration I had felt in the taxi was gone, I was close to tears. I don't know what I had expected; perhaps I had wished for something more memorable, some thing festive, some thing in celebration. The minutes passed. Cars and trucks whirred by. Neither one of us spoke. Finally I grabbed the handle of my suitcase and pushed it towards the front steps of the building.

"Let's go in," I said.

❧

THAT WAS OUR ENTRANCE to the New World and the beginning of our new life.

It must have been devastating for Mother to be dropped off so hastily in such an impersonal place. I could tell how sad she was; how she felt let down, even angry. Hadn't her own mother, many years ago, lovingly taken care of the little boy, cousin Joel, whom his parents had put in her care, so that they could more easily establish themselves in America?

We dragged our suitcases into the building and along the marble floor to a desk near the entrance. There was no one around except for the bored-looking young woman at the desk who addressed us in Yiddish, assuming that it was our common language. Mother looked offended; in those days she was of the opinion that only Jews from Eastern Europe spoke Yiddish.

"You can speak English to us," I interrupted. The woman seemed relieved and rattled off questions and directions in what I realized must be an American accent. I understood enough of it to be able to answer her questions.

What kind of a place was this? Our steps echoed in the empty building as we were led up a wide flight of marble stairs to the second floor. There, along one side of the huge space, divided off by flimsy temporary walls was a row of small rooms. One of these cubicles was to be our home for the next few weeks. It was tiny, and appeared even smaller because of the very high ceilings of the original room. It had no window; light came from a bare bulb and from the hall. There were two cots, a scratched maple dresser topped by a small mirror, and a small open closet.

We unpacked some of our things in silence. I don't know what we had expected, but I can feel even today how acutely depressing the place felt, how cold and inhospitable. Even our room in Lisbon had been nicer. Was this what we had waited for so long?

Mother tried to explain. "Joel means well; after all he and his brother Frank laid out a lot of money to get us out of Europe."

"Hm, hm," I said not convinced.

"I think he's just a typical American businessman, who doesn't have the slightest idea of what we've been through," she added. I realized reluctantly that our arrival was not such a momentous occurrence as to disturb his routine.

"Anyway, we should be forever grateful to him, don't forget that."

Later Mother made more excuses for him. After all, he had never met me, and he hadn't seen her since they were both small children; how could we expect a warmer reception?

"I know he means well," she said again. "Without his help we wouldn't be here."

"He could have invited us to his house for the first night at least," I ventured.

Mother kept silent.

I was so disappointed that I almost cried; and when Mother saw that, she too became teary. But then she pulled herself together

"Let's see whether we can get something for these," pointing to the flowers.

It was very hot, the room felt close and stuffy. I was glad to go in search of a container. I noticed the institutional smell of disinfectant in the halls, the impersonal, aseptic feel to the place; the fact that we saw no one else who seemed to live there. This was our promised land? The girl at the desk had told us to be sure to lock the door to our room, because "you never know . . ."

We walked down the wide marble stairs to the basement cafeteria for our first meal in America. As our steps reverberated in that very empty place, that at one time must have been elegant and sumptuous, I felt like a little child who had been deluded by a promise of a treat that never materialized.

Mother and I looked at the handful of people who sat at two of the many green Formica tables in the dining hall. The old men and women were hunched over their plates gobbling down their dinner from plastic plates. We had dressed in our best clothes, not wanting to look poor, while they, to judge by what they wore, were obviously poor. Many wore house slippers I noticed. They spoke Yiddish with each other, and now and then they looked at the two of us as if they wondered what in the world we were doing there. I don't remember that we ever spoke with any them. Were they refugees too and if so, where had they come from? Or were they just poor immigrants who had come to better themselves and never made it here in America?

We did not think of ourselves as immigrants. We were refugees, a clear distinction in our minds. What did we mean? It was an illusion, of course, for we were as poor as the immigrants who had come before and would come after us; like them, we brought nothing, we had nothing, perhaps even less than many. We meant, I think, that we had not come of our own free will, that we would not have chosen to leave our country if our lives had not been threatened, that it was not only out of economic necessity that we were here. At least I felt that the grown-ups thought so. Somehow that salvaged their egos; somehow it meant that we did not have to end up like the people in the cafeteria. Somehow it made us feel a little more optimistic, more determined, maybe even a little superior, in spite of our cool reception.

Like other immigrants we brought with us our own notions and prejudices. Like others, we changed and would later look back at those ideas we had held with wonder and shame.

Since we only had twenty dollars, for the next few days we took all our meals in that cafeteria. Mother told me one evening that during the taxi ride, Joel had mentioned, almost as if in passing, that in America people had to make it on their own. He had done so, and so had everybody else, and so would we. It was clearly a lesson we were not yet ready for. To me it seemed a callous thing to say when we had just arrived. But perhaps that was the American way, Mother said. And again, this time with a little disdain in her voice: "A typical American business man."

As promised, we spent the weekend in their house in Lawrence, a residential suburb on Long Island. As I picture the house with today's eyes, it was a pleasant upper-middle-class Long Island house, but then it seemed very elegant and grand. As Joel led us to the front door, I noticed ornamental bushes and trees and a small, very green lawn on which a black-face statue wearing a red uniform and cap stood holding a lantern. I remember the many rooms through which Joel guided us, and that he proudly explained how the different gadgets in those rooms worked: the dimmer light switches, the short wave radio, the electric toaster and built-in oven in the kitchen, the sliding doors which, when opened, revealed large lighted closets.

"Look at this," Joel would say, pointing at yet another miracle of American ingenuity, "isn't this great? You don't have that in Europe, right?"

That evening, as Mother and I prepared for bed, we wondered how Americans pictured the Europe we had come from. Perhaps they thought of it as primitive and backwards, the way we pictured places like New Guinea or deepest Africa. Our laughter about their ignorance was tinged with bitterness. Did they see us backward and ignorant as well?

Bea, Joel's wife, dressed in a brightly colored, thin summer outfit, which contrasted sharply with our worn, dark, too heavy clothes, was welcoming and friendly. She too seemed not the least bit interested in what had been happening to us; instead she told us about how much work she did raising money for her various charities. She invited Mother to come to the next fund raising event at the Waldorf Astoria Hotel, one of the most elegant hotels in New York, she pointed out. As her guest of course. How strange it all was!

The message was clear: here in America one looked forward, not back. I don't know what my mother felt; I, on the other hand, was ready to put away all memories of the past years, even perhaps the sweet memory of Gert.

Was that wrong of me? Was I that unfeeling? As I think back, as I look at that sixteen-year-old girl, it seems to me that it had to be that way; that the Atlantic Ocean had not only physically separated me from the first part of my life, but also succeeded in separating me from its memories. I think that's the way I had wanted it. Those memories disappeared deep inside me; so deep, that they continue to be very difficult to bring to light.

On Sunday our cousins took us to the beach. It was still broiling hot outside; "With weather like this, here everyone goes to the beach on weekends," Joel explained.

"Another thing one only does in America?" I thought, wondering again at their ignorance of other places.

We drove to the beach at Far Rockaway. I couldn't believe my eyes when I saw the crowds, packed body to body on the sand. Some sat under colorful striped beach umbrellas tilted against the sun; others lay motionless, face down, working on their tans. Candy wrappers and paper cups were everywhere, radios blared popular music and children were digging in the little areas of fine sand visible between the blankets, or running around chasing balls or each other. No room for sand castles here, the way I remembered them from our visits to the beach when I was little.

Bea insisted that I put on the bathing suit she had lent me and go in the water. In her own way she tried to make me feel comfortable, to treat me like one might an American teenager, who of course would want to do that. I didn't want to go, but found no way to say no. I trudged reluctantly to the women's bathhouse, while the others waited for me on the boardwalk.

There are a few scenes that stand out in my memory and that appear in my dreams; stark, indelible, frightening. The scene in that bathhouse is one of those. Not only that everything seemed strange and different from what I knew, but what I experienced with my senses, what I saw, smelled and heard became interlaced with what I saw in my imagination.

As I entered the women's changing room I was struck by how crowded it was. There was no privacy, there were no partitions. Women and girls of all ages—there must have been thirty or more—were changing their clothes, talking, laughing, and shouting. A toddler cried. Voices echoed against the cement walls. It smelled like chlorine and disinfectant, sweat and salt. Women were everywhere, naked or in various stages of undress. I looked around furtively, at breasts and buttocks and stomachs, at thighs and pubic hair. I was shocked. How could women be so unconcerned? Didn't they care how they looked? Didn't they have that sense of privacy and esthetics I had thought all women possessed? Certainly most of them were not beautiful, with hanging breasts and fat stomachs and buttocks. A few of the younger women, I noticed, were thin with good figures that passed what I had imagined American women must all look like. I looked furtively at some of their faces. No one seemed to be shy or care what others thought. No one seemed embarrassed. Everyone just went about their business of dressing and undressing and chatting with their friends. I had never seen anything like it.

Reluctantly I too changed into my suit, facing the nearest wall, all the while hoping no one would see me. I carried my rolled up clothes under my arm and started to leave. I wasn't quite sure which way to turn for the exit, and as I turned to my left, I stood in front of the shower room: A narrow entrance, dark gray cement walls, an overpowering chemical smell, naked women standing everywhere under jets of streaming water, their voices made raucous by the echoing walls.

I did not see that the women were stretching their bodies to enjoy the warm water running down their backs. I did not see that their bodies looked healthy; I did not hear that their voices were ordinary conversation and the chemical smell was chlorine. What I saw was the death camp, the shower room, the women, each one holding a small cake of soap. What I smelled was Zyklon B. What I heard were cries, and then a deep silence.

This event took place in the summer of 1943. I now wonder whether I could have known then about the gas, about Birkenau and Auschwitz, about the ovens. Where did that image come from? Was it there in the Rockaway bathhouse or later when knowledge and memory coalesced into one image which embedded itself so clearly and firmly in my mind that I had no hesitation to write about it as authentic? Perhaps that trickster we call *remembering* had played one of its tricks on me, erasing time and rational thought to superimpose on my experience in the bathhouse pictures of the camps seen or imagined at a later time.

That is the image I have carried with me. That's how it must have been.

I walked slowly out of the building and joined the family.

"I don't feel like going in the water," I told them. I put my clothes on over the borrowed bathing suit right there on the beach.

After we left the beach at Far Rockaway, our cousins drove us a short distance to their private beach club. I don't know what was in their minds; perhaps they wanted to show us different ways of living in the United States; perhaps they wanted to let us know that naturally they never had to go to such a crowded beach, to which anyone could go. Was this meant as a kind of object lesson in what could be achieved in America, if one only worked hard enough? Perhaps they thought of the scene at the public beach as an interesting and colorful slice of American life they wanted to show us. In any case, the contrast was striking.

We entered a fenced-in compound after being greeted by a guard. On the large, spotless white beach about a dozen people were sunning themselves in various positions. A fat-bellied middle-aged man, sporting a straw hat, was smoking a cigar and reading a newspaper: two thin female bodies in very small two-piece bathing suits were sunning themselves face down on beach towels. Two other women were sitting on beach chairs under an umbrella talking and drinking cokes. I was still in shock from my last experience, so that this scene, although quite ordinary, seemed strange and exotic as if from a different world. The women looked up when they saw us coming, and exchanged a few words with our cousins.

"I know everyone here," Joel said. "I was one of the founders of this club twenty years ago. It was easy then, but now it costs a lot to belong." He added some dollar amount, which I have forgotten. "They are all nice people here." This almost as a sort of apology. Three little boys were digging in the sand, building a castle and an elaborate network of canals and tunnels. The waves were rolling in steadily, one after the other, broke with a soft swish and receded. The same waves as those we saw on that other beach a little distance away. The same fine white sand. But here no one was in the water and it was very quiet.

"This is a Jewish club," Joel volunteered, "Almost everyone here belongs to the same temple. When you work very hard all week you need a place to relax on the weekend. It's nice here, isn't it?"

Mother asked how many people belonged to the club and did you have to be Jewish to belong?

"We are not welcome in other clubs, so we have to have our own," was the reply.

I could see my mother nod her head at the answer. Even though she didn't say anything in response, I knew what she was thinking. I knew she was so grateful to the cousins for having helped us that she did not want to feel, let alone say anything, which might be critical. In addition, I knew that she had warm family feelings towards Joel from the memory of the year they spent together as children in Germany and from the occasional letters they had exchanged.

I on the other hand had no such feelings. Did I feel gratitude toward the cousins? I don't know. Gratitude was probably not in my teen repertoire. However I felt a total sense of bewilderment. In America Jews were not allowed certain things? Why was that? Was that something ordinary and acceptable? As far as I knew, in Germany, in my family and among my mother's friends, it had not been important as to who was Jewish and who was not. Until the Nazis, of course. Nor had I known anyone who belonged to a temple. I wondered.

I didn't like that fat man on the beach and those women under the umbrella who were wearing too much make-up. I didn't like that these few people were sunning themselves in luxury on a quiet empty beach, while not very far away thousands of people were crowded together, also seeking some relaxation and fun after a week's work. If this was America it was certainly different from what I had imagined!

On that day, although I was not even aware of it, my social conscience was born.

～

WHAT MAKES an immigrant's story unique? The historical period in which it takes place certainly, but most of all it is the balance of memories of the past combined with expectations for the future that individuals carry in their hearts that shape the story. Being young, even though I had of course absorbed certain German attitudes and standards, I did not look back with nostalgia at the way the adults did. Since I wanted to become American as quickly as possible, but also was not sure of what to expect, my experiences of the first few days and weeks in New York proved to be seminal for my future outlook.

I was restless. I didn't want to spend more time than necessary at the HIAS; better to get to know the city by walking its streets. Mother was too tired, too worn out by the heat to walk around, she said. I suspected that it was more than that. She slept a great deal, while every day I put a map of the city into my pocket and took off early in the day to learn my way around.

I walked up the Bowery under the El as far as Forty-Second Street, and down Second Avenue. I walked into Chinatown and to the East River, west into Greenwich Village and down to the Financial District. I had no idea what I would find in each of those places, and so I was left with the impression as I walked on Third Avenue that the city was made up of Irish bars, with names like Shamrock and Blarney Stone, with drunks sprawled on the steps of dingy apartment houses; of "Rooms for Rent" signs and cheap hotels that reminded me of those in the poorest parts of Barcelona. The elevated train roared overhead, cars and buses spewed exhaust, and the heat was unbearable. Men in white shirts and dark suits were rushing around in the Financial District, and on Second Avenue one antique store tried to undo the next one in bizarre objects and bric-a-brac for sale. I loved it all and just kept walking and walking. Often I forgot to eat, even though Mother had given me a few dollars to buy something. I usually did without, since I didn't know what I could buy and how much it would cost.

The narrow streets of Chinatown were crowded with people rushing around every which way and almost everyone was Chinese, a strange and exotic sight for me. I had never before seen any Chinese, nor Japanese, nor Africans except in pictures. I didn't like the plucked ducks and other animals hanging upside down in front of the little shops, but I would have liked to find out what some of those things in barrels and sacks were, with their signs in Chinese characters. I was too shy to try to ask and probably would not have understood the answers. Instead I acted as if I too were doing my errands and had to hurry.

In a playground near the river, groups of older boys were playing ball, trying to throw it through a net suspended from a metal ring. I had never seen basketball before. It too was interesting. Sometimes I sat on a bench in a little park at the river to rest my feet and to watch the boats and barges passing by, but usually my rest didn't last too long, because sooner or later some man would sit down next to me, look me up and down, and start a conversation.

One Sunday I walked once more to the financial district. Where had all the people disappeared to? The empty streets felt eerie as if a great disaster had made the people flee. It scared me and I hurried out of that part of town as quickly as I could.

I took the subway, just to see how that was. The weather

was still incredibly hot and humid, and as the wooden escalator took me down, and down some more, until I finally reached the platform, it seemed that I had reached the true bowels of the earth. It can't be any hotter there, I thought. I had figured out from the map that I could transfer at the Times Square station and take a different train back. Arrived there I was totally at a loss as to where to turn. It was rush hour and the station was full of people hurrying everywhere. I couldn't figure out what all the signs meant and I was sure that no one would be willing to stop their rushing to direct me to my downtown train, especially asked in halting English with a German accent. I went this way and that, up and down the long hot corridors; I looked at my subway map again and again. Not a clue. Finally in desperation I decided to take any train that said 'downtown' and take my chances. I guessed where to get off and then walked to the left—counting on the regular grid of Manhattan streets—until I got back to the HIAS. By now the sky was dark and Mother was frantic. I had to admit to myself that I too had been pretty worried.

CHAPTER TWENTY

I THINK OF the words of Käthe Kollwitz: "What capacity human beings have to endure . . . and go on . . . and start again, with hope." What did my mother hope for now that we were safe, now that everything was new—a new continent, a new language, new people and living conditions? When we arrived my mother was 49 years old, an age when one expects to be well settled into the life one has chosen. She now had to start all over again. I marveled at her valor. She knew only a little English and was worn out from all that had happened in the last few years. Since we had no money, a job had to be found quickly. The war was on and jobs were plentiful, except for someone like Mother, new and not so young, with only a little English. The people at HIAS eventually found her a job for the summer working at a children's summer camp near Hudson, New York. She was told that it was a "charity camp" for poor Jewish children from the city, and that the pay wasn't very much. "Better than nothing," Joel said. "Besides, it will be nice for Elizabeth to be with American kids. She'll have a good time, swimming and tennis and she'll improve her English."

There was a dairy farm attached to the camp, which in part supported it and where a group of boys in their late teens worked. It was those farm boys whom Mother was supposed to take care of; to cook for them, to wash their clothes and clean their rooms. "That's all," they told her. The work would not be too hard, and I would get a chance to be with the other campers and have a good time. Besides we would get out of the hot city and be in the beautiful countryside.

It was indeed beautiful as I saw recently when, to refresh my memory, I decided to go and see whether the camp still existed. I stopped at the little general store in the village.

"Yes, Camp Tranquility is still there," the woman behind the counter told me, and directed me to the camp.

As I drove up the dirt road to the white and green buildings scattered about the grounds of the camp, as I passed the tennis courts and the new swimming pool, the ball field and finally the little lake where the children had gone swimming, it struck me how little I had seen when I was there more than fifty years ago. I thought I recognized the farm house where our room had been and where Mother and I had worked from five o'clock in the morning till well into the night.

It was an impossible job for one person. The fire in the wood stove had to be started at five in the morning, so that the boys could have their pancakes, eggs and oatmeal breakfast at 5:30; their lunches had to be packed, their beds made, their rooms swept and their dirty clothes from the day before had to be washed in huge kettles and hung outside to dry. Later a hearty evening meal had to be prepared and served to those tired, ill-mannered boys. Mother had never done much cooking and certainly never on a capricious wood stove, whose firebox had to be continuously stoked, nor was she familiar with many of the dishes she was asked to cook.

The rooms used as camp infirmary were located on the second floor of the farmhouse. Somehow the director of the camp had neglected to hire a nurse; the nearest doctor was in Hudson, some twenty miles away, and soon kids were coming to the infirmary, with all sorts of complaints, dirty and tired. There was no one to take care of them. What else could we do but do the job ourselves! The infirmary beds were filling up and Mother and I became nurse and caretaker, seven days a week, all day and way into the night.

Many kids had poison ivy sores. I remember painting some of them with Gentian Violet, used in those days to treat the infected pustules. That little seven-year-old girl, violet from head to toe, wrapped in a sheet and miserable, stands still vividly before my eyes. There were those kids, who from pure exhaustion asked to stay in the infirmary where it was quiet and where the meals Mother cooked for them were better than camp food. My task was to amuse them and keep their spirits up when they felt homesick.

Kids sometimes cried out feverish during the night. I, roused from sleep, would get up groggily to comfort them and give them half an aspirin from our own supply. When Mother complained that there wasn't even a thermometer in the dispensary, the answer was, "We'll see what we can do." We were reminded that there was a war on, and didn't we know?

Every now and then Mother would tell me to go to the lake for a swim or join one of the camp activities as I had been promised. But I never did. I knew there was no way she alone could do everything she had to do. Here we were together in strange surroundings, with people whom we often didn't understand and who didn't understand us, but this time, out of necessity, we were a team. We felt very close that summer. I admired her strength and resourcefulness as never before and she was grateful for my help. There was no one else to talk to; the farm boys looked at us with disdain because of our poor English and our

European ways, and the counselors were much too busy to concern themselves with our well-being.

One morning when Mother told the boys that there was no more wood for the cook stove and asked them to split some and bring it in as they were supposed to do, they told her they were too busy. When she objected, one of them said, "Stop complaining. Do it yourself." And then he added, "If you don't like it here, why don't you go back to Germany where you came from!"

I couldn't believe my ears, and as I saw tears forming in Mother's eyes, I really hated those boys in their hurtful ignorance. They were Jewish themselves; didn't they know anything? I have never forgotten those words. As I write this, I can't help but think of all the others, wherever they came from and whatever their reasons for coming, uprooted and lost, being looked upon with disdain by those who came before.

We were exhausted; we didn't get enough sleep; we worried, we couldn't think about anything except what needed to be done next. We felt isolated, stranded, trapped. We worked so hard and such long hours that now and then Mother thought of leaving. She had been hired through the end of August, and this was only the third week of July. But she needed a job, and she didn't think she could get another one in the middle of the summer. Besides, what would happen to the sick kids in the infirmary? And so we stayed on.

I remember how, one late evening, both of us started to laugh about something trivial. We laughed and laughed; we were hysterical, we couldn't stop laughing. We looked at each other and laughed even more, with loud guffaws, until our sides ached and our eyes watered. We forgot what it was we were laughing about; we no longer cared. What made us lose control like that? Exhaustion certainly, but also the sense that we were in this together. That new feeling of being a team, equal and needing each other, mother and daughter carrying the same weight, felt to me as if we were the same age, that we now depended on each other in a new and different way than before. Maybe I was really growing up.

The head counselor told Mother that I really should attend the Friday night services which were held every weekend. I didn't want to go, but Mother persuaded me that since it was practically a command, I'd better do it. She couldn't go, she pointed out, since someone had to stay with the kids in the infirmary.

Reluctantly I trudged up the hill to the main building. When I arrived at the dining hall, I noticed a big black shiny Cadillac parked in front. A stout man, the president of the charity organization, his overdressed wife on his arm, was about to enter.

The campers, washed and combed, were assembled and the Service began. The president talked in a monotone, on and on, endlessly—I understood only half of what he said—and I soon stopped listening. The room was stifling hot in spite of ceiling fans that whirred and creaked. Big black flies buzzed around our heads. The kids started to get restless, fidgeted and whispered to each other, while the young counselors tried to keep them quiet. Mr. President droned on and on.

Like the kids I wanted to get out of there. I was worried about Mother and about the little boy in the infirmary who had a high fever and stomach pains, but there was no way for me to leave unnoticed. When the service was finally over, I raced back down the hill to the farmhouse. Sammy's fever had gone up and he was crying from pain. By now Mother had guessed that he had probably appendicitis, but she couldn't convince the head counselor, who thought that she worried too much, like all Europeans. We were foreigners who didn't know how Americans thought, she said. That night he got worse, and in the morning Mother finally threw a tantrum, yelled and screamed at them in German and broken English and told them she would leave immediately unless someone called a doctor. She had been right. Sammy was rushed to the hospital, his appendix was removed and he recovered. Mother had saved his life.

In desperation she now decided that she had enough of the place, even though there was no other job waiting. She gave them notice and they let her go. We left two days later.

BACK TO THE HIAS. This time we knew it would only be for a little while. Our first American experience was behind us and we were ready to move on. As far away from New York as possible, Mother hoped. Maybe somewhere else life would be easier.

The money we earned at Camp Tranquility was just enough for two train tickets to the West Coast. It had not been difficult for Cousin Alice to persuade us to come to San Francisco. She had arrived there two years earlier, and since the death of her husband, Cousin Alfred, who never recovered from his experiences in Buchenwald, worked for a wealthy family as the upstairs maid. The climate in San Francisco was wonderful, she told us, and that there were plenty of jobs, even for someone with only a little English.

Again we packed our two suitcases. This was going to be the last time, Mother said hopefully. We said good-bye to Joel and Bea by phone and Mother thanked them once more for having helped us to get started. This time there wasn't anyone I was sad to leave behind.

The train was crowded with young soldiers and sailors on leave, many with their girlfriends or wives. It smelled like beer and whiskey and cigarette smoke. At night the lights in the train were turned down low, and as I walked up and down the aisle to stretch my legs, I noticed that most of the couples sat very close, their arms around each other, kissing. Some of the girls were sitting on a boy's lap, moving up and down. What were they doing? Mother had seen it too and urged me to stay in my seat.

"Don't bother them. They are trying to sleep," she said. "Why don't you sleep too?" I was wide awake and curious, but I stayed in my seat and tried to sleep sitting upright as best I could.

On the second day of the trip, as the boys walked around in the narrow aisle, some of them would stop at our seat to talk to us. When they heard my accent, they wanted to know where we came from. Spain, I said. Of course I didn't want them to know that we were actually from Germany.

Mother had brought a box of crackers, some cheese, and a small bottle of orange juice, assuming there would be food to buy on the train. But there was none, and on the second day we started to get hungry, especially when we smelled the others eating. The young sailor sitting opposite us, noticed that we weren't eating, got up and offered to share his sandwich with us.

"No thank you," Mother said quickly, "we are not hungry." He didn't believe her.

"Come on," he insisted, "here, take this," handing me half his sandwich. "I've got lots more."

I could see Mother was embarrassed, but I wasn't too proud to accept the offered sandwich and bit into it ravenously. He must have told his buddies, for suddenly he brought us all sorts of things to eat and drink. "Everyone chipped in," he said.

Mother declined the beer, but we ended up being grateful for the rest

"Thank you, thank you," was all we were able to say every time he brought us more things to eat.

"That's OK," he would answer, smiling. There was something about that easy generosity of the young men that impressed us. Maybe not all Americans were as mean and unfeeling as the boys at Camp Tranquility; maybe we had gotten the wrong impression after all.

One of the boys played his guitar, and many of them joined in, singing army songs, camp songs, and popular songs. The beer flowed in abundance and spirits were high because they were alive and on furlough. We were made happy along with them and started to look forward to our arrival on the West Coast of America.

It took the train four days to arrive in San Francisco. Mother pointed out that it was about the same length of time it had taken us to get from Berlin to Barcelona.

CHAPTER TWENTY-ONE

FALL 1943. I am a junior at Lowell High School in San Francisco. Every morning I leave our room on the third floor of a big house in Pacific Heights, one of the old elegant sections of the city, and walk to school. Cousin Alice, who thinks she is an expert on American customs, chides my mother for letting me carry my lunch in a green, waxed lunch bag instead of a plain brown paper bag.

"Here in America everyone uses a brown bag," she says. "You can't let Elizabeth go to school like that."

Reluctantly, Mother complies, although she doesn't understand why that is so important. But who knows? So many things are strange and different from what she is used to.

Language, for one. She answers the telephone in her employer's house. "I'm sorry," she says. "Mrs. Brown can't come to the phone. She is in the bathroom."

What Mother meant was that she was taking a bath. How embarrassing. Mrs. Brown is angry, when she finds out what Mother said. Mrs. Brown is often angry, although she tries to hide her anger and act reasonably. Mother was hired as a housekeeper. I am to take care of their two small children on some afternoons and Saturdays when their Irish nanny goes home.

There is also Mattie who rules in the kitchen. She is from the South, and is an excellent cook. At first she is not overly friendly towards that white, middle-aged intruder with her teen-age daughter with whom she is to share her domain. Often she can't understand what Mother is trying to say in her broken English, and ignores her, but gradually she begins to feel less threatened and becomes friendlier. Mother has trouble understanding her Southern speech as well, and sometimes they both get really annoyed at each other's misunderstandings. Eventually Mattie becomes my mother's friend and cooking teacher. She shows her how to use the many gadgets in the kitchen and initiates her into the art of Southern cooking.

I wait in the kitchen and watch the two of them negotiate. Once in a while Mattie lets me taste something special, but I don't eat dinner until the Brown's have been served. I'm always hungry, so waiting is hard, especially with all those delicious smells around me.

At dinner time, Mother changes from her white housekeeper outfit into a black dress and a small white lace-edged apron and sets the table in the dining room. She refuses however to put on the little white maid's cap that Mrs. Brown wanted her to wear to complete the outfit. *"Lächerlich!"*—ridiculous—she says. I can see how it offends her dignity. On ordinary days, when there is no company, Mr. and Mrs. Brown sit opposite each other at the ends of a long highly polished table in the dining room, separated by two tall shiny silver candlesticks and a bouquet of flowers. In the kitchen, Mother wonders out loud whether they ever talk to each other across that immaculate expanse and whether they enjoy the elegant place settings: silver chargers under Wedgewood plates, heavy six piece sterling silver place settings and damask napkins in silver napkin rings. Mattie doesn't say anything, but I can tell from the look on her face that she has her own opinions about her employers.

The first time Mother set the table she did it the European way, but that was all wrong, and Mattie had to show her that the soup spoon has to be placed next to the knife and not horizontally above the charger plate. She often loses her patience when Mother doesn't know how to do something the right way, but gradually she shows Mother how Mrs. Brown likes things done.

After I eat dinner and we have finished cleaning up, we walk the two blocks to the house of our landlady who is one of Mrs. Brown's friends. Her husband is overseas in the Navy and she lets us occupy a spare room on the third floor.

As we enter by the front door, I glance furtively into the living room where she is usually entertaining a good-looking young man, and not usually the same young man, and I notice how she always looks very glamorous in her long gown or lounging pajamas like a movie star, and how the next morning there are always empty bottles and dirty glasses and lots of cigarette butts. I like to speculate about the wonderful exiting life she must be leading, and how it would feel to be rich and beautiful and American like her.

Upstairs in our room I take my books out of my school bag to do my homework. But I can't concentrate, so instead I get a box of Ritz crackers from the shelf, sit down on my bed and start a letter to Gert in Barcelona. There is so much to tell, about San Francisco and school and the Brown family, but mostly about how I miss him and how some day we will be reunited. It is bittersweet that letter writing. I don't yet know that gradually all my new impressions will supplant my longing for him. I don't know yet that eventually our letters will stop and we will each go our own way. The box of crackers is empty by the time the letter is finished.

On Saturday mornings I usually take Hobbie, the charming three-year-old, and his six-year-old sister Sandra to the playground. They are dressed in white outfits as always; their mother insists on it. They are not allowed to get dirty, especially Sandra, because she is a girl. Even their white shoes have to stay clean. How can they play like that, I wonder? They stand at the edge of the sandbox and watch other children play. Then they run around on the grass, chasing each other. Sandra stops now and then, having outrun her brother and looks longingly back at the other children. It upsets Mother that Sandra is so serious and sad and jealous of her little brother who charms everyone and is preferred by his parents. She asks me to be especially nice to her to make her feel a little better. Sandra is brittle and anxious and rejects my attempts to humor her. Perhaps it is because she senses that I too am brittle and anxious and a bit jealous. Do I resent my mother's concern with that little stranger's feelings? I don't really like Sandra much.

TODAY I HAVE shaved down the daily walk from our room to Lowell High School to twenty-five-and-a-half minutes, thirty seconds faster than yesterday. That walking faster and faster is something I focus on, a manageable task, something I do for myself, something that engages my attention. Inside my head there are melodies, there are snatches of Mozart arias, repeated over and over, or bits of popular songs I have heard in school at recess. They help me go faster. I know that if I pass the middle-aged man who wears a plaid cap before I cross Geary Boulevard, I'm going to be late for the first bell, and I have to hurry. There are not many pedestrians on my way to school, so everyone counts. I look down at the ugly brown oxfords on my marching feet. I would like to have a pair of penny loafers or brown and white saddle shoes like the other girls, but there is no money for that yet, and besides Mother believes that those hand-me-down shoes are alright, provided I polish them well. I try to stop looking at my feet to get my mind off the subject of shoes, and concentrate briefly on the fact that I now have a long, light blue "sloppy Joe" sweater and a white blouse to wear under it, whose pointy collar, even though it is not quite the right shape, is a nice contrast against the blue.

"*In diesen heil'gen Hallen*"—in these sacred halls.—I hum silently in my head as I hurry past the cemetery on the hill. Mozart's melody fills me up completely, so that there is no room left for anything else, not for the school day lying ahead, not for last night's argument with my mother, not even for the wondering about others, those lucky kids and adults, Americans all, who seem to know exactly who they are and where they fit in and what they have to do. My feet propel me automatically towards the day in school. Only once in a while do I look at my watch to make sure I won't be late.

I really like school because I like learning new things. It is something simple, uncomplicated, something that makes me feel good, that I don't have to question. Like the music inside my head, it engages my attention and leaves no room for worrying. In between classes, at lunch and recess, I skirt along the fringes of the community of my schoolmates and look at their strange behavior and rituals. It is a kind of learning, also. The gulf between them and me seems too immense to ever be crossed, and I am glad when the next class begins and I can focus on the teacher in front of the class and the material to be learned.

In English class we are reading a Victorian novel, *Cranford*. by a Mrs Gaskell. It takes place in the English Midlands. The teacher, Miss Gillie, all in brown, brown hair parted in the middle held back in a small bun, brown dress, sensible brown shoes and brown tortoise shell glasses, seems to be a part of that novel which she has chosen for us. She looks ancient to us, although she is probably no more than fifty. The students hate the book and dislike her pedantic, old-fashioned ways, but she is enthusiastic and praises the author's beautiful language. I struggle to understand the story with its many words and expressions that I don't know. What I like about it is the way the story has nothing to do with me, and is at the same time a challenge to my still limited knowledge of English.

The handsome blond chemistry teacher juts out his cleft chin and flirts with the pretty girls in the front row. He teases them about their boyfriends and hints at what they might have been up to. I don't know why he makes me uncomfortable. He is very popular among all the students, especially the girls, who don't seem to be at all interested in chemistry the way I am. I would like to learn the periodic table and the properties of the elements, but I also realize that the teacher reminds me of that English teacher in my German school, who would come to class in his Nazi uniform to mock the way the English soldiers marched.

When the teacher asks a question, I usually know the answer, but even as I'm about to raise my hand, I hear my mother's voice telling me that I mustn't show myself, that I must not let the world see what I know, what I can do and especially who I am. And so I keep quiet and even lose interest in the subject. I can't wait for the period to end.

I WOULD LIKE to join the student orchestra, and I bring my recorder to the try-outs. After a moment's hesitation the teacher says that maybe a recorder would be OK, but she is looking at me in such a funny way that I feel peculiar and out of place. My recorder and I don't fit with the other instruments, I understand that. Disappointed at being rejected, I let myself be a little sad, but not too much. I half expected it anyway, I tell myself.

This morning, after social studies class, a dark-haired girl catches up with me in the hall and approaches me shyly. I'm hurrying, alone as usual, to my next class.

"Elizabeth," she says, walking along with me, "you are from Germany, right?"

How does she know? My German accent be damned!

"My family came from Germany too," she continues. She smiles at me. I notice how her dark eyes are warm and how her shiny brown hair frames her round face in soft waves. Her hair is not scraggly like mine, and her pink sweater is soft and fluffy. The points on the collar of her white blouse are just right, and so is her plaid skirt. Rolled matching socks and, of course, sparkling white and brown saddle shoes. I see all that in a flash and think she is perfect. I can't believe that she spoke to me, that plain, dumpy-bodied girl, the foreigner. For one instant I wonder whether we could become friends, whether she might like me. But no, she is too perfect. I smile back self-consciously and I sense that she doesn't mind when I turn to walk the other way, mumbling that I have forgotten something.

We never talk again I think that perhaps her mother might have asked her to be friendly to the new refugee girl. I look for her every day in class and try to smile at her, because she had spoken to me. She usually throws me a quick smile back. I notice that all her friends are also perfect, although they don't talk to me the way she did.

When Mother and I are alone together in our room, after her workday is over, I will only speak English, and I urge her to do the same. She objects, says she is too tired in the evenings for that. I remind her of what Cousin Joel had said to us in

New York a few months ago, extolling the virtues of living in America. He predicted that Germany would soon be defeated and be totally wiped off the map of the earth.

"German is a dead language," he had said. He had wanted Mother and me to become instant Americans and to forget about the past. Oh yes, I want him to be right, and I want especially to kill everything German in me too. I want to eradicate all traces of my German background. I will never speak German again, I say to myself, never, never, and I will never look back.

I'm not German, but neither am I American; so what am I? Again I ask myself that question. Again, my sense that I don't fit in anywhere. I am not part of the group of my mother's refugee friends, some of whom bring daughters to their occasional gatherings over tea and cake, who compare employers and living conditions as they speak German in their various regional accents: Berlin, Frankfurt, North-German, Vienna. They talk about how hard it is to learn English, and they laugh about the mistakes they make and they tell each other how they manage their lives. They reminisce about the old days in the old country, when they were somebody, when they had money and didn't have to work so hard at menial jobs. I notice that Mother doesn't say very much, yet she seems to feel comfortable in their company. I now refuse to go with her to these gatherings. I don't belong.

Since I won't speak German and Mother is usually too tired at the end of the day to struggle with English, we talk a mixture of the two languages with now and then a Spanish word or two thrown in. After a while I'm no longer aware of which language is which. Mother on the other hand is very much aware and the need to learn the language better is very much on her mind. I become her teacher; I teach her new words and try to correct her pronunciation and syntax. Just like cousin Joel I want her to become an instant American. She is not yet ready to do that; she wants the English language to help her get along in her new world, while her thoughts and dreams will continue to remain in German. I get impatient, "It's REST-o-rant, *not* rest-au-RANG," I repeat again and again. "Why can't you remember?" I don't understand why she can't learn English as easily as I.

Perhaps in self-defense she starts to nag me about not forgetting my Spanish. I agree with her, but how? Too much homework to read books in Spanish, so I decide to go to the theater on Fillmore Street which shows Spanish language movies on Sunday afternoons. I can walk there, it's not too far and it's cheap. Mother and I don't go to regular movies because they cost too much. She says she can't understand what's going on anyway with their rapid-fire American language. On Sundays we usually take a walk or visit her refugee friends or I do my homework while Mother does our laundry and rests. I'm ready to do something different. I ask her whether I can go.

"Alone?" she hesitates.

"Sure," I say, "so I won't forget Spanish."

She's not sure, hesitates some more, but finally gives her OK. I think she is glad that I'm doing something else besides sitting in our room doing homework and eating Ritz crackers.

The theater is empty the first time I go. It's a beautiful sunny day; everyone must be out somewhere. The man in the little booth who sells me my ticket looks at me in a funny way. Isn't going to the movies a perfectly ordinary thing to do? I try to ignore the musty smell and the dirty carpet, the gum wrappers and spilled popcorn, and find a seat in the middle of an empty row. The movie starts, and I'm pleased that I understand what the characters are saying.

About halfway through, I notice that some men have found seats quite close to me and are looking at me. One of them is now sitting next to me. A hand is touching my knee. It feels kind of nice, so I try to ignore it, but as it moves up my thigh, I reluctantly get up and find a seat in a different section. The film ends, and as the lights go on, I notice, that there are several couples sitting here and there, but no one else. Oh well, I think, maybe I made it up.

The next few Sundays I go again. I'm a little more cautious and move my seat several times in case anyone like that sits next to me. Mother has told Alice, her almost-American cousin, how I spend my Sundays. She is aghast, and chides Mother for letting me go alone to the movies.

"Especially this kind," she says. "You can't do this sort of thing here," she insists. But I go again anyway.

One afternoon as I leave the theater– it is another beautiful day– a young man approaches me. "*Habla español?*" he asks.

"*Un poco,*" I answer. A little.

He walks along with me, tells me he is from Mexico and that he knows only a little English. He wants to learn more.

"Can you teach me?" he asks, smiling shyly.

I look at him, surprised. His hair is light brown, he has no mustache and his eyes are hazel-green. Not at all the way Mexican men look, I think. He tells me that Sunday is his day off and that he goes to the movies because he is lonely. He has seen me there and he wonders whether I am lonely too. I like it that he thinks I'm American. I like it that he doesn't know that I speak English with a German accent.

"You teach me English?" he asks again and I don't say no. I don't say anything, as I listen to him. He tells me about his family in Mexico, about his mother who is a wonderful cook and how he misses them, especially his mother. We are speaking Spanish. I'm glad I haven't forgotten.

"What do you do?" I ask him. "Where do you work?"

I can see he is too embarrassed to tell me, but I insist.

Finally he tells me, looking down at his shoes, that he is a dishwasher in a restaurant. "As soon as I learn English I'll get a better job," he says as he looks up at me again.

I want to tell him a little about myself too, only not that I am also new here and am not an American. I tell him that my mother works as a housekeeper for a rich family, and that I am a junior in high school.

"You seem older," he says.

When he asks me, as we are standing in front of the door to the house in which I live, whether he can walk me home from the movies next Sunday, I nod yes. He looks at me, looks up and down the house, and tells me that he doesn't have much money, so maybe . . . I interrupt to tell him again that my mother is a housekeeper and that we just live here. Maybe he didn't understand before that we are not rich either. He smiles and reaches out his arm to embrace me, but I turn away and open the door.

"*Hasta Domingo,*" he says and I nod my head. "Until Sunday" I say.

Mother wants to know how the movie was. "OK," I say. I don't tell her about Juan. Not yet. But, I know that sooner or later her keen mother-sense will make her aware that there must be a reason why my mood has changed, why I'm less sullen and sometimes seem even happy.

After three more Sundays, Juan suggests that we go to the amusement park at the beach instead of meeting at the movies.

"I'll pay," he says proudly.

I concur, but I have started to be a little uneasy. I don't want him to fall in love with me, even though I have come to like his arm around me as he walks me home. I like our goodnight kisses too, but he is only nineteen and we really have very little

286

to say to each other and not just because of the language. I'm not teaching him much English, but he doesn't seem to care.

I tell him to pick me up next Sunday so that he can meet my mother. He comes wearing his best shirt and trousers with a sharp crease. He presents my mother with a large bouquet of daisies. I don't know why I am embarrassed, but I am beginning to think that maybe I made a mistake; maybe he thinks that inviting him to meet my mother meant that I was ready to be his *novia*.

Sure enough, no sooner are we seated in the bus to the beach than he puts his arm around me, kisses me lightly and tells me in rapid-fire Spanish how happy he will be once we are married. How his mother will really like me and how we can have the wedding in Mexico with all his family and friends. After a while we would live in San Francisco so that I would be near my mother. He would become a citizen and go to school, for he has never had the chance to finish school in Mexico. We would have a little house near the beach at first, until he made more money, and then a bigger house. We would have many children, for he really loves children. Many boys but also some girls. He'd be a good father and provider. Of course, before he could get married, his mother would have to give him permission and approve his choice of wife, which of course she would. That was their custom. We should plan to go to his village soon; or maybe his mother could visit here and could stay with my mother . . . On and on he goes, breathlessly in such rapid Spanish that I only understand half of it. He is so happy that I don't dare say anything to him.

The next day I compose a letter in Spanish, telling him that I am sorry that he has misunderstood me, but that I cannot marry him.

CHAPTER TWENTY-TWO

I'M SURPRISED when a girl with long flaming red hair approaches me at recess.

"I'm Alison," she says. "I play violin in the orchestra. I saw you there the other day. Aren't you coming any more?"

I hadn't noticed her, even with her remarkable bright hair. She must have seen my disappointment when my recorder and I were not accepted. I tell her that I don't really care, because I had already realized that the teacher thought that a recorder didn't fit with the rest of the instruments.

"That's not fair, she should have managed to arrange a part for you," she says.

She's standing up for me, and she doesn't even know me!

She is casual and friendly in an offhand sort of a way and we chat a little about our classes and teachers. We aren't in any of the same classes together we discover, because she is a half a year behind me, and is just starting her junior year. She asks me where I live.

"That's not far from my house. Let's walk home together," she suggests, just as the bell rings to end recess.

Sitting in social studies class I wonder about what might have made her search me out. Could it be that she has seen that I am different, and sensed my aloneness, just as perhaps she too feels herself to be different from the others? Or could it be that mysterious something that makes one notice a stranger in a crowd as a potential friend?

At the end of school she is waiting for me.

"Hi," she says, and we start walking. She is much taller than I am and she seems very American to me in the casual way she speaks and moves. I answer her questions in monosyllables, reticent as usual to talk about myself, too shy to reveal how excited I feel. She doesn't blink an eye when she finds out that my mother is a maid and that I have to baby sit to earn money. I had thought that of course Americans would look down on someone who works as a domestic. Neither does she say anything about how interesting it is that I come from Europe. I am glad that she doesn't ask questions about that, and I don't volunteer any information about my past to her.

We start walking home together regularly and she invites me to come to her house after school and on Sundays whenever I can. I can hardly believe it: I have an American friend!

Her house, her big family, all their many activities, and the way they talk with one another: it's all new and exciting to me. It quite overwhelms me and I love it. The house is old and in need of a paint job, the furniture is equally old, and there is stuff lying all over the place. Her five younger brothers are always asking, "Bunny, have you seen my mitt?" or my notebook, or my jacket, or my sneakers? Bunny is their mother. Nobody says Mom or Mother.

"Bunny?" I ask Alison.

Her name is Florence, but no one calls her that, Alison informs me. "Bill is away in the Navy," she adds, and for clarification, "Bill is my father. My oldest brother is Bill too."

Gradually I meet all of her brothers. They look at me with

289

curiosity and then pay no further attention. I'm their sister's friend, and there is a hard line of demarcation between theirs and hers. No wonder she wants girlfriends, I think.

"You can call me Ardie," Alison says. "Alison is too formal."

I have noticed that a lot of Americans have nicknames; Bunny and Ardie, Bob for her brother Robert, Micky is her youngest brother Michael, the chemistry teacher is Mr. G. I've always been Elisabeth except that now I spell my name with a *z* instead of *s*, to make it more American. I hate my name now; it's too long and too foreign sounding.

One Sunday afternoon, when Ardie, her friend Joan from across the street whom everyone calls Jill, and I are up in Ardie's room on the third floor, they decide that I need a new name too. They go through all the variations of Elizabeth: Liz and Betsy and Lisa and Liza, among others. They look at me and decide that none of them fits me until they hit on Beth; so Beth I become. I like it and I feel flattered that they take an interest in making me more American. My new name cements our friendship.

It's a noisy place, Ardie's house. Everyone is always practicing on one instrument or another. The sounds of trumpet and trombone, cello, clarinet, piano—scales, arpeggios or snatches of melodies—usually at least two at a time—a cacophony that even closed doors can't prevent—I find it wonderful. Sometimes Bunny sings in a high, clear soprano voice while doing housework. She is slim, with ash-blond hair, which usually hangs untidily around her thin face. She limps slightly and her face is slightly pockmarked. Ardie explains childhood polio and acne. I think she is beautiful in spite of it. I especially love her blue eyes which look calmly at all that young life around her. She helps with homework where needed and supervises everyone's music practice, answers all the questions thrown at her without ever getting impatient, takes the boys to baseball or football practice, arbitrates their arguments, and amidst all that chaos she finds time to sit at her easel and paint.

When I am there I am always invited to stay for dinner. Huge bowls of spaghetti or baked beans are served, and there is always a green salad. The rest of the time everyone goes to the refrigerator or the kitchen cabinets for snacks whenever they want.

I love being in Ardie's house.

I tell Mother that Bunny has asked about her and wants me to bring her over some time. When Mother looks doubtful I insist.

"I know you would really like each other." How can I be so sure?

"She is very nice and very unusual," I say. I want Mother to have an American friend too. She hesitates; she feels her English isn't good enough, and besides, she would need a real invitation.

That invitation comes, and Mother dresses in her best. She wants to make a good impression; she doesn't want to look like a poor newcomer. I tell her that for Bunny that isn't necessary, that she doesn't stand on ceremony, that she doesn't dress so well herself.

But Mother can't believe me. "It's a dinner invitation, and for that you dress well," she says.

When we arrive, it is I who is embarrassed. Mother is wearing her best dress, and has put on bright red lipstick, while Bunny is her usual casual self in slacks and a man's shirt and no make-up. She is much more accepting than I am; she doesn't seem to find it strange that my mother is so formal, and extends her a warm welcome. At dinner, the boys wolf down their food and disappear as always, and after a while Ardie and I ask to be excused too, leaving the adults to themselves. I am glad to leave the table, because I see that my mother is giving disapproving glances around the room, even while she and Bunny are talking with each other in the friendliest way. Why have I forgotten that Mother likes things neat and clean? Have I made a mistake by bringing them together?

"Mrs. Cary is very nice," Mother says on the way home in that to me too familiar voice that denotes disapproval while saying something pleasant. "She sure isn't a good housekeeper though," she adds. "It's a nice house, but so disorderly and not very clean."

I hate it that Mother is so critical. Why does she think that order and cleanliness are so important for everyone? I guess I made a mistake. I should have known. I am disappointed.

We walk a few blocks in silence when suddenly Mother says, "I saw some of her paintings. I like them. They are good. She is really talented." After further reflection, "I suppose she doesn't have much time for housework with all those boys and painting too. She does so much."

I am relieved. Maybe I wasn't too wrong after all? "You should call her Bunny. Everyone does," I suggest as a kind of peace token.

Bunny becomes Mother's first and best American friend. She talks to her about other topics besides how hard it is being a refugee who has to work as a maid. They talk about art, about gardening, about bringing up teenage kids, and about the war. Bunny teaches Mother to cook some American dishes like baked beans, and in exchange Mother shares some of the southern recipes she learned from Mattie. They are happy in each other's company and remain connected long after Ardie and I have drifted apart. I congratulate myself for having been right in the first place.

It was through Bunny's influence that later, when she was in her early sixties, my mother took up painting. I had urged her unsuccessfully for a while to get involved in something of her own. I knew that as a young woman she had spent some happy weeks at Worpswede, a famous German art colony. There in the company of other artists, she had learned to use her artistic talents in new ways. I never forgot, through all those long years that those had been some of the happiest weeks of her life. I also hoped that she would find something more enjoyable than telling me how she worried about me. I think she understood my motives. Later as the joy in her own creative endeavors became stronger, it became the mainstay of her daily life. I was able to feel good that I had helped her in that way, even though my motives had not been totally unselfish.

Painting led to ceramics and ceramics to sculpture .Until she became too old and her body too frail, her art activities gave her a great deal of pleasure. Yet she would often say in her letters, or later when I visited her and she showed me the things she had created, "It's not really very good; I'm not very talented. I just like doing it." As if to say, don't take it too seriously, it is really not what I am about. As if to say that painting and working with clay are only a substitute for the pleasure of our being closely, lovingly connected, mother to daughter and daughter to mother.

I was proud of her and liked many of her paintings and glazed pots and clay sculptures. After she died, I brought back with me a few of her paintings, a few bowls but no sculptures. I knew that her clay figures were the works to which she was most connected, but I felt in an only half-understood way that those three dimensional, often life-sized heads and busts, that looked so much like her, would have been too palpably her presence in my house.

For many years several of her paintings hung on my walls, until they were replaced with others and put away, but to this day I take pleasure in using her bowls and plates. "This is the first bowl my mother made," I think when I put rice or potatoes into a heavy, earth-colored bowl, my hands cupped around its circumference.

❦

TODAY WE ARE again in Ardie's room on the third floor. She bolts the door securely against invading brothers, and stands in front of the mirror and brushes her long wavy red hair endlessly with tender loving strokes. Then she lifts the back of her hair, twists it around and drapes it over her head for a chignon. She experiments with all sorts of other hairdos as well and puts on make-up. I stand next to her and try to figure things out. She wants me to do stuff with my hair too and offers to brush it, but I resist. My brown hair, which just covers my ears, is very ordinary, not like hers, and there is really very little one can do with it. Besides I am too fascinated watching her. Up here in her room, she is different than when she is with her family or in school. She doesn't talk much and is absorbed in admiring herself. After a while I get bored just watching her and decide to go home.

"I guess I better go," I venture.

"Don't leave," she pleads, "I am almost done." She really wants me there.

She tells me that she and Joan are planning a party. It's a birthday party for Joan. "Of course you'll come," she says.

Joan lives with her old grandparents. Somewhere in a boarding school there is a brother, but her parents don't seem to exist. Did they die? Are they somewhere in a foreign country, where they don't want to bring their children? I'd like to know, but I don't dare ask. I'm given to understand that it's very important that there be a birthday party for her, which only confirms the mystery of her family situation.

They both want this party to be the best ever There are endless discussions as to the decorations, the food, the music and whom to invite and whom to leave out before the actual work begins. Every day for several weeks, we three meet after school for planning sessions. Long lists are made, which at the next meeting get changed. No more than thirty kids, Alison says, but Joan wants no more than twenty. They settle on twenty-six. They want to invite all the cute boys, but they can't agree on who is cute and who is a dope.

All their best girl friends will be invited; the list stretches and shortens as they discuss the pros and cons of each. It all seems very strange to me. Don't the grandparents have anything to say about all this? Doesn't Ardie's mom? Apparently not. I just listen, having no experience with teenage parties. The seriousness with which my two friends go about all this is astonishing. I try to go along with it all; I want to be just like other American teens, I don't want to put in my suggestions, let alone seem critical. I haven't forgotten what the farm boys at Camp Tranquility said to Mother when she complained about something: "If you don't like it here, why don't you go back where you came from." Not that I think that Ardie or Joan would say that; but still, best to be cautious.

When it finally comes to transforming the dingy damp basement, stuffed full with old junk, into the equivalent of a fancy place in which to have a party, I become useful. I marvel at the amount of discarded stuff: sports equipment, toys, games, books, magazines, tools, pieces of furniture. How can people have so many things? How can there be such a surplus of things to throw out? We string lights, cover the walls with colorful cloths, hang miles of streamers, and inflate balloons and more balloons until we collapse on the sofa completely exhausted. Fuses blow several times, balloons pop, we nibble potato chips and drink cokes and all the while popular songs blare from the radio. Joan and Ardie are having a great time as they sing along. I don't know the words, but as the music carries me along, I get into the swing of things and hum the melodies. It feels wonderful to be involved in their party as their friend, even though I know that I am not quite like them. I hope that they don't think so as well. Maybe they don't care that I'm different. I am starting to have a wonderful time.

The big day has finally arrived. Lights are dimmed and the chosen guests are streaming in. Presents are piling up on the corner table. Someone keeps changing the records. The noise level increases. The girls are standing together in a tight knot on one side of the room chattering away while the boys congregate across from them on the other side of the dancing area, which has been marked off with tape. I don't know any of the kids and I don't know quite what to do and what is expected of me. I stand aside against the wall, observing.

The girls giggle and snicker and as unobtrusively as possible glance over in the direction of the boys. The boys fidget and whisper until finally a courageous boy asks Joan to dance. They are off! Others join them and soon there are only a few kids not dancing.

I look at the left-over boys, and think, who would want to dance with them? They all seem so young and babyish. I feel so much older, so much more experienced in ways that they are not, because I have come from Europe and have been through a lot of stuff, because someone actually wanted to marry me, and because once I was truly in love. I think about Gert and wonder: if he would suddenly appear at this party, would I still be in love with him? Would he think that this party is silly?

No one seems to want to talk; at least no one talks to me. I don't know how to start a conversation the way they do, or what to talk about, or how to tell jokes the way they do. I wish I knew better how to behave at a party like this. Besides, I don't know all the dances the others do. How did they learn?

Potato chips and popcorn are all over the floor by now, and there are puddles of coke here and there. No one seems to mind. Ardie is dancing with a boy who comes just up to her shoulder. She is having a good time. Here she seems to be different from the Ardie I know. I can't figure it out; I can't figure her out.

I am not having a good time at all. Pretty silly all this. I'd like to leave, but I promised to help clean up afterwards; so I stay.

Finally, one of the left-over boys sidles over to me and asks me to dance. I don't know how, I say, and he admits that neither does he. We both laugh at that. What a relief! He is standing next to me, but neither one of us can think of anything to say. I feel awkward, but I suspect that he is too. He walks over to where the drinks are. "Want any?" he asks. I shake my head, "No thanks."

One of the kids dims the lights, and in the semi-darkness I see that several of the couples are kissing. They seem playful and lighthearted in a way that I can't be. Perhaps I never was? Yet I am no older than they are.

When Joan blows out the candles on the oversized pink and green birthday cake, and all have dutifully sung '"Happy Birthday," the boys crowd around the refreshment table. They can't wait to get their slice of birthday cake, which they gobble up in a minute flat. One of them has decided to use his sticky plate as a Frisbee, and soon green and pink frosting-covered plates are sailing through the air. The kids all think that is hilarious. They holler and laugh and one of them smears his face with frosting. It seems pretty disgusting to me, and I look in the direction of

Ardie who is still dancing, this time with a boy who is as tall as she is. She has seen me and rolls her eyes to let me know that she agrees with me. But she lets it go on and continues dancing.

Someone brought rum to the party. "Drinking Rum and Co-ca Co-la" the popular song blares from the phonograph. I only notice now, that many of the kids are tipsy. At the refreshment table I pour myself a glass of ginger ale. The rum bottle is empty. I find a place to sit in the corner of the room and wait for the party to end. Is this what American birthday parties are like? If I could go back and start all over as an American child, would I feel different, not so out of place? I don't know.

When finally the party comes to an end and everyone has drifted away, Ardie and Joan sit down on the old sofa exhausted and I come out of my corner. I feel more comfortable again, just being with them. They decide to leave the cleanup for the next day. "Just too tired," Joan says

"A great party," they agree, "the best ever." I remain skeptical. What strange customs they have here in America.

IN THE SUMMER Ardie invites me to spend a week with her family at their vacation cottage in the mountains near Lake Tahoe. It's a beautiful place and I am thrilled to be there. We hike to a waterfall, go canoeing on the lake, take short swims in its freezing cold water and play badminton with her brothers. It is still an amazing thing to me, being so casually accepted as a member of this large family. I notice that even though there are a lot of arguments and disagreements, a lot of shouting and banging of screen doors, there is a cohesiveness and true family feeling that I admire.

What I admire even more is that all the children express themselves as if they knew that they had a right to be themselves. Their mother accepts them and loves them just the way they are, even though there are times when they exasperate her. At times they all seem like some exotic foreign tribe to me. I wish I could be like them, but I can't. To make up for it, I try to be as helpful as I can. In the mornings I make sure the cabin gets cleaned up and after meals I help wash the dishes .The boys are thrilled; they don't object when I do the work assigned to them. They hate to do chores around the house, and if their sister's newcomer friend actually wants to do them, why not let her!

There is a small resort down the hill at the lake shore.

"Let's go down to the lodge," Ardie suggests one afternoon.

"What's there to do?" I ask innocently.

"We'll get something at the fountain. Mike and Bill work there. You'll see."

I am being introduced to an American teenage ritual, called 'Hanging Out.'

Mike is there behind the counter. He is tall and blond. Maybe sixteen, I guess.

"Hi," Ardie says.

"Hi," Mike answers back.

"I'll have a strawberry soda," she says and I say I'll have the same. We perch on the stools in front of the counter as Mike squirts syrup, scoops ice cream and finally splashes seltzer into our glasses.

"How's it going?" Ardie asks.

"OK, busy," he answers.

That seems to be the end of the conversation for now. Some customers come in, order various drinks and snacks and put some coins into the jukebox. Mike is busy. We slowly sip our sodas, tap our feet to the rhythm of the song and sing along with its refrain, "Don't Fence me in."

"This is Beth." Ardie nods in my direction when Mike is finally free. He has poured himself a coke.

"Hi," he says, giving me a quick glance over his right shoulder.

"Hi," I reply.

We have finished our sodas but remain seated at the counter. I am getting bored, but Ardie has no intention of leaving. I don't know why she wants to stay, but she must have her reasons. After a while some adult customers come in and Mike motions to us that we better vacate our seats at the counter. We get up and Ardie puts a dime into the pinball machine in the corner and plays a game. I watch. Some kids come in. Ardie doesn't know them, but they seem to know Mike, and a short conversation ensues about the upcoming Saturday night dance.

"You going? Ardie asks Mike.

"Nah, can't. I'm working." At least he has something to do, I think.

"I'm not going either," she says after a moment's hesitation. "Got to baby sit my little brother. So long." She has decided to leave.

The next afternoon she declares that we should check out the lodge again. Maybe Bill will be there. He's nicer than Mike, she says.

Bill is Mike's duplicate except in a different color scheme. He is dark haired with almost black eyes, whereas Mike's are blue, and he sports a deep tan. He has the faintest mustache on his upper lip, which he caresses now and then furtively. We order chocolate shakes. "To match Bill's coloration?" I wonder with some irony. The conversation is about the same as with Mike.

A group of girls in bathing suits show up. They and Bill seem to know each other. They laugh and tease each other as Ardie and I watch. I feel out of place, a foreigner, a displaced person.

We spend an hour or so there, not doing anything in particular, before we leave.

When Ardie asks me to go to the lodge again the following afternoon, I demur and she goes alone. I take my book to the porch and lie down in the hammock to read. What is it that makes my friend want to go there, day after day? No one has anything interesting to say and it makes me feel stupid just to sit there on a stool sipping a soda. Maybe she is looking for something exciting to happen? Maybe she has a crush on Mike? Or on Bill? I can't figure it out. I don't understand the point of "hanging out"; no, not one little bit.

CHAPTER TWENTY-THREE

WHEN HOME is a cot in the tiny maid's room behind the kitchen one's mother is assigned to by her employer, where is that girl that was me to be? School, of course, and after that selling shoes at Chandler's downtown. Then walking the streets and getting something to eat at a cafeteria, and then back to that narrow cot, hoping the mother would be asleep already so that she wouldn't want to talk.

That is the outline of my days, now that my mother has a new job as housekeeper for a different family, whose lifestyle is less ostentatious and whose house is less grand. There are no little children for me to take care of; there is only an overweight teenage son, whom I almost never see. I don't see Ardie as much any more either. I live far from her now, and with working at the shoe store and waitressing for a caterer on Sundays, there is little opportunity to meet. I miss the fun we had together, but I have to earn money for college.

The war is raging on both fronts; some of the senior boys in my class have enlisted. Mother rolls up aluminum foil into balls to recycle for the war effort, and a few foods are rationed. But all that is somehow only peripheral to my existence. The many new experiences I have leave little room in my mind for the state of the world. When on rare occasions I find myself starting to think back about Germany or Spain, I quickly put it out of my mind. Mother looks at the newspaper to know what is happening in Germany, but there is little except news from the fronts; she doesn't know what the fate of the remaining Jews has become.

Hamburg and other German cities are under heavy Allied bombing attacks she has read, and she wonders whether her German friends, Lili and Paula and their families, are alive or dead. I see red-bordered banners with a gold star in the center appear in some of the windows on the streets I pass. Some mother's son has been killed in the war. I can't understand why these mothers are supposed to be proud when it is so sad, all that killing, even though I know that Hitler and the Japanese have to be defeated. It's too confusing. Better not think about it too much.

FRIDAY AFTERNOON and all day Saturday are the busiest times at Chandlers shoe store; then we really have to hustle. When I ask why, one of the salesmen explains, "Friday is payday in the shipyards. Some of these women from the South have never had so much money in their pockets to spend." He adds with a sneer, "You can sell them almost anything. They don't even care whether the shoes fit or not. They just want to spend their money right away and go dancing."

I don't like the way he says that, but then I have noticed too that these women seldom leave without buying at least two pairs of shoes at a time, and sometimes even more. Having more than one pair of shoes at a time still seems pretty extravagant to me, but then, why not buy more if you have the money? I try to sell each customer as many pairs of shoes as I can.

"More commission for me," I say to myself. "Even if they don't fit, as long as she is happy," watching my customer wobble out of the store on her too small, too high-heeled, brand new dancing shoes.

The rest of the week I don't have much to do. Then I have fun trying on some of the latest styles: sandals called 'ankle straps' which are held on with a thin strap wound around the ankle and thin four inch heels, scuffs with thick wooden wedge soles, and shiny patent leather shoes which come in all colors of the rainbow. Eventually I buy myself a pair of much needed, sensible house slippers.

MY OTHER JOB is working for a caterer. Compared with being a waitress, selling shoes is easy. The caterer, Mrs. Rubin, is a Jewish refugee herself—that's how I got the job- she's a friend of a friend of Mother's. I think she is trying to get rich quick. She pays very little and doesn't hire enough helpers. Besides she is never satisfied, even though I try my best to do what she says. At wedding or anniversary dinners in someone's house I carry trays of hors d'oeuvres to the guests, who are standing around with drinks in their hands, talking and being happy. I'm not supposed to serve drinks because I'm not old enough, but when she is shorthanded she lets me do it anyway. Mrs. Rubin tells me I should be friendlier to the guests, but it is too upsetting to be a servant in an elegant home with all these happy people celebrating, when I don't have a home myself. It's funny that I don't think of Mother in this connection. I am not meant to be a waitress, even though I am efficient and work hard. But I won't smile and be gracious to perfect strangers in someone's fancy apartment or house. No way. At dinner many people don't even finish what's on their plates; huge chunks of steak or chicken are left untouched and have to be thrown out. When I come home late on Sunday night from yet another party, I am exhausted and angry. I'm glad when I get fired.

My next job is at a country club. I am more experienced and the place is a more neutral ground for me. The kitchen staff jokes around a lot and we waitresses get along well. I eat large quantities of steak and baked potatoes with lots of ice cream for dessert. I even get some tips!

❧

I AM NOW in my senior year in high school. My English has improved and I am taking physics instead of chemistry. There are about twenty boys and two Chinese girls in my class. The girls are very hard-working and get good grades. I eat at the same table with them at lunch and stay close to them during recess and during the many football rallies and school dances that still seem like strange rituals to me. They are friendly enough, but somewhat cool and aloof; they too are strangers in a foreign environment. I envy them in a way, because they have each other and return home every afternoon to their families and a life that I know nothing of and can only imagine. When I notice that they like to play basketball at recess, I try to join them, but I am an inept beginner, and I see that they don't really want me there. Again I retreat and wait for recess to end.

"I'll be seeing you in all the old familiar places . . ." the P.A. system blares in the courtyard. And then "Begin the Beguine." Couples are dancing, and those girls who have not yet been asked to dance by a boy, are whispering to each other, waiting. I stand on the sidelines in the shady part of the courtyard and watch. I like the music; it makes me feel lonely, and I long for something wonderful to happen, although I don't know what really.

I fix my eyes on a couple, who are dancing very close. They have no eyes for anyone else, only for each other. They are not in any of my classes, and they are not part of the "in" crowd. I have noticed them before and I also notice that the boy is overweight and not particularly handsome, and the girl wears glasses and is quite plain. They are different than the other dancing couples: a familiarity with each other's bodies, in the way they lean into each other, in the way they look at each other. I can see that they are in love, but there is something else too. I have never thought, let alone said the word SEX, but of course, that's it! They have sex! I am very interested, as if by watching them intently I can learn something I need to know. Watching them move against each other makes me feel uncomfortable, but I can't look away. I had imagined that to be desirable, a girl had to be beautiful, or at least pretty, and this girl is very ordinary looking. I'm very ordinary looking too, especially now since I gained so much weight, eating Ritz crackers. I very briefly think about Gert in Spain, how we too were in love. I watch the couple leave as soon as the song ends. I would like to follow them and ask them, "How did you know?"

At six o'clock, after the shoe store closes, I walk along the streets of downtown San Francisco, clutching my schoolbooks under my arm. I am heading for Fosters, the cafeteria where I will eat vegetable soup and green Jell-o, cut into cubes, topped with Cool Whip. Every day, when I have finished my Jell-o dessert, I stay seated at the green Formica table, take out my books and do my homework.

I usually have breakfast at the kitchen table at home before I go to school, but the rest of my meals I have to have somewhere else. That is the arrangement now. I can sleep where Mother works, but I can't eat there. It was something Mother very reluctantly agreed to, but I urged her to accept those conditions.

Sometimes Mother offers me something to eat when I come home, but I usually decline.

"Come, have some cake," she might say. "I made it from a new recipe. It's delicious. They all liked it." She then looks at me, pleading.

I always say no. "I'm not hungry, thanks," I say. "I'm really tired. The store was crazy today."

Am I too proud to accept her offer? I know it makes Mother sad, but what can I do, that's how I feel.

Today, after the shoe store closes, I'm not in a hurry to eat. I take my time. As I cross Union Square I am aware of the old people sitting here and there alone, each to a bench, and I wonder where they might go later, when the cops patrol the square to clear it of bums and hobos and dirty drunks. I pass quickly, for they make me uncomfortable and I really don't want to know about them.

It is getting dark, and all the city noises are muffled by the soft air The streets are crowded with late shoppers hurrying home, with couples standing in front of restaurants, with young soldiers in groups who wear their army caps at jaunty angles, with young sailors laughing boisterously before entering one of the many bars that line the brightly lit streets. I see all that, and I think that everyone is going somewhere, that everyone has a destination, that everyone else is with others.

I'm pretending that I'm going somewhere too, that I am window shopping, that I am waiting for someone to meet me. My eyes wander up and down the façades of the old buildings. When I see a lighted window I imagine people there, talking, laughing, touching each other. I especially like the windows whose dirty shades are only half drawn, behind which the lights are dim and where sometimes I see a figure moving. There is something deliciously, sensuously sordid about those rooms behind those old, dirty windows, the way I imagine them. I can feel it in my body, a

307

tingling down my spine, a stirring in my groin. My hands, holding my schoolbooks feel clammy, and I am suddenly very hungry. I don't try to understand what is going on, but I don't reject the feeling. I feel vaguely that anything is possible from now on.

A group of young sailors is swaying towards me. As they pass, one of them puts his arm around me, pushes his white sailor hat back on his curly brown hair, leans his face close to mine, and invites me to have a drink with him. He is really cute, I think, as cute as some of the most popular boys in school. Wouldn't it be great if I too had a romantic story to tell the next day? But I turn away, saying "no thanks," and cross the street. His alcohol breath still clings to my nostrils.

Every evening now I walk the downtown streets. I don't talk to anyone, and I no longer pretend that I'm looking in shop windows or that I am about to meet a friend for dinner. I now imagine myself to be a streetwalker; that I am glamorous and desirable, that men yearn for me, but that I am also very choosy and therefore won't just go with anyone.

I avoid looking in darkened shop windows so that I won't see my true reflection, a rather dumpy looking girl carrying her school books under her arm. I walk with a firmer, more determined step, I swing my hips just so and I hold my head high and let a slight smile play my lips. Suddenly I am in one of those rooms with the half-pulled shades, on a narrow bed, seductively poised in the direction of someone, whose shadowy body is leaning towards me. This person has no recognizable face, no physical body, and yet he—for I believe it is a man—it is like a specter whose palpable sexual desire evokes in me a delicious feeling of being sensual and powerful.

My fantasy always stops there. It is enough. In any case, I don't really know much about sex, and in a way I am not really interested in finding out.

I walk the last few blocks to the cafeteria, where I put my meal on a tray, open my books and do my homework while eating. Usually the place is quite empty, because it is late for the dinners of the lonely people who eat there. Tonight I am later than usual. It is almost closing time and there are no other customers. There is very little food left on the steam tables, a few grey pieces of meat are lying on the bottom of the stew container, some green peas are floating in water; the shelves behind the glass partition hold a couple of slices of soggy lemon meringue pie. The vegetable soup is almost gone too, but what sits on the bottom of the container is thicker than usual.

"I'll have some of that," I say to the woman behind the counter, "the last dinner roll and lemon Jell-o." There is no green Jell-o left. She recognizes me and says hello. Other women are already cleaning up. One of them is mopping the floor with a large string mop. As she nears my table she stops for a minute, leans on the mop handle and smiles at me.

"Late tonight, right?" she says.

"Hm hm," I respond with my mouth full of yellow Jell-o and look away. "I'm about to leave," I add. I finish quickly and decide against doing homework, gather my things together and stand up. I pretend that I am there only for a snack and that I have an important place I must go to as soon as I am finished.

"Bye," I say, "I've got to hurry."

Do they ever wonder about that high school girl who eats her dinner every night in a cheap place like this instead of at home with her family? Probably not.

❦

COUSIN ALICE tells Mother that Elizabeth really must start to have a social life and not just go to school, to work and to sleep. Cousin Alice Knows. She has been here longer than we, her daughter is engaged to a medical student and her son is becoming an accountant. She has very strong opinions about what's proper and what is the "American Way." Mother has opinions too, but they don't lie in this realm of thinking. I overhear Alice telling her that I should wear a girdle; that she has really let me gain too much weight, that all girls who are overweight wear girdles here.

On Saturday I go to Lerner shops and buy a long stretchy girdle and a dress to wear for social occasions. It is navy blue, with a slightly flaring skirt, narrow sleeves and a high neck. I can't see myself in anything too flashy, besides it is all-purpose. Mother thinks it's OK, but Alice shakes her head.

"Too conservative. Probably meant for an older woman," she says. Still it's better than nothing. She insists that I borrow her fake pearl necklace to dress it up.

All decked out I wait for Gerda, to be taken to the Jewish Center for a dance. Gerda's mother had found me with the help of the unofficial German refugee network and had invited me to go with her 16 year old daughter as a companion.

As I think about it now, I wonder how I could have been so compliant, so accepting of plans others made for me. I didn't know how to dance; I wasn't eager to go; I felt foolish being all dressed up. There was also something about going to a Jewish Center, with the implication of separateness and religious flavor that I didn't like. I could have said no, but I didn't.

We leave our coats in the cloakroom and enter the dimly lit room, where couples are dancing to the music I am familiar with from school recess. I feel shy as I look around and notice that most of the people there are older than we two. Gerda is off dancing already; she knows the ropes because she has been here before, and I am left standing alone, feeling uncomfortable in my three-inch heels and girdled body. I want to leave, but this place is across town, and I have to wait for Gerda's mother to pick us up. Two more hours!

Just then I see a blond young man separate himself from the dancing crowd. He walks over to where I am standing, resigned to my fate. He asks me to dance. He looks at me through his rimless glasses, smiles a friendly smile and tells me that he has been watching me for quite a while. I watch him as he talks and I notice that he is rather squarely built with a head that seems equally square. He smiles again and says that he thinks I am pretty. We stand up and he leads me to the dance floor.

"Sorry," he says, as our legs get entangled when the music rhythm changes. "Sorry, I'm not such a great dancer."

"Let's sit down," he says when the music ends, "so we can talk." Obviously, he prefers talking to dancing. That's OK with me, under the circumstances.

He is a European refugee too, from Vienna. The inflection in his voice gives it away. He is twenty-five and a graduate student at Berkeley, soon to be drafted. He thought at first that I was much older than seventeen. Still in high school? He is astonished; I seem to be so mature.

"Can we see each other again?" he asks me as the evening ends.

"I don't have a phone and the people where I live don't like to take messages," I say.

"So next time here?"

I nod. I don't find him attractive, but he seems friendly and he is so much older and thinks I am pretty and smart. That's flattering. Besides it's an adventure. Dating a university student when I am only seventeen seems daring, and yet dating at all makes me the same as all the other girls. I am all mixed up, but I say yes, we'll meet here next Sunday to talk some more. He squeezes my arm as I leave, and I notice a slight, ever so slight, leer as he looks at me. Or is it just a friendly smile? In the bright light of the foyer I notice that there are two large almond-shaped bumps on his neck, one on each side. Some sort of a disease, I think. They seem to be a more serious flaw than his nearsighted eyes and his fleshy fingers.

Why do I say yes? Why do I meet him the next week and the week after and the week after that? We talk and we walk long distances along the San Francisco streets and in Golden Gate Park; he buys me perfume and kisses me. I think that maybe I might fall in love with him, though not the way I was in love with Gert. Still, he is nice and intelligent, and seems to like me a lot, and that's something. He tells me laughing that his studies are suffering on my account. I like that and I squeeze his arm back. He wants to meet my mother.

"Why?" I ask. He has no real answer to the question, only that perhaps my mother might want to know with whom I am going out. I am reminded of the Mexican boy who had asked to meet my mother because he had wanted to marry me.

"I'll have to ask her first," I say. "Maybe the following Sunday? I'll let you know." I feel uncomfortable about the prospect, perhaps because he is not handsome and so much older. Yet I am also pleased that he chose me; after all, I am still in high school.

I know Mother will worry because of his age and because he is Viennese. She hopes that he isn't smooth and oily and a little dishonest the way in her opinion so many Viennese are. I know she means seductive, a word I find in the thesaurus Alice has given me. I tell myself that I am lucky to have a boyfriend who is really very nice and protective of me, and I like the fact that he is interested in ideas and books. He says he doesn't know very much about music, but he is willing to learn from me. I relax a little and look forward to our dates. I have learned to look at him from the side in a certain way, so that I don't see both of those bumps at the same time. Then he is almost good-looking. He tells me jokingly that they are the remnants of his having been fish-like with rudimentary gills when he was a fetus.

He invites me to a party in Berkeley where he introduces me to all his friends. Everyone there is much older than I. Graduate students and their wives and girlfriends are lounging around on old broken-down couches and chairs, listening to Jazz or talking excitedly about things I know nothing about. I sense that Fred is proud of his prize, me, and as he leads me to the tiny space cleared for dancing, he tells me that everyone thinks I am cute and simply loves me. I look at the posters on the wall, drink when drinks are handed to me, until I no longer know how many drinks I have had. I feel light and giddy. I laugh at the men's jokes, even if I don't understand them, as I take another drink someone is handing me.

I let Fred and his friend Joe lead me to the bedroom where they lay me across the bed. I feel their hands warm on my body. No one says anything. They are unbuttoning my blouse and I close my eyes and I let them take it off. I feel sleepy and too warm, but I like their caressing hands. I become vaguely aware that Joe has left the room and that Fred is pulling at my bra.

Suddenly with a jerk I wake from my befuddled foggy state and sit up. My mother! She had made Fred promise to get me home by midnight. It must be past midnight now! I panic and wonder what I have let myself get into.

Calls are made and I am driven home. Mother, in dressing gown and slippers, has waited up to scold me, but I am too sleepy and drunk and contrite to listen.

I promise myself the next morning that I will never again drink too much and will only let things happen that I choose myself. But of course I forget my resolutions and really nothing changes for a long time, as I go from moment to moment, letting others call the plays.

When Fred is drafted and sent to boot camp, I am not too unhappy, even though at first I miss our dates. He phones me when he can, but we have little to say to each other and only talk about when we might see each other again.

In the meantime I date others, boys more my age. With them I fly model airplanes in Golden Gate Park, go horse back riding on the beach, ride the cable car up and down California Street, go to amusement parks in the Sunset, and play pinball machines in the arcades on Market Street. It is all a lot of fun, and not at all serious. I'm beginning to feel more lighthearted. Maybe I'm becoming more American? More what I think American girls my age are like?

On my class graduation picture, spring 1945, I look almost like the other girls, with shoulder length wavy hair, the collar of a white blouse showing above a Shetland wool sweater. I am smiling slightly. My feet don't show in the photo. Maybe I'm even wearing saddle shoes now.

In February I start my first semester at Berkeley. I have a scholarship and I move into a boarding house near campus. Mother and I will never again live in the same place—we will never again share a bed, a room, an apartment—we will never again even live in the same city.

She asks me to phone her nightly. She is lonely without me, she says, and worries about me, although she won't tell me what she is worried about. I understand about lonely but I can't accept the other which feels like a too heavy burden on my new-won independence. It's as if the tables had suddenly been turned and I had become responsible for her well-being rather than she for mine. I try to comply with her wishes, but I am resentful just the same. I ask my friends as to what I should do.

Their opinions are divided: call her, don't call her, be kind, be independent, she loves you, she is too demanding. I go back and forth between feelings of anger and guilt. She phones me when I skip a few nights: I must not love her enough to give her a few minutes every day.

"Can't you understand?"

Yes I do, but I don't want to keep thinking about her when now there are so many other matters I need to think about: chemistry and roommates and politics and sex. I teeter back and forth. Sacks full of self-accusations: I am callous, unfeeling, ungrateful, worthless, hurtful. Piles of self-justifications: too busy with classes and studying and friends, the pay phone in the hall is seldom free, her demands are unrealistic, I have no extra money for phone calls, I am doing the best I can. Finally I am struck by a different idea: if I succeed in separating myself from her, am I not also helping her to separate from me and to rebuild her own life? It becomes a wrenching process for both of us, but in the end we both succeed; each in her own way.

SOME TIME AGO, I went to the library to verify some dates about which I was not sure. I hoped that reading historical accounts of the period between 1939 and 1943 would help me find my way back. I can only guess why in more than sixty years I had never once taken any steps to learn the how and why of our last minute escape. Whenever I was asked about the events that put in motion our rescue from Germany, our two-year sojourn in Spain and Portugal and finally our arrival in the U.S., I would answer that I really didn't know. Why had I not taken this step before? I think that I had wanted to know only what I remembered, the places in which I had found myself, the memory of the people whom I knew then, the landscape, the weather. I would acknowledge that yes, our flight from Germany in 1941 and from Europe in 1943 in the middle of World War II, had truly been remarkable, but in a way that always precluded all further questions. I was not interested in exploring the details; I wanted to put all that safely behind me to get on with life. Did I think there was a stigma to having been a refugee? Was there a sense that if we had only been smarter, we would have left Germany earlier and would have been able to come to America with more than the clothes on our backs? I did not want to question or think about all of that; I wanted to believe that my European past was no longer of consequence. I wanted to be an American, I wanted to belong, to fit in, and I was determined to make it happen.

And so I lived my life, married and divorced, became a mother and grandmother, held jobs in science and education for which my training qualified me, formed close relationships with others, until finally it became clear to me that my hitherto suppressed memory of childhood events needed to be brought into the light of day.

AS I NOW look at the tiny black-and-white photos taken of my mother in Barcelona, or at the old studio photographs of her and her sister as children, or the ones that show the young mother and the little girl that was me, I realize how much I missed by my desire to be separate from her. Later, during our yearly visits, after I was married and had children of my own and she was married as well, we would both try over and over to bridge the gap between us, but after a brief period of closeness I would always fall back into my old ambivalent wariness of her, while she would experience again her disappointment in me. We were not able to tear down that barbed wire strand between us which we would both approach and try to cross and on which we would both be caught again and again. Finally thirty years later, when I had found my own place in the world and she was content in hers, when I no longer needed to drive her away, and she no longer needed me to be close, I was able to tell her that I loved her. It was almost too late, for she was dying.

AFTERWORD

EVER SO SLOWLY, I have tried to unwind the thread of re-membering the events of my early years. I have taken hold of the outside end, and have let the yarn run through my fingers in starts and spurts, stopping often to untwist tangles and loos-en knots. I discovered in the process of writing, that often these tangles and knots contained the most significant parts of those years; events which for so long lay hidden, sensations which were buried in a fallow field because they were too confusing or too painful to think about. Often as I wrote, all my unasked questions hovered above me like hungry vultures, waiting for an answer, a revelation, a vision of what I didn't remember. All the questions I should have asked my mother while she was alive, all the conversations we could have had which I believe now she had wanted and would have welcomed, I would like to have had with her.

I can no longer ask her, she is no longer there to remind me. I have had to search for myself. As I wrote, a word, a phrase, an old photo became the incantation to bring back past people and events; sometimes a mnemonic helped to shake loose forgotten images; some self-imposed bribe would occasionally lure the misplaced events back into my consciousness.

I think of this story of my early years as two tightly inter-woven strands: The teller, myself as I am now, and the tale of the events that occurred in the life of the child and young girl who I was then. Memories filtered through the teller's eyes, forgotten events recalled almost by accident, images retained as they were or perhaps altered by associations with current views, feelings remembered but words no longer recalled the way they were spoken, that is the fabric of my story: THE TELLER IN THE TALE.

ACKNOWLEDGEMENTS

For years I resisted looking back at my early years in Germany and as a refugee. On being questioned I would only say, "Well, that's a very long a story." Finally my daughter-in-law Arlene urged me to put my story on paper, even if only for my grandchildren. Thank you, Arlene. Thanks also to the members of my Southampton Herstory Writers group, who helped me shake loose long-forgotten memories. To son Wayne and daughter-in-law Cynthia my deep-felt gratitude for surprising me on my eightieth birthday with a gift from my family – a beautiful hand-bound hardcover book of my manuscript, formatted and designed by them. Thanks also to the many friends whose thoughtful comments on early versions were very helpful. I am grateful to my son Ken for taking such a keen interest in the historical background of our escape and our sojourn in Spain. I am indebted to Jim Tent, Professor of History at the University of Alabama, whose book of oral histories of German children of mixed marriages during the Nazi period, along with his correspondence with me, helped me to realize that my story might be likewise of importance. Friend Marion Sullewsky helped with some of the necessary steps for publishing. Thank you, Marion. Warmest thanks go to Alan Gold who, through his expertise, patience and interest provided the design that made my manuscript into a book.

Above all it is to Erika Duncan, artistic director of Herstory Writers Workshop, that I am most deeply indebted. Without her continued encouragement, generous guidance, and wise criticism, this work might never have seen the light of day. Thank you, dear friend.